Boomer's Guide to

Dating (Again)

Laurie A. Helgoe, Ph.D.

ALPHA

A member of Penguin Group (USA) Inc.

For Becca, who always believed

Publisher: *Marie Butler-Knight*
Product Manager: *Phil Kitchel*
Senior Managing Editor: *Jennifer Chisholm*
Senior Acquisitions Editor: *Randy Ladenheim-Gil*
Development Editor: *Tom Stevens*
Senior Production Editor: *Billy Fields*

Copy Editor: *Sara Fink*
Cover Designer: *Doug Wilkins*
Book Designer: *Trina Wurst*
Creative Director: *Robin Lasek*
Indexer: *Angie Bess*
Layout/Proofreading: *Becky Harmon, Mary Hunt*

Contents

Introduction

We were conceived out of post-war passion and optimism, and born between the years of 1946 and 1964. We are a generation defined by our numbers—numbers which have helped us forge movements, influence trends, and feel less alone. We've been through a lot together, from The Twist to the anxieties of Vietnam. Whether we were echoing the message of Martin Luther King Jr., or handing out *Nixon/Agnew* buttons, we cared. We were "out there" with our hearts and minds—and with our fashions. We evolved from skinny pants and mohair sweaters, to space-age minis and go-go boots, then bell-bottoms and headbands, and on to the "night fever" look. We listened to the same songs, munched on popcorn in front of the same movies, and watched the same idyllic sit-coms. We were stunned by John F. Kennedy's assassination, and held our breath as Neil Armstrong took his first steps on the moon.

We've come a long way since then, taking diverse paths and becoming involved with our individual lives, careers, families. Yet we still share a unique history and identity. The *Boomer's Guides* are written just for us. They draw on the experiences that shaped who we are, and speak to the challenges we face today.

Boomer's Guide to Dating (Again) addresses what it means to be out there, probably on the heels of an old relationship, facing the prospect of dating again. We'll talk about how dating has changed since we did it the first time, as well as how we've changed. The book will take you through the stages we encounter as we venture back into dating. And all along the way, we'll be inspired by the authors, songwriters, movie stars, television characters, artists, comics, and activists of our generation.

In Part 1, we discuss the challenges of leaving a familiar relationship and opening ourselves to something new. We address your fears and anxieties, from concerns about getting hurt to the question of whether you still have it. As you start to get excited about the prospect of dating, we'll move to Part 2, and explore the rich resources available for finding and connecting with potential dates. In Part 3, we get down to the nitty-gritty of meeting, asking someone out, being on a first date (again!), and becoming a couple. Part 4 is the troubleshooting section, and will address conflicts you may face along the way, from whether to settle down or keep looking, to what sex means to you now, to how to balance the passions of dating with the responsibilities of parenting.

Entertainer Danny Kaye once said, "Life is a great big canvas; throw all the paint you can at it." Through the Boomers years, we have thrown a lot of color on that canvas—pink angora, blue suede shoes, army green, women seeing red, black-is-beautiful, purple haze, flower power and tie-dye. Even as television and film were coming out "in living color," we were colorizing our world. This richness is what made writing this guide so fun. The passion and optimism that gave us life continues to infuse our generation. We are Boomers!

Acknowledgments

To Barron, thank you for reading every line I write, for paying the bills while I shifted gears and, above all, for being as in love with me as I am with you.

To dear Bjorn and Josh, thank you for inspiring me with your faith. And thanks for the computer help, Bjorn!

Much thanks to sister Rebecca, for living this book, giving me feedback, and believing in happy endings. You and Julie make the journey so much easier.

Thanks to my writer's group—Maschelle, Cindy, Jim, Patti, Beth and David, who cheered me on and fed me ideas. Thanks also to my consultants, Luke, Jessica, Sylvia, Dee, Cathy, Jeff and Deb, Susan, Beth and Bernie, Suzanne, Patrick, Bonnie, Joyce, Wayne, Aila, Lisa, Thrace, and April. Catherine, thanks for helping me get here. And thanks to all my clients who humbled me with your wisdom and courage.

Gratitude and love to my big, wonderful family: Andy, Steve, Andrea, Rebecca and Luther, who expanded on my memories of the boomer years; Dan, the pioneer author in the family who helped me learn the ropes; Carolyn and Art, and my dear little sister and buddy from childhood, Julie. Thanks to Jen and Matthew for helping to make all this possible.

Dad, thanks for feeding my desire, telling me I could do anything, and being oh, so proud. Mom in heaven, thanks for teaching me to write and seeing talent in my little fifth grade story, "Goupie."

Thanks to my agent, Jacky Sach, for the love you give to your work and the support and friendship you have given to me. Thanks to my editors, Randy Ladenheim-Gil and Tom Stevens, for helping me make this book better.

And thanks to my Creator for taking away all my excuses for not writing.

Moving On (or, Leaving the Past Behind)

When you were a teen-ager listening to the Beatles sing "Yesterday," your troubles may have felt very far away. Today, those troubles could be getting in the way of your desire to date. The chapters in Part 1 help you unload baggage from old relationships, confront fears of dating and concerns about the kids, tap into your own desires, and free yourself to experience dating again as a fresh, new adventure.

chapter 1

Free as a Bird!

Expose yourself to your deepest fear; after that, fear has no power, and the fear of freedom shrinks and vanishes. You are free.
—Jim Morrison

So maybe we never planned to be dating at this stage in our lives. Been there, done that. Whether your dating experience reflected the innocence of '60s sitcoms or the wildness of "sex, drugs and rock 'n' roll," dating is something we associate with youth—and energy. Back then, many of us couldn't imagine trading the single life for marriage and a house payment. But that was then.

Now we're supposed to be the adults we swore we'd never trust—settled, secure, and maybe even a little boring. So what's the bad news here? Being unsettled is a bummer, as we might have put it back then, but if we think about it, unsettled means free. Freedom defined us once. And, as Mick Jagger reassures, "it's all right letting yourself go, as long as you can get yourself back."

But maybe you're not interested in reliving the '60s and '70s—all that swingin' took a lot of energy! And even if dating brings back great memories, not all our dating experiences were fun. The good news is, we are actually more free now than when we were at Woodstock—screaming about freedom until our voices were gone—because life has shown us numerous options to choose from.

Yes, it's scary. Freedom always is. But if we can embrace it, we might even enjoy ourselves!

Getting Another Chance

Of all the pleasures in life, it is hard to top the "firsts" in relationships. Why do you think the flirting between Elvis and Ann-Margret took up most of the movie? Even today, popular movies such as *Sleepless in Seattle* and *When Harry Met Sally* also keep us waiting for the firsts. Remember how it felt to slow dance in junior high, to let your bodies touch and communicate secret messages? To finally get to kiss? To passionately "neck" for the better part of an evening? (How did we *do* that?) Remember when you first exposed your skin to the one you loved (or thought you loved), and felt those first reactions as your bodies met? Okay, I'm ready to go back—how about you?

But there are other reasons we fantasize about going back. Haven't you had times where you wanted to go back to your dating years, meld your adult brain with your teen body, and do it better? Granted, it's much easier to feel such confidence when we're just imagining. Now that we need to actually get out there, we might feel a little more shy. And, unfortunately, we don't have Jeannie, the genie or Samantha, the witch to bring back our teen bodies. Yet, we do have the magic of a second chance and the potion of all we have learned. Let's go back and see what we can mix up.

That Was Then, This Is Now

Before we move forward, let's reflect back on your dating experience and indulge in your enlightened perspective. Try to generate a list of the people you dated. High school yearbooks and old photos are great resources. The main point of this exercise, however, is for you to reflect on how *you* were. Put yourself back on one of your dates. Were you nervous, cocky, superficial, open or shy? Which dates were fun and which have you tried hard to repress? The more you get into this, the more you'll remember.

I Found My Thrill

Use the following triggers to help you revive your date memories:

- On TV. *77 Sunset Strip, Leave it to Beaver, Gunsmoke, The Brady Bunch*
- On the Radio. "Cherish," "Satisfaction," "Hey Jude," "Light My Fire," "Bohemian Rhapsody."
- Make Out Places. A Chevy with fins, Daddy's station wagon or a decked-out Trans Am; the drive-in; at home in the rec room; back seat at the movies.
- Date Places. Roller skating rink, movies, ball games, sock-hop, drive-in eatery, cruising' around town, rock concert, protest rally.
- What you were wearing? Angora sweaters, letter jackets, penny loafers, then bell bottoms, minis and maxis. Hair ala James Dean, Jim Morrison, Cher, and Farrah. ID bracelets, go-go boots, mood rings.
- In the News. JFK and MLK, Vietnam and Watergate, Apollo 11, Roger Maris hits 61.
- What you were saying? Groovy, far out, boss, what's your bag?, peace (may have included two-finger peace sign), keep on truckin'.

Now, think about how you would like to be this time. More confident?, relaxed?, picky? Maybe you have a specific date you'd love a second shot at. In date redo fantasies, we are not likely to put up with treatment we settled for back then. Today, we have a shortened sense of time, and are less willing to spend it with people who treat us poorly.

From the Mouths of Baby Boomers

"I wore long white gloves with a prom dress that was purple velvet in the bodice and lighter purple in the skirt, empire-waisted, scoop neck, and sleeveless. The guys wore dark suits usually. The big girl's hairdo for prom was hair in ringlets swept up on top of their heads, although this was pretty daring. Not a lot of girls chose it—a lot of boys didn't like it this way."

—Class of '69

"Our first date was a 'Sadie Hawkins' dance scheduled for November 23. It had to be rescheduled because of the assassination of John F. Kennedy. Finding the perfect place to park was a lot of the fun. It's amazing how many "secret" places we found. Cars were made for lovers back then with comfortable bench seats that encouraged closeness and intimacy. Today's generation has no idea how convenient lovers had it back then."

—Class of '65

"I have had many fantasies about how I would now respond to the date who came to my door on prom night—*drunk*. Instead of stuffing my disgust and passively going along, I would have left him at the door and driven separately, convinced my best friend to ditch *her* drunk boyfriend and had better conversation, a better dance partner, and a prom photo with her (which *wouldn't* have been torn up). So, I would have missed out on the opportunity to make out with a slobbering drunk. I think I could live with that."

—Class of '79

And what about those times we were dumped? Rejection happens, but it's what we *did* with the rejection that we can change. If you were rejected by someone you were crazy about, maybe you decided that passion wasn't safe and "settled" with someone you felt lukewarm about. Or maybe you started rejecting before you could get rejected. Dating this time around, we can decide to embrace the risk of rejection in the pursuit of excitement and passion. And, when rejection happens, Chapter 34 will help keep you in the game.

While some memories make us cringe, others make us smile, and yet others make us just plain horny. You may have forgotten about that boy you made out with on the bus, that girl you first kissed, or a person you dated that you can still feel love for. You may be surprised to note the things you did *right*, the risks that paid off and the fun you had. Use these positive memories to feed your confidence. If you did okay when you were that clueless, just think what you can do now!

Speaking of now, dating is different today than it was during that revolutionary time when we came of age. We're less idealistic, maybe a bit jaded, more set in our ways, and we might feel more vulnerable right now. A survey of 40 to 69-year-old daters by *AARP The Magazine* (Nov/Dec 2003), reveals a trend toward dating for fun and companionship rather than either casual sex or marriage; and notes that a significant percentage of women are dating younger men, challenging the traditional idea of men being the elder member of the couple. We can bring experience forward, but we can't really go back. We know too much. And yes, we are older.

Although our drugs of choice today may be Botox or Rogaine, we are not "old." Because of our numbers and money, we boomers have been catered to by experts in health, fitness, and beauty. We're actually a pretty attractive bunch! Look back for inspiration or memories of lessons learned, then take stock of that fact that you have a new adventure ahead of you. You've got so much to draw from, and before you lies the opportunity for the ultimate do-over.

> *"You have brains in your head, and feet in your shoes. You can steer yourself in any direction you choose. You're on your own and you know what you know. And you are the one who'll decide where to go."*
>
> —Dr. Seuss

You've Come a Long Way, Baby

At the age of 40, I decided to try out modeling. After getting my weight down to the required range (ouch!), I attended a screening in my town. I was the only person over 30, and the majority of the candidates were under 20. Despite my status as a minority, I realized I was much more relaxed than most of the others. Like the younger candidates, I was hoping good things would happen. The difference was, I already had an identity. I was not looking for the judges to decide who I was. This difference freed me up to have fun, to check things out, and, ultimately, for *me* to be the judge of the experience.

This is the attitude that gives us an advantage as we approach dating. When you were 16, you were only beginning to define who you were. Like the wide-eyed model candidates, the world's definition of you carried a lot of weight. But, as the Virginia Slims commercial proclaimed back then, "you've come a long way, baby." Now you have an advanced degree in life, and here are some ways it will pay off:

You carry yourself differently. This difference is subtle, but very powerful. You feel more comfortable in the world, because you've been here longer. You talk to other adults as peers rather than as authorities. You have places in the world where you are known and respected. This sense of belonging here not only frees you to enjoy the ride, but it looks good, too.

You have more to talk about. Do you remember suffering through times where you and your date had absolutely nothing to say? Once you got past the school gossip, there may have been little left. Now you can talk about fascinating places you've seen or funny situations you've been in or the business you helped build or the unique way you have come to understand the world. Think of how interesting you have become, just by being here and by being you.

You know what you want. If you've recently left a relationship, you may be more in touch with what you *don't* want, but that helps, too. You are less likely to stick around in situations that are unsatisfying. Knowing who you are, what you want, and what turns you on will make it easier for you to find people you enjoy and want to spend time with. And, as a bonus, knowing what you want is attractive.

You know your limitations. A late night now might be eleven o' clock, but at least you know your limitations and boundaries. You are less likely to apologize for what you don't like, and what turns you off. That makes you less likely to get yourself into situations where you feel out of your league.

So savor this opportunity you have for a sequel to your dating story. This book will help you minimize dating anxiety, increase your confidence, find people to date and, mostly, to approach dating as an adventure which will enrich your life.

This book is broken down into four sections which correspond to what you will encounter on your dating journey: "Moving On," to help you leave the past behind and get set to date; "Finding People," because you need them in order to date; "Embracing the Adventure," your dating manual; and "Troubleshooting," which helps you get through difficulties and make important decisions. So, start hearing that music that makes your heart pump faster, think about touching someone new, dancing, feeling the intensity of the chemistry between you. We once were going to change the world with love. It's not too late to reclaim that power.

chapter 2

The Voice of Old Loves

*Revolution is not something fixed in ideology, nor is
it something fashioned to a particular decade. It is a
perpetual process embedded in the human spirit.*
—*Abbie Hoffman*

Although you are free to date, you may not *feel* free if your ex
keeps calling and telling you how awful life is, if your parents
are still asking you to explain what went wrong, or if you're
still grieving the death of your partner. Even when these
holds loosen, some voices still linger. These can be the tough-
est ones to deal with, because they have lodged themselves
in our heads.

My Mama Told Me ...

Why does it seem that every time we feel liberated, Mom or
Dad's voice creeps in? It's not a coincidence, you know. Whether
you initiated it or not, your life is going through a revolution,
and we know from the '60s that revolutions stir things up—
especially parents (including the internalized ones!). Whenever
I take on a new challenge, my mama's voice plays the soothing
words in my head, "you're tired." As well meaning as those

words may have been, they got inside me as a message that I couldn't handle challenges—I was too tired. We all have voices that got inside us when we were little and still threaten to limit our range.

We took in these voices when we were learning how to woo our important caretakers. Whether positive or negative, we memorized their words: "You're selfish," "you're so cute," "you're just like your father." These voices became an internal guide to how to be loved or unloved in relationships.

But it seems we've come so far since then. We were a part of the generation that challenged everything—our parents' voices didn't daunt us then, and since then, we've come into our own in the world. So, we may feel silly when old voices haunt and make us feel insecure all over again. Yet, it is natural that when we lose our footing and need to grasp something, those voices tend to fill the void. Let's say you took in the voice that said "you're selfish." When you approach a new relationship, that old voice may advise you to be careful about expressing what you want. After all, your "selfishness" cost you points with your parents, and you certainly don't want to lose points with your date. Let's take this voice out on a date, and address the fears that give the voice power.

Fear of being unattractive. So you want to tell your date that you'd really rather go to a nice sushi bar instead of his (or her) favorite burger joint. The Voice interrupts, "you're selfish." Now you start to worry that your date will find you unattractive if you express your preference. You are unconsciously registering: "Better to be agreeable and easygoing, because that's how my parents liked me." Problem is, your date is not one of your parents, is hopefully not related to them, and may not have even met them yet. Your date may actually be suggesting burgers because The Voice in his head is encouraging frugality. (Sometimes it's heartening to remember you aren't the only one hearing voices.) Anyway, your date might actually find your suggestion liberating and be turned on by your individuality. After all, we are most likely to be attractive to others when we are real, when we allow what is unique about us to be seen.

Fear of the unknown. Let's say your date is not impressed with your suggestion and even responds, "Yuk, I hate sushi." The fact is, your date could respond in any number of ways. *You don't know.* Once you relinquish the "you are selfish" belief, you venture into unknown territory. You exchange the certainty of The Voice for the adventure of discovering your date's response. Voices from the past help us organize our world: "If I am this way, I'll be loved." Even if the voices are negative, they are predictable, and that can be comforting. Allowing the unknown opens up a world of possibilities and, as scary as that can be, it's the only way to find out what is true.

Fear of losing support. So, you push for sushi, and everything goes fine. Problem is, you feel rather "out there" and even alone. By alone, I mean you have proceeded without the approval of The Voice. (The voice that says "you're selfish," would have approved if you had kept your sushi suggestion to yourself.) Now you're on your own and responsible for your own actions. It's a lot like leaving home. Yet, this separation is the only route to finding true support. True support comes when we are seen and known and get backing for who *we* are. As you may have discovered, even parents have been known to eventually provide such support. And real parents often turn out better than the ones in our heads.

> "*Vulnerable to my irrational fears,*
> *Vulnerable to giving you the power to define me,*
> *Pain I've known these past few years,*
> *Clouds my ability to see.*"
>
> —From "Vulnerable" by
> Rebecca Aadland-Schoper,
> Dating-again baby boomer

Blue is My World

Quick—how many of you had "Love is Blue" as your prom theme? Back then, the blue side of love made for a good slow dance and resonated well with our teenage angst. But from where you stand today, love may have become not only blue, but hurtful to your sense of who you are.

Even if Mom and Dad no longer inhabit your head, what about that person who has shared much of your adult life? Former partners also tend to linger in our heads. Even though you are divorced, you might find yourself continuing an unresolved fight inside your head. Remember how George and Martha thrived on their fights in *Who's Afraid of Virginia Woolf?*" If you suffered an unwanted loss, you may cling to last exchanges and memories, anger or guilt. Let's discuss some common voices that can keep us stuck:

- "You're selfish" and other judgments. Sound familiar? Yes, often the voices of our chosen lovers tend to echo the criticisms of Mom and Dad. (Another tricky way we keep them around.) See "My Mama Told Me…"

- "You have destroyed me." This kind of message is a form of emotional blackmail: "If you don't stay, I'll fall apart." Your partner may have been depressed or an alcoholic, and you came to share the belief that you were holding him or her together. Even after freeing yourself of such a relationship, guilt-inducing voices can linger.

- "I don't love you anymore." The withdrawal of love stirs up a core fear and can leave us feeling abandoned and helpless. What is particularly difficult about this message is that you may be given no clue to the "why?" You feel desperate to recover the feeling of being loved, to make sense of the loss, to regain some control over your world.

From the Mouths of Baby Boomers

"If you are dating divorced people, or are divorced yourself, you are bound to encounter what I call 'buried land mines.' These are things the ex used to do, say, topics for arguments, that you will undoubtedly encounter and learn to identify. It works like a Vietnam flashback and sooner or later you find yourself in the middle of an argument with your ex, even though they moved to Alaska six months previously."

—Class of '76

"It was totally unexpected. My husband told me he was leaving me, that he no longer loved me. I didn't understand. My whole world was destabilized. I thought, 'if this can happen, anything can happen.'"

—Class of '82

- "There's someone else." The echo of these words can linger and even become an obsession. You may try to achieve a sense of mastery over the situation by comparing yourself to the other lover, pressing for details and mentally replaying scenes of them together. If this voice is generalized, you will anticipate betrayal in other relationships.

The Sound of Silence

When a partner dies, dating again becomes complicated in unique ways. Guilt is a biggie, and comes in different forms. If things weren't going so well in the relationship, or if chronic illness preceded the death, secret feelings of relief may induce guilt. If the relationship was cherished, it may be hard to imagine loving anyone else. And we may fear loving again and risking another loss.

Excitement about dating may feel incompatible with feelings of grief. Old voices may interrupt the silence and comment on how we are supposed to grieve, how we are supposed to feel. You need to find safe places to explore *your own* reality and whatever feelings come along with it. The wisest advice I was given about the grieving process is that "it takes as long as it takes." Give it the time it takes, and you—and only you—will know when you are ready to move on.

Talking Back

Old voices maintain power over us when they keep us engaged. So, if our response is to get hooked into an internal fight, it doesn't matter if we win the fight or lose it. The voice is winning. We are preoccupied with something old, and it is preventing us from living in the present. We may want to deal with the old voices in a deliberate way, such as working with a therapist, talking to a trusted friend, or writing in a journal. But at some point, we need to deprive the voices of their power.

Let's go back to "you're selfish." A predictable response would be "am not!" and possibly a list of reasons why you are not selfish. You are on the defensive, and you are expending your effort convincing the voice—and yourself—that you are indeed the person the voice wants you to be. Wait a minute! Your argument has actually become an effort to appease the voice.

What if you responded, "Yes, I'm selfish. I like to get what I want. Period." What would the voice have to say then? If it's hard for you to respond this way, you are probably conflicted about the part of you that *is* self-interested, even selfish. Practice embracing that part.

But let's make it harder. What if the message is, "You'll never be a success." You don't want to respond, "You're right, I'll never be a success." Or do you? Maybe you can respond, "You're right, I'll never be a success in your eyes." Or even better, "You don't believe I'll be a success." Both responses separate you from the voice and free you to have your own opinion.

Even the stinging "I don't love you anymore" voice is better responded to with "you don't love me anymore" than the translation "I am unlovable." The need to make it about us is one way we try to secure a sense of control over the love of another. The thinking goes something like this: "If I say I am unlovable, at least the abandonment makes sense, and I can fix myself and become loveable again."

> "I haven't a clue as to how my story will end. But that's all right. When you set out on a journey and night covers the road, that's when you discover the stars."
>
> —Nancy Willard

This does not negate the importance of understanding our own roles in relationships that didn't work. Actually, quieting old voices will help us more objectively view the situation. And letting go of old voices means letting go of a false sense of control. It means venturing into the world without knowing how things will turn out. And it also means opening ourselves to possibilities beyond the limitations of our imagination.

chapter 3

Letting Go Is Hard to Do

Beautiful! Beautiful! Magnificent desolation.
—Buzz Aldrin, on the first moon walk,
July 20, 1969

"I'm clearing my head of old voices, breathing some fresh air, feeling ready. Yeah, right. Why am I still stuck at home? Why did I end up sleeping with my ex? Why haven't I removed the old pictures?"

When you find yourself asking questions like these, go easy on yourself. Letting go, one of the easiest physical acts (think of holding onto monkey bars), can be one of our biggest emotional challenges. Let's look at what might be in the way.

The Comfort Trap

Remember when we could stand in line for hours to get tickets to hear Peter, Paul, and Mary or the Stones, and then actually look forward to being mashed up against each other at the concert? I knew I was getting old when I went to a popular bar and felt indignant that there was no place to sit. Let's face it, we've become accustomed to comfort, and relationships are no exception.

Whether relationships work or not, we get used to them. The fights are familiar, lines well rehearsed. We know which side of the bed to sleep on. We also tend to get comfortable with the feelings the relationship generates, even if those feelings are negative. If you were always angry in your last relationship, that feeling will be hard to relinquish. If you felt like a victim, you may cling to that role.

As we enter the unknown, it is natural to want to step back at times. That is why change often happens in patterns of "two steps forward, one step back." Sometimes, the stepping back reminds us of how bad it was and helps us to take a leap forward. Sometimes we get caught up with the old voices, the old roles, the old fights. This old stuff keeps us preoccupied and helps us avoid the unknown.

Letting go is an act of faith. It involves giving yourself over to the unknown, but also trusting yourself to negotiate whatever comes.

To let go means to endure a temporary state of emptiness. Some of you will enjoy the emptiness, the freedom from old burdens, the sudden lightness, the fresh air. For many, it will feel frightening, like being out in the wilderness with the old behind and the new still off in the distance. Yet, the emptiness itself can be healing. When we were challenging our Western values in the sixties, Eastern mystics taught us to see emptiness as a "fertile void," where new inspiration could be discovered. Our generation has embraced many practices to foster emptiness, such retreats and meditation. Maybe it's time to take our own advice and let the emptiness be.

That Annoying Feeling Called Grief

Staying tied up in the past not only keeps us in known territory, it helps us avoid the awareness of grief. The grief I am talking about is not just grief about the loss of a relationship. Especially in the case of divorce, our grief may be about having spent so much time in a bad relationship, about the years we can't get back, about what we let ourselves put up with. As long as we're still in it, we can maintain illusions that we can fix things—make good on a bad investment. In letting go, we are giving up, calling a loss a loss, and feeling the grief.

Another type of grief is the loss of your childhood vision of married life. Television shows from *Ozzie and Harriet* to *The Waltons* fed us images of happy, forever marriages and supportive families. Even if we were more entertained by *Peyton Place, Leave it to Beaver* somehow stuck. Internalized images of changeless relationships can leave us with feelings of failure when our stories turn out differently.

> "*Life doesn't imitate art, it imitates bad television.*"
> —*Woody Allen*

Changes in relationship status can also mean a loss of identity. You may feel more like a married man or woman than a single person. If you are a woman leaving a marriage, you may be faced with choices about your name and the possibility of having a different name than your children. If you have left a straight relationship to acknowledge a gay or lesbian sexual preference, the identity shift is even more dramatic. Surrounded by people who assume you are straight, you face the multiple challenges of getting used to your own identity, educating others about who you are, and finding your place in the world—a world which still threatens ridicule, loss of relationships and discrimination.

Usually it is not only your partner you lose when a relationship ends. You may feel alienated from people who were a regular part of your circle, such as your partner's family and friends.

Hanging on keeps grief at bay. Moving on allows grief. We cannot change without feeling loss. So don't end your therapy or support group right after you pave the way for change. Don't feel shy about calling friends after things start going well. I remember coming into therapy after implementing the changes I had been talking about. I was miserable. My therapist inquired about my mood and I said mournfully, "I'm getting everything I want!" She helped me understand that I really had moved on, and I was feeling grief. So, keep in mind, when you notice that annoying feeling called grief, it's a clue that you are out there, risking change and moving on. Gather a lot of support and give yourself credit for your courage.

Ozzie and Harriet was not only the prototype for the American postwar nuclear family. Before *The Osbournes*, it was the Boomer's version of Reality TV. Ozzie and Harriet Nelson were Ozzie and Harriet Nelson in real life. Their sons were really their sons, and even the sons' wives were real additions. This fact may have enhanced the impact of the ideals they created. But reality only went so far. The scripts were written and acted, and the set was only "modeled after" their real home. And did you ever question how real it was for the breadwinner of an upper middle-class family to hang around the house with no defined source of income? Ah, television.

Becoming a Novice

Dating again means allowing yourself to be a novice, to start at the beginning. This can be hard, especially if we convinced ourselves that the point of growing up was to "arrive," and be all set up with our happy marriage, house, 2.5 kids (how does that work?) and two cars in the garage.

Returning to dating can feel like going back to school. We feel rusty and out of touch. Yet, there are some very good reasons to become a novice at this time of our lives. For one, new challenges help us stay young. In the early '60s, some of your Boomer peers from Berkeley (Rosenzweig and associates), demonstrated that rats who were continually exposed to new tasks developed more brain mass and performed better on tests compared with rats in static environments. Now scientists are exploring parallels in humans. I bet you hadn't considered that dating again might actually help your brain grow!

Becoming a novice also opens up a new world to you. Dating again challenges us to tune into current trends, to find interesting places to meet people, to discover new entertainment options. You might even become "Web fluent" as you explore Internet dating. And, most of all, you will discover people and open yourself to the richness of new relationships.

The downside to becoming a novice is, well, being a novice. You may feel uncomfortable and out-of-place at first. Don't get discouraged by this: Your discomfort is evidence that you are venturing into new territory, working those brain cells. If it isn't fun right away, that doesn't mean it won't be fun. Just as we need to listen to a song a few times to pick up the tune, dating a few times helps us get into it. Meanwhile, here are some tips for negotiating as a novice:

1. Read the rest of this book. You will get a preview of what you are about to encounter, so it won't all feel so new.

2. Remember what you know. You probably have dated before, even if it's been awhile. You have much better social skills than you did when you were 16. You have probably accumulated some sexual experience. And, as we discussed in Chapter 1, you feel more comfortable in the world.

3. Find other novices. Get connected with other people in your situation and share tips, support, and stories. If you can't find a support group, start one!

4. Appreciate what you are learning. Notice the ways in which your world is becoming larger.

5. Give yourself room to make mistakes. Mistakes are shortcuts to learning, and if they are really stupid mistakes, they make great material for entertaining friends.

6. Enjoy the adventure! Explorers are always novices.

From the Mouths of Baby Boomers

"I have more experience on life with a 'cheating, lying spouse,' than on life after divorce. It took me two years to actually go through with my divorce. I kept giving the sap more chances to *change* and *prove himself*, and discovered the old saying is very true, a leopard does not change his spots. So, after two-and-a-half years of walking around with my head down and my spirit broken, I let go and let new people into my life. Things are looking up. My sun is shining again."

—Class of '77

"The first day I led a 'coming out' group for lesbians, I thought I was in the wrong room. Everybody looked like everybody else. I was astounded by the variety of women. I particularly remember a woman in her late '60s. She fell in love with her best friend after both of their husbands had died. She was a bit unnerved by it. It was so touching to see the intergenerational reaching out, the younger women mentoring her and vice versa."

—Class of '63

chapter 4

Deciding for Yourself

I decided to start anew—to strip away what I had been taught, to accept as true my own thinking. This was one of the best times of my life. There was no one around to look at what I was doing, no one interested, no one to say anything about it one way or another.
—Georgia O'Keefe

As you approach dating again, you are embarking on a whole new phase of life. What's exciting is that you get to decide how you want it to go! You can write the title and cast yourself as any character you want. You even get to audition the supporting cast.

Rediscovering You

So here you are, alone (for now). Take this time as a gift, because you could be in a new relationship before you know it! Here is your opportunity to check in with yourself, to think about what you want to happen and who you want to be.

You have always been the star in the drama of your life, but you may not have always felt like the director. Remember *I'm OK, You're OK*? This pop psychology book, written by

Dr. Thomas Harris, hit the shelves in 1967—the same year hippies were rushing to Haight-Ashbury for the "Summer of Love." The book became "one of the most extraordinary self-help bestsellers of all time" (Ingram Books), with over 15 million copies in print. Harris popularized an approach called Transactional Analysis (TA), founded by Eric Berne, which described the way we become entrapped by scripts.

When we were little, our parents attended to certain attributes of ours more than others. We each started playing out a script. Maybe you were the cute one, or the comic, or "so smart." Siblings may have reinforced your role, and you found you got "strokes" by keeping with the assigned script. Let's say your role was caretaker. Your script involved tuning in to what other people needed, providing looks of concern and physical care, and acting like an adult before your time.

As you grew, you became more proficient in your script and found supporting characters who needed you and allowed you to enact your role. You may have even found a career in the helping professions. (Oops, this sounds familiar!) At each stage of your life, other people—your boss, your partner—contributed to the direction of your script, and your income and identity may have kept you stuck in an unwanted role. According to Harris, such scripts have power over us to the extent that we maintain the belief that others are "Okay," but we are not.

> "My one regret in life is that I am not someone else."
> —Woody Allen

The positive side of working a single script is that we get good at it. We can derive a great deal of self-esteem from being a good helper, an entertaining comic, an intellectual, and so on. And your script does capture a *part* of who you are. The problem is, the script limits you, and it may not actually represent who you really feel yourself to be. Remember, the script was initially assigned.

When something happens that doesn't fit with your assigned script, you give it less credence. For example, if your script says that you are unattractive, you may not notice that person who is flirting with you, even if he or she is coming on strong.

From the Mouths of Baby Boomers

"I had made concert choir, and was nervous about proving myself. I was going over the music in a practice room late at night. The president of the concert choir, who happened to be the hottest guy on campus, knocks on the door. He comes in, says, 'Whatcha doin'?' I can't look at him. He puts his arm around me, tinkers on the high keys, and says, 'maybe you need a little help.' I can see my body language—I'm practically doubled over. I couldn't even respond. What I was thinking is that he must be checking on me to see if I'm learning my music. It never even occurred to me that he was hitting on me.

I think of how my life went after that. I could have responded to him, believed he was attracted to me. Who knows—I might have married him. I remember when he got engaged to someone else, and the huge diamond on her finger. Instead, I married a guy who told me I was worthless. I guess that's what I expected to hear."

—Class of '72

Whether you chose to be single at this time of your life or not, the reality of your single status has probably already altered your script. Use this complication as an opportunity to take over the direction of your own drama. For many of us, it takes a long time to realize that we actually get to decide who we want to be. I remember the day it occurred to me that I didn't have to practice as a therapist anymore. I could choose something completely different. It was up to me. Wow.

> *"They always say time changes things, but you actually have to change them yourself."*
> —Andy Warhol

So let your mind go. How would you like your life to be? Where do you want to live? How do you want to spend your time? There are no limitations in fantasy, so take it as far as you want. Think about what you value the most, as well as what you would like to eliminate. If you haven't done so already, this may be a good time to clean out closets and storage areas and decide what to keep and what to throw. Doing so gives you a concrete way of deciding what you value and what no longer fits. Take this sorting attitude into your life. Reevaluate everything: "Do I like this? Why do I still have this around? Is that working anymore?

What if I tried this?" Don't worry about practicalities for now, just identify what you like and don't like, and free yourself to consider new realities. You are the director. You get to decide.

Let's play with some different roles for your character in the next chapter of your life:

- This time, I get to sow my wild oats. I pick up a leather bomber jacket and try my hand at aviation. After a tough day of negotiating stormy skies, I hit the bar and down a shot of tequila. The men/women are all over me, and I get to pick who I take home.

- I find serenity. I get a smaller, simpler home, plant a little garden. I sit outside with my easel or writing pad, breath the fresh air, and indulge my freedom to express myself. I make friends with other recycled hippies, and we share poetry and music at the local coffee shop.

- I go for it. After holding back my ambition, I decide to start taking some risks. I invest in the business I've harbored in my mind for years. Instead of just thinking, I act. I get the information I need, hire a lawyer to set things up. Before long, I'm on the phone with contacts in New York and Paris, I'm making important decisions, I'm making things happen.

Do any of these spark something in you? Write your own scenario, and make it as extreme and dramatic as you want. It's your script—have fun with it!

Time Out or Time to Date?

The advice to "take time off" has become so common, we don't think much about it anymore. Yet, the decision whether to take a break before starting to date is a complicated one. For example, even though you were married for years, you may have felt very alone and disconnected from your mate. You may feel like you've already taken considerable time off. For you, taking a break may feel like further punishment, not a gift. On the other hand, if your life and identity has felt very tied-in with your relationship, you may need a stretch of time to disentangle and sort out who you are. Here are some questions to ask yourself as you decide how much time you need:

1. Do you *want* to date? This is the key question. Sometimes the need to date right away comes out of fear. We may fear we won't find anyone, or fear being alone, or fear getting in touch with what we are feeling. Fear puts pressure on us, and can cause us to make poor choices. Fear is also not very attractive. On the other hand, if your choice to date comes out of *desire*, you will look and feel ready. You still may be a little nervous, but dating is about dating, not avoiding something else.

2. How much do I know about how I got to this place? Of the few things I remember from high school, I'll never forget hearing the words of George Santayana: "Those who cannot remember the past are condemned to repeat it." This statement applies to relationships as well as it does to war. (Sometimes the two are not that far apart!) You may have already gained a great deal of insight into why you chose who you did and what happened in the relationship. Maybe you have been through individual or couples therapy. In fact, the ending of your relationship may be a *result* of insights you have come to and changes you have made. If so, you are less likely to repeat history in your new relationship. On the other hand, if you know it didn't work, but don't know why, give yourself some time. Talk it through with a therapist, get some input from a support group or from friends who have observed your relationship. It is easy to focus on your partner's role, but it is crucial to understand your own steps in the tango.

3. Do I know who I am? You don't have to know the whole story, but it helps to know what you want and what you don't want (see "Rediscovering You"). If your identity was derived largely from your relationship, you may feel out of touch with who you are and what you want. If you date too soon, you could relinquish your identity again (see question 2).

Getting to "I Would Date Me!"

The really great thing about tuning into your own story is that you start to get really jazzed about yourself. I remember writing an autobiography as a part of my therapy process. Before writing it, I thought my life (and I) had been rather boring, even depressing. By the time I completed it, I fell head-over-heels in love with myself! I found the thread of the real me that wove through my life, and saw how I was evolving and how far I'd come and that I didn't want to be anyone but me. This is your chance to tune into your lifeline. As you explore your desires for the next phase of your life, you will recognize signs of those desires that have been there all along.

If there is only one thing you do to prepare for dating, learn to love yourself. This does not mean seeing yourself as perfect. Loving yourself means loving the unique way you are put together, including—and maybe *especially*—your quirks and vulnerabilities. When you accept and love yourself, the world is compelled to love you, too.

chapter 5

Dating Fears

*Life is what happens to you while you're busy
making other plans.*
—*John Lennon*

As we get closer to the reality of dating, we are likely to encounter some fears, which often come in the form of "what
if?" questions. What if I don't find anyone? What if I do find
someone? What if I get rejected? Chapter 8 addresses the
worry that there aren't any good ones left, and Part 2 is
devoted to helping you find people. Let's look at some other
common fears about dating:

Dating Fears, Then and Now

Then	Now
Parents ask where you've been	Kids ask where you've been
Hair looks bad	Enough hair to look at?
Boobs not big enough	Boobs not high enough
Enough money for a date	Date wants your money
Zits	Wrinkles

Then	Now
Meeting his/her parents	Meeting his/her kids
Ashamed family has money	Ashamed of credit card debt
Pregnancy	No more babies

I'll Get Hurt Again

If you've recently been cheated or mistreated, you may fear being hurt again. It is natural to feel cautious and self-protective. Problem is, acting out of this fear can actually keep you in the hurt position. For example, you might avoid engaging in a relationship. The logic here is, "I could end up alone again, so I'll just stay alone." You create the outcome you fear—you just skip right to the end. Or else you date, but are constantly on the watch for signs of rejection or betrayal. You see your date talking to someone else and imagine betrayal; your date has plans one weekend and you imagine rejection. Here again, you have created in your mind the scenario you fear. So how do you deal with this fear without sabotaging your love life?

"Owner of a lonely heart much better than the owner of a broken heart..."

Look at what you haven't lost. If a hurtful relationship has become your focus, you may have lost sight of people who have stayed true, treated you well, and still love you no matter what. Scan your life and you may be surprised to recall how many people you have been able to count on. You also may be taking for granted friends, family, and associates who are there for you right now. *These* are the people to look to as examples of what to expect in new relationships. Surround yourself with these people and let them remind you of what is continuous in life. You may even be moved to look up your old glee club pal or fellow flower child. At times of change, there's nothing more reassuring than an old friend.

Acknowledge the possibility of being hurt. You take power away from your fear when you say, "Yes, I could get hurt again." I know you don't want to go there, but let's say it happens. What are you afraid of? What you really might fear is that you can't *tolerate* being hurt again, that another hurt would do you in. At the bottom of every fear is concern about your ability to cope. The good new is, getting to the other side of this hurt can actually leave you stronger and less fearful. When you've encountered your worst fear—let's say you found your partner in bed with someone else—it is very empowering to discover that you can not only survive, but thrive, afterwards.

From the Mouths of Baby Boomers

Before: "Fear of rejection was large for me in high school. I remember several attractive girls routinely sitting on my lap in study hall (one of which was particularly well endowed and positioned them in such a way as to render me completely helpless and confused) and the same girls blocking my path in the hallway. Still, while I thought there might be a chance that they would go out with me, the possibility that they wouldn't was usually too much of a barrier to make the call. The call was a borderline terrifying prospect and I remember my heart racing like I was about to wrestle a grizzly bear."

After: "I was substantially more confident the second time around. I moved in on Jamie pretty quickly. I asked her out shortly after she started work here. I even unloaded my previous marital problems on her on the first date. I figured that if she was still interested after that there was potential. After our first date, I found out she had another acquaintance of mine pursuing her. He was a jock type who kind of acted like he was God's gift to women. He had been bragging that he hadn't found anyone in the area that could beat him at racquetball. I, as fate would have it, beat him (note my humility here). I later asked her about my competition. She assured me I didn't have any.

—Class of '74

Live in the present. Fear is based in the past and oriented toward the future. It has little to do with the present. Living in fear can actually keep us from seeing what is happening now. The solution to fear is to acknowledge our lack of control over the future and wake up to what is happening now. If you don't like what's happening in a relationship, talk it over, address it, change it. If it's good, enjoy! Since nothing is guaranteed, all we have is what is now. And the good news is, the better you deal with the now, the better chance you have of securing a happy future.

I'll Feel Out of Place

Maybe it's just the idea of dating that sends chills of terror down your spine. We all know what it's like to feel out of place. It's scary. You may be asking yourself, "What if I have no one to talk to? What if I look stupid? What if I'm dressed wrong?" Chapter 9 will help you get ready, but here are some other things to keep in mind:

- You are not alone. At the time of the 2000 U.S. Census, 82 million men and women in the United States were unmarried.

- Almost half of all U.S. households were headed by unmarried individuals, and about 40 percent of the workforce was unmarried. Nearly 20 million of you were divorced, 13.6 million were widowed, and more than 48 million had never married. Believe me, you are not alone.

- Keep in mind that there are millions of you out there, and they may be feeling out of place, too. Maybe you can even think of the world as "your place." After all, the married ones are probably at home, and the younger ones are in their own world. And, when you're a Boomer, there is always comfort in numbers.

- Start where you're comfortable. If you don't feel comfortable in bars, don't go there. As you will find in Part 2, there are many places to meet people. The best places are the places you like to go anyway.

- Transform your fear into excitement. When I took public speaking in college, I learned that my anxiety could be an asset. It got my adrenaline flowing, and when I thought of it as excitement, it gave me the energy I needed to deliver a dynamic speech. You also learn in speech class that people do not notice your anxiety as much as you think. And, for most people, dating isn't as scary as speaking in front of an audience. So try thinking of your fear as excitement. Let it sharpen your senses and enliven your attitude. You might be surprised at how well you do.

I'll Get a Disease

When you dated as a teenager, your concerns for your health may not have extended any further than the possibility of catching a cold. Today, as you are inundated with warnings about AIDS and other sexually transmitted diseases (STDs), dating can feel as risky as a swim in the Amazon. If you have been in a monogamous relationship for most of your adult life, these concerns can feel foreign and unmanageable. Here are some ways to alleviate your concerns:

- Get accurate information. There are many myths out there about STDs, especially AIDS. We keep learning more, and the medical community is working hard on developing vaccines and treatments. Talk to your doctor about what the real risks are, and what you can do to prevent them. If you're not up for abstinence, usually your advice will come down to one word: condom.

- Talk first. Having to talk about it may actually be one of your fears. It may help to remember that STDs are a concern everyone is familiar with, and your date is likely to expect (and have) questions. A good rule of thumb is that if you're not ready to talk, you may not be feeling comfortable with each other yet. Give yourself time to feel assured that it truly will be good for you both.

- Carry condoms. Whether you're a man or a woman, don't leave home without them. There's no greater letdown than being in the heat of passion and finding you have no protection. Actually, there is a greater letdown: continuing anyway and later finding you have an STD.

- Keep your sense of humor. Disease is a heavy subject. It may help to relieve anxiety to just acknowledge your discomfort. Joke about the challenge of being seductive while checking out each other's diseases. The more real you are, the more it will put you both at ease.

I'll Fall in Love

This may seem like an odd subheading to the topic of fears. Yet, falling in love can be scary. Why do you think we use the word "falling"? You may fear losing hold of who you are, being vulnerable, and risking a broken heart.

"Do you want me to tell you something really subversive?

Love is everything it's cracked up to be.
That's why people are so cynical about it.
It really is worth fighting for,
Being brave for,
Risking everything for.

And the trouble is,
If you don't risk anything,
You risk even more."

—Erica Jong

Beyond these concerns, however, is the fear of getting what you want. If this seems odd, take a moment to imagine having the love you want. For many of us, having what we want means brushing off that chip of resentment, relinquishing anger, giving up the power in being a victim. No wonder we avoid success! To the extent that we have learned to wield power through suffering, a good relationship can feel like a threat.

If a loving relationship is a threat to suffering, bring it on! Risk being happy. See what it feels like to have nothing to complain about. Entertain the revolutionary notion that there doesn't have to be a downside to love.

chapter 6

What About the Kids?

Being forced to seek balance within ourselves, we can make our unsteady, stumbling days feel less and less like disaster and more and more like a joyful dance—the dance of a wildly, wonderfully, perfectly unbalanced life.

—Martha Beck, author and life coach

When you have children, dating is not as simple as looking for what you want. You may feel like two people at once: a single person interested in dating, and a protective parent looking out for the kids. And the two of you may often feel in conflict.

Using Kids as an Excuse

When you're a parent and you've ended a relationship, you know you aren't the only one that has been through a lot. Whether your children are young or on their own, their world has changed. So how can you put them through the emotions of watching you date?

Taking things at a pace that allows ourselves and our children to grieve and adjust is important. However, kids can also become an excuse to avoid dating. Sometimes it is easy to stay preoccupied with our responsibility for others and overlook our responsibility for ourselves.

Ironically, parental protectiveness has become a Boomer priority. After all, we have first-hand knowledge of the kind of trouble kids can get into!

In February of 2002, Sociologist Elaine Bell Kaplan published the results of her interviews with a group of middle and upper class Boomer parents. Her findings came out in a CBS News report, which indicated that many of the parents "said they neither respected nor understood the current teen culture, particularly hip-hop and its often violent lyrics, and believed the world was much safer in the 1960's." These parents were found to be very conservative regarding drugs and sexual activity. Have we become our parents?!

I was impressed when a friend of mine shared with me what she said to her kids about her divorce. She told them, "This is *not* the best for you. I'm doing this because it is best for me." On the face of it, this may seem like a selfish statement. Yet, it freed up her children to have their own reality, separate from hers. They could be mad or sad. It also freed her children from the burden of feeling responsible for their mother's happiness. Their mother was taking care of herself. Finally, her acknowledgment made her more available to help them with what they were experiencing. They were not required to smile and pretend this was "best."

When our attempts to do what is best for our children come at the expense of our own self-care, it hurts the kids, too. There is no greater burden a child can bear than to think that he or she was capable of destroying Mom or Dad. If you as a parent become depressed and lonely, you are less and less available for your children. And remember, we are showing our children what they can expect from life. When we take responsibility for our own happiness, we give them permission to do so as well.

Staying a Parent

When the other parent isn't around, children will often try to fill the void. This can even feel good for kids. They feel important in a new way: Mom or Dad needs me more. They can even feel a kind of triumph in knowing they are preferred to the other parent and may compete to be the better caretaker, the better partner. Even if that is what they seem to want, it is not what they need.

While dating can be hard on kids, it actually maintains a boundary between adult relationships and parent-child relationships. Adults' needs get channeled into dating, and kids get to keep their roles as kids.

But when you're dating, you may not feel like an adult, much less a parent. You'll be spending more time in the bathroom, checking your face and hair, in dreamland reviewing your last date, on the phone making plans and, of course, off on dates. Sounds like adolescence? Well, get ready.

Allowing ourselves to indulge in the experience of dating while being responsible as parents is a tricky balancing act. At times, you will feel resentful that parenting restricts your freedom. At times, you will be ridden with guilt over being a rotten parent. Often, you will feel like you can't win. You may ask yourself why you're doing this. Here's why: It's what a good parent does. You are not giving up yourself for your kids, and you are not giving up your kids for yourself. You are keeping everyone in the room. Maybe your life will feel more chaotic when you're all there, but it will also be much richer.

Helping Kids Adapt

Talk to them. When I was training to be a therapist, my colleagues and I were often humbled by this advice from our supervisors: "Ask the client!" Somehow, we felt we were supposed to magically know what our clients were feeling and what they needed from us. The thought to ask the client did not even occur to us.

As parents, we often make the same mistake. We assume what our kids are feeling, assume what they need, all without consultation with the source. Ask your children how they feel about you dating. Remember that you are not asking them for *permission*, rather you just want to know what it's like for them.

You may have noticed that formal, sit-down conversations are not real attractive to kids, especially boys. Kids who resist talking on de-mand will often naturally open up while involved in a mutual activity.

So instead of announcing that you want to "talk," try coloring together or going for a walk.

Even if your kids don't talk to you, you can keep them posted about what is happening and the changes they might expect. How much you share with your kids will naturally vary depending on their ages. For kids at home, being able to predict changes in their day-to-day life will help them feel more in control and less anxious. The more lead time you can give them regarding your plans (and who will care for them), the less likely they will feel abandoned in favor of your date.

The main thing that distinguishes parent from child is that the parent is the one "looking out" for the child. Being present enough to know where our children are and what they are experiencing provides them a sense that we are always there. The more our children feel this overseeing function, the less they have to look out for us, and the freer they can be to just be kids.

How Your Children May be Reacting to Your Dating

Age	Task	Reaction	Tips
0–7	Trust	I'm being replaced.	Talk through play, reassure.
8–12	Competence	I'm not good enough.	Clarify your need for adult friends and reinforce what your child does well.
13–18	Identity	This is weird.	Maintain structure. Don't compare dating stories!
Adult	Adjustment	Home ain't home.	Preview changes. Maintain holiday rituals to provide continuity.

Let them feel. This isn't always easy. Sitting with your child as he cries can be very trying. Being the object of her anger isn't fun either. Yet, the more we are able to tolerate the range of our children's feelings, the easier it will be for them to release those feelings and move on. Premature "cheering-up" can actually interfere with the resolution of feelings. I hate every minute of it, but when I have the strength to wait out my kids' emotional meltdowns, I find they often begin to cheer themselves up. Having had the opportunity to wail about everything that is bad about the situation, they are then freed up to look at the situation from other perspectives.

There is a difference between understanding feelings and being manipulated by them. If you agree to stay home because your child is crying, or begin to allow abusive behavior from your angry teenager, you put your child in control and relinquish your responsibility as a parent. While we might be afraid that our kids can't tolerate their feelings without having them indulged, it may be just the opposite. Feelings are most threatening when they have the power to destroy.

From the Mouth of a Babe (of a Boomer)

"Suddenly, the high pitched ring of his mother's cell phone made Rob snap out of his fog. This was the most irritating sound in the world to him. And guess who it was? Of course, her damned new boyfriend. She was always gabbing to him on that annoying piece of plastic. And every time, it was a pretentious sting in the back of Rob's mind, reminding him of the divorce. He felt jealous of his mother, sorry for his dad, and hate for himself. He began to blame himself. Rob and his mother used to be so close. He yearned for the days before the divorce.

'Were they so great, Rob?' his mother suddenly asked. He thought of the loud arguments and tears.

The conversation began to take a new turn, and the mother he used to see in despair pulled Rob out his despair. When they got home, Rob walked to the piano, rested his fingertips across the pattern of white and black ivory, and began to play. He suddenly felt unafraid, not full of regret. He was free in the music, creating beauty.

His mom came down and smiled at him. Rob just smiled back. He continued playing."

—Class of 2005

Make time for shared pleasures. If you haven't done so already, now might be a great time to schedule a regular outing with your child. If you have more than one child, try to free up time to be alone with each of them. As Anne Morrow Lindbergh writes in *Gifts from the Sea*, "We all wish to be loved alone." A child needs to feel a special love from you that can't be replaced by anyone else. One-on-one time away from all the distractions of home is a gift to both of you. When it's just you two, a different kind of intimacy develops, and that goes a long way to helping the relationship feel solid and secure in the face of change.

7

"I Hate Dating Games"

Every game ... is basically dishonest.
—Eric Berne, M.D., from his 1964 bestseller,
Games People Play.

Oh, the games we used to play. In junior high, we played the Message Game. Messages got passed around—"Do you like her?" "He likes you." Friends acted as scouts, and relationships began without the need to speak.

As you began to feel safe enough to talk to people you "liked," new games were at your disposal. The best known of these is Hard To Get. In her movie roles, Doris Day was a master of this technique (of course, we now know that she never really had a shot at Rock Hudson!). The idea behind Hard to Get is to disguise your attraction as indifference, to distance yourself as a way of increasing the other's desire. If you are hard to get, after all, you must be more valuable. It's the supply-and-demand theory applied to dating.

Then there's the Jealousy Game. Here again, you disguise your desire. But this time, you transfer your affections to someone you are not really interested in. The hope is that the person you are really interested in will get jealous and want you more.

If you are playing the Hard to Get or Jealousy Games, you will be a perfect target for Chase and Conquer, which involves being pursued relentlessly until you respond, only to be dumped for a more challenging target. The Chase player works hard for the goal, but never fully indulges in the payoff.

A subtle but familiar game that doesn't end with dating is the game of Mind Reading. In Mind Reading, you harbor a wish, but don't express it. At the same time, you expect your date to fulfill the wish, and are likely to become angry if he or she doesn't. What can be especially tricky about Mind Reading is that you may consciously work against your wish, saying, "no, no, I don't want a birthday present," and later become furious that your wish for a gift was not responded to.

Notice the irony here? Except for the Message Game, dating games require you to act exactly opposite of what you're feeling. Now, multiply this deception by two (or more)—maybe your boyfriend is using *you* in the Jealousy Game—and the dating world becomes a house of mirrors. No wonder you're reluctant to get back into it.

> "... *You may know more about vintage wine than the wine steward, but if you are smart, you'll let your man do the choosing and be ecstatic over his selection, even if it tastes like shampoo.*"
>
> —*From* Always Ask a Man, A. Dahl, 1965

The Good News About Dating as a Grown-Up

Take heart—you aren't the only one who hates dating games. Your Boomer peers are fed up, too. Like them, you have learned to be more straightforward, and get to the point. You know that life is short and games take time.

Yet, even the most evolved Boomers run into situations where a dating game seems useful. Just as you have reevaluated other habits, now is a good time to sort out what is salvageable about dating games and what you have no use for. Let's take a look.

The Message Game

This is a game more in the sense of a fun activity, and there is much to be said for it. Getting advance information on someone's feelings for you, and vice versa, protects the ego as matches are made. I include the Message Game here because communication occurs indirectly and, if overused, the game can become a substitute for direct communication. (I remember being asked out via my girlfriend!) When this happens, facing your date can actually become more difficult and awkward.

If the Message Game worked well for you, a dating service may provide you similar advantages. The service does the "who likes who" research by matching profiles, and you can be assured that your date is looking for someone like you. Just as you would be reluctant to send a friend you didn't trust to gather information on your desired date's feelings, you want to feel in good hands with your dating service. Check out Chapter 19 for help.

If you hated message-passing and who-likes-who intrigue, you can choose to bypass the game and find out for yourself. You'll save time, avoid the distortion that can happen as messages are passed, and may just turn on your potential date with your boldness. After all, you're no longer confined to a school environment where messages fly whether you like it or not.

From the Mouths of Baby Boomers

"One time a girl called me and asked me if I liked this other girl. I said I kind of liked *her* (the caller). Turns out, the other girl was on the line. I didn't get to go out with either of them!"

—Class of '76

"I notice these control games. What is it with some guys—does a man feel 'whipped' if he gives a woman what she wants? For example, he knows I like to have Diet Coke around, but he never buys it. Then he makes jokes about it. Somehow, he can't see it or frame it as being loving—if he does what I say, then he's whipped. It's especially bad if they have controlling mothers!"

—Class of '69

"She calls me all the time, wants me to come up. When I do, she turns around and ignores me. If we're at a party, she goes and talks to someone else. It's as if she can feel she's worth a lot by watching me coming after her."

—Class of '72

Hard To Get

The Hard To Get game is a lot of work because it requires you to act in opposition to your own feelings. You are probably busy enough to want to avoid this extra effort. And, if you've been making headway toward that thing we call authenticity, playing a game may feel like a setback.

But what do you do when you start to feel devalued or neglected by the person you're after? Or if your date is acting too cocky or in control of the relationship? We'll discuss this more in Chapter 32, but for now, let's extract what is good about the Hard To Get game—the part about *valuing yourself*. Thankfully, you don't have to disguise your feelings to pull this off.

Valuing yourself means seeing your time and company as valuable and worthy of good treatment. Valuing yourself means carrying an attitude that "I am good for you," and expecting that others want to be around you. Now maybe you don't always feel this way, so if you have to do some acting, here's a good place to start. Acting *as if* you are valuable begins to instill that belief in you—others are prompted to treat you well, you feel more valued, and so on.

Carrying yourself with a sense of value is different than playing Hard To Get because you remain free to express your desires. Instead of gaining power by denying what you want, you express your power by asserting what you want. You can say "I want to be with you" in a way that communicates "aren't you lucky?" And when you think of it, who isn't lucky to be the recipient of desire?

The Jealousy Game

This game is related to Hard To Get, in that you are trying to increase your value in someone else's eyes. Think about why you might want to make your date jealous. You probably want to keep him or her from feeling too comfortable in the relationship; to remind your date that you could make another choice.

The awareness that you could make another choice can be a benefit. It is a way to avoid settling for treatment you dislike or a relationship that doesn't excite you. Being aware of the options can help you notice what behaviors you like and don't like. This can be helpful information for the relationship you're in, or possibly a clue that you want to get out.

What distinguishes this attitude from a game is that you are focusing on your desires, rather than on an attempt to manipulate your partner.

Chase and Conquer

Although this game is most associated with men, any of us who have witnessed a Beatle's concert know that women can play, too. The fun of the chase game is in the pursuit itself. Whether we are screaming for a blown kiss at a concert or going after someone who seems inaccessible, part of the allure is in the challenge. This game matches up well with "hard to get." The tougher the resistance, the stronger the pursuit. Yet, when the conquest is made and the date begins responding, the satisfaction gives way to the desire for a new challenge. A new chase begins.

While the chase *can* be thrilling, it is a very one-sided thrill. If we go from one chase to another, we exercise our power to attract someone, but don't allow ourselves to *have* someone. And we don't allow ourselves to take in the desire of another. In a way, we keep ourselves hungry without allowing ourselves to be fed. While we act confident, we don't acknowledge our fear of truly having what we desire.

Yet, the willingness to go after what we want is an asset as we date. We've all heard stories about how persistence paid off: The "you want to date me" attitude of the chaser eventually sunk in, the reluctant party went out with the pursuer, and was conquered—for good! If we can allow ourselves to go after the relationships we desire—and enjoy them, too, chase can be even more fun.

Mind Reading

The wish to have your mind read is tied to the desire to be taken care of. There's actually nothing wrong with this desire. The only problem with the Mind Reading game is that it so often fails. The part of the Mind Reading game we can pay attention to is our wishes. What is it you are hoping he or she will do for you? If you're expecting to be disappointed about something, what wish is behind that feeling?

If we can read our own minds, make our own wishes conscious and then start to communicate them more directly, we are much more likely to get what we're hoping for. A friend of mind shared a great way to help her partner select gifts for her: "I just go around to a bunch of stores, pick out what I like, leave the information at the sales counter, and tell him the stores to visit. Last time I did that, he got everything I had selected!"

Honesty Is an Aphrodisiac

The need to play games comes out of a fear of honesty and its implications. We make all kinds of contortions to work *around* the truth. Throwing out a line somehow feels safer than honestly sharing, "I'd like to get to know you." Yet lines and games are often transparent. Telling the truth can be not only refreshing, but sexy. And being honest reveals confidence. Even when you admit feeling awkward, you are more likely to come off as charming than foolish. You also give permission for your partner to be real.

When we recite lines or play old games, we are hiding. If you want someone to like you, *reveal* yourself. The more you are able to use your own voice, the more life and energy will come through. Notice how you respond to the person in the room who cuts through the b.s.—I usually wish I were the one who had spoken up! Truth is a great turn-on. Practice saying it like it is. Admit what sucks. Start by being more truthful with yourself, and more open with your friends.

We all have to identify our own style of engaging with others. If a game works for you, it might just fit your way of flirting. If coy and seductive is your ace in the hole (no pun intended), then use it! Just know that you have options—and the choice it yours.

Friendship First

My best romance was one that started out as a friendship. In fact, my friend was dating someone else when we met. After kissing his date goodbye, he would come over to my dorm room and we would sit up and talk philosophy, religion, or whatever was on our minds. Although we were attracted to each other, there was no pressure and we could be real together. It was a year before we started dating, and by that time we had developed both an attachment and a backlog of sexual tension. The first kiss was amazing …. I digress. My point is: One way to avoid dating games altogether is to start as friends.

Imagine yourself looking for a friend to hang out with rather than a lover to date. Doesn't that feel different? With a "date" you think of dressing up and inventing clever conversation—and playing games. With a friend, you can let down your hair, have fun, and be real. Just this subtle shift in attitude can be a great asset as you meet people. Beyond that, there is no better basis for a relationship than a true friendship.

> "In the sweetness of friendship let there be laughter, and sharing of pleasures. For in the dew of little things the heart finds its morning and is refreshed."
>
> —*Kahlil Gibran*

chapter 8

"All the Good Ones Are Taken"

Never marry a man before he's had at least one midlife crisis. Never get married again unless you've had at least one of your own.
—*from* Boomer Babes *by Linda Stasi and Rosemary Rogers*

If you're worried that all the good ones are taken, look in the mirror. I hope you believe you're a good one! This book wouldn't have gotten published if we didn't know there are a lot of you out there. Fortunately for you, almost half of adults heading households are now sharing your single status (see Chapter 5).

The idea that the "good ones" have been taken assumes that good ones attract the right person early on, get hitched, and stay committed—and off the market. While this assumption has some logic to it—and there are many good ones in committed relationships—it only goes so far. Healthy people change and grow, and if a partnership is truly good, that evolves, too. Not all good ones are lucky enough to find that kind of relationship the first time. Some good ones find the right relationship, but become single through the death of a partner. And many of us have become good ones—or *better* ones—through the process of making changes in our relationship status. Think of the benefit of hooking up with someone who has already been through therapy!

When we think that the good ones are taken, we forget about this key element called *change*. As we discover at any class reunion, some people we thought were hot back then become bores, some geeks become Microsoft millionaires, and some people we barely noticed have come to life. We now have the benefit of history, and can observe how our Boomer prospects have evolved over time. Because midlife is a time where we really come into our own, you might do even better than finding a good one—you could find the *best* one.

Nipping Hopelessness in the Bud

As much as we try to convince ourselves that there are good ones out there, we may feel hopeless. The prospect of finding someone new might feel overwhelming and futile. Often, these feeling are temporary and vacillate with feelings of excitement and hope. But when negative feelings persist, they need to be attended to. Hopelessness is a primary sign of depression, especially when coupled with other symptoms, such as loss of pleasure, feelings of guilt, physical signs—such as changes in eating, sleeping, energy, and thoughts of suicide. Talk to your doctor or therapist about what you're experiencing, and get some help. Antidepressants and psychotherapy—together or alone, have been consistently found to be effective in the treatment of depression.

Even if you are not depressed, it is natural to wrestle with your sense of hope. Some days just feel bleak, and the prospect of anything good happening seems nonexistent. At times like this, it is helpful to remember that your vision is limited, that there is blue sky beyond the clouds, and there are more possibilities than your mind can comprehend. Your feelings are temporarily ruling your sense of reality, and just knowing that can help. In the meantime, here are some tips for dealing with the occasional crisis of hope:

Be Good to Yourself

Have you ever noticed the tendency to rub salt into your own wounds? Here you are, feeling bad already, and then you turn on yourself with questions, accusations, and blame. When the world feels unfriendly, it makes a big difference whether you choose to turn against yourself or stay on your own side.

Staying on your own side isn't always easy. Start by noticing what you say to yourself when you're feeling low. You may be surprised at how harsh you can be with yourself. Then practice interrupting the running critique with a deep breath and statements of self-love. Learn to soothe your hurts rather than salt them.

Go Easy on Yourself

Acknowledge that you are handling some scary changes. Concentrate on the basics for now: eat good food, seek comfort, get rest. Look to people who carry a hopeful vision for your future, and borrow their perspective for awhile. Know that the bad feelings will pass.

Misery Loves Rodney

Through the years, Rodney Dangerfield has been there to make us feel better by letting us know he has it worse. Here's some of what he's said about life, marriage, and sex:

"My wife and I were happy for twenty years. Then we met."

"I'm at the age where food has taken the place of sex in my life. In fact, I've just had a mirror put over my kitchen table."

"We sleep in separate rooms, we have dinner apart, we take separate vacations— we're doing everything we can to keep our marriage together."

"If it weren't for pickpockets, I'd have no sex life at all."

"Life is just a bowl of pits."

Revive Your Desire

Scratch the surface of hopelessness, and you'll find desire. Desire turns into hopelessness when we fear we can't have what we want. Hopelessness conveniently closes the gap between desire and fulfillment:

we just conclude we can't have it. Staying with desire and hope means allowing the gap—allowing the tension while desire is unfulfilled. This is a skill that comes with practice, but it's worth nurturing. Because the more we allow desire, the more we attract fulfillment.

So try shifting back from hopelessness to desire. Acknowledge how much you want what you want. Get used to how your desire feels, and stay with it for longer and longer stretches. Desiring is a wonderful habit.

Act Hopeful

It is possible to act out of hope even when you don't feel hope. You are acting out of hope when you don't go running back to the security of the past, when you proceed forward without knowing how it will turn out. If you read any adventure novel, times of despair are a part of the story. Even heroes and heroines feel like giving up—they just don't.

Expand Your Thinking

You may feel hopeless because things aren't going according to your plan. Maybe someone you thought was meant for you just got serious with someone else. Maybe being single right now was not in your plan to start with. Or this process is just taking longer than you planned (doesn't it always?). You had a certain idea about how things were supposed to go, and it hasn't worked out that way. If this is the case, the hopelessness you feel may say more about the limits of your plan than about your potential for fulfillment. Consider that life may have much *more* in store for you than you planned. We have all had situations where a failed plan becomes a blessing because it opens the door to something new and better.

> "To work magic is to weave the unseen forces into form; to soar beyond sight; to explore the uncharted dream realm of the hidden reality."
>
> —Starhawk, Boomer activist and author

Grieve the loss of your plan, and let it go. Transfer your hope onto possibilities greater than what you can imagine.

An Attitude of Abundance

The concerns that the good ones are taken—or, at least, are rapidly being snatched up, comes out of an attitude of scarcity. Scarcity thinking is based on the belief that there is not enough to go around. When motivated by scarcity, we are driven by fear rather than desire. Applied to dating, you may want to go on a date with *anyone*, rather than look around for someone you want to date. You may be inclined to settle, rather than evaluate. You may fear letting go of a relationship that isn't satisfying because, at least you found someone.

On the other hand, an attitude of abundance assumes there is enough to go around, that there is a multitude of options, and that you can afford to take your time and be choosy. If you see someone happy in a relationship, you don't conclude that their success takes away from your chances. Rather, you use their success as evidence that good relationships are available for all of us.

In our culture, there is a myth that we all desire the same things and are competing for the same limited resources. The media promotes this myth of sameness. Commercials ring in our heads, suggesting that everybody wants a Chevy or needs Mr. Clean. Movies and magazines provide prototypes for who is sexy. The reality is, your desires are yours. They cannot be replicated. I am often surprised to find that a guy I'm drooling over is just okay in the eyes of a friend, and vice versa. Consider the possibility that you are not competing with anybody—that your match is as individual as you are.

An attitude of abundance is a great asset to dating. When you're not worried if there is enough, you are free to think about what you really want and to let go when something isn't working. My friend is a perfect example of this attitude. She broke up with a guy she was crazy about, but whose incessant flirting (with other women) didn't stop even after many conversations between them. She then decided, since she was free, she wanted a guy who was kinder, richer, better educated, and better endowed. The next man she met qualified on all counts. Talk about abundance! Practice walking around with this attitude, and note how you carry yourself, how you interact. Looks good, doesn't it?

From the Mouths of Baby Boomers

"There are good men out there. My e-dating experience proved it. I was 41, single, and professionally relocated to a city with a population of about 300,000, so I gave a paid Internet dating service a try. The results were overwhelming. Over the next 11 months, I met or went out with 17 different men: 3 attorneys, 1 gynecologist, 2 college professors, 4 engineers, the owner of a chain of car dealerships and assorted other interesting characters. I remember the professions of most of them; I only remember 4 of their last names (who could forget Mr. Clapp), and have forgotten 5 of their first names even though it was less than 2 years ago. (And we think men are shallow!)

Most were courteous, bright, relatively interesting men looking for serious relationships. My e-adventures only stopped because I became involved in a 15-month relationship with an e-intro. It ended in a marriage proposal I declined. I wasn't in love, and I can afford to expect that."

—Class of '77

chapter 9

"I Can't Go Out Like This!"

Besides the bouffant babies in their stretch pants, furry sweaters and Dick Tracy eyes, there would be the boys in Presley, Big Bopper, Tony Curtis and Chicago boxcar hairdos. No one ever seemed to notice how maniacally serious they were about their hairdos, their flesh-tight pants, puffy sweaters, about the way they walked, idled, ogled or acted cool.
—*Tom Wolfe, from* The Kandy-Kolored Tangerine-Flake Streamline Baby.

Okay, we haven't dated since polyester was hot. So what if it's been a decade or three? Yes, we've gotten out of the habit of "primping" in front of the mirror, and have probably put on a few pounds (ten pounds a decade is the norm, so they say!) We haven't had time to study the fashion magazines since Twiggy was hip, so maybe we're a little behind on current trends.

Let's see what we can do to get ready for dating in the new millennium.

An Honest Inventory

When you ask someone, "Do I look fat?," do you really want the answer? Or are you grasping for a little reassurance? Now is the time to get real with yourself and answer truthfully. Look in the mirror as if you're looking at someone else. What do you see? I know Bob Dylan told us never to trust anyone over thirty, but if you have a close friend that dares to be honest, get input. Some changes require very little adjustment. You may be wearing a color that makes you look dead or a style that makes you look heavy. Is your hair flattering? It's easy to become attached to a look that worked for us back then, but—be honest—is it working today? If you use makeup, how skilled are you at applying it? Not everyone has the inborn surgical skills to draw eyeliner on straight!

Simple Shape-Up Strategies

- Lay out workout clothes and sneakers by your bedside at night. Put them on in the morning or immediately after work. Whether or not you have a workout planned, the uniform will get you moving.
- Keep in mind that the flavor of food is most intense during the first few bites. Practice relishing the initial bites, then quit. It doesn't get any better than that!
- Go through your cupboards and refrigerator and dispose of mediocre food. Practice tossing food that doesn't satisfy you. Then stock up on food that satisfies. You'll need less of it. Learn to be picky.
- Try this: Buy your favorite candy bar next time you are out shopping. Take a nice, satisfying bite, and toss the rest in the nearest trash can. Very empowering!
- Front-load your calories: Eat breakfast, snack midmorning, eat a big lunch, snack midday, eat a small dinner. People who wonder why they aren't losing weight when they don't eat "all day" actually tend to consume most of their calories after 6:00 P.M.

Don't just pick at what isn't working. Notice what is the most attractive about you. Proud of your height? Your long hair? Your biceps? Your eyelashes? Get specific about your assets and think about how you can enhance them.

Taking inventory doesn't necessarily mean you will choose to change your look—you might look great already, just that you're taking the time to honestly see what everyone else is seeing. If you'd like to buff up or slim down, you need to decide whether you're really prepared to change. If not, accepting your body as it is and dressing it well is going to look a lot better on you than wishing for a different one. I remember getting fed up with dieting in college, and giving away all of the too-small clothes waiting expectantly in my closet. The weird thing was, I felt so much better about myself in clothes that fit, I naturally lost weight! (But then again, that was college, when my metabolism—along with my brain at times—was running on high!)

Walk This Way

How we carry ourselves can make the difference in whether we are seen or ignored, and in *how* we are seen. Do you slump and unconsciously hide yourself? When I ventured into modeling in my forties, standing and walking became a new challenge. I realized that I had been moving through life with my head down and my shoulders slumped. Walking tall and looking straight ahead not only felt odd, but downright frightening!

Remember the time when you were proud to walk into a bar, when you felt young and sexy and available? I vaguely remember feeling that way. But there I was, forty-something, in the world, facing forward—and it felt weird. As I adjusted to my new posture, I began to feel more confident, as if I had a right to be in the world. I soon came to enjoy being seen. Just as confidence can affect how we carry ourselves, how we carry ourselves affects confidence. Just walking and sitting *as if* you own the world will help you feel more self-assured. Think of yourself as Stevie Nicks on stage or Elvis strutting his stuff. You still have a helluva lot of sex appeal, I bet. Your attitude is half the equation!

Now that we've looked at you, let's visit your wardrobe.

Stayin' Alive! Updating Your Look

Young people pay attention to fashion and trend, in part because they are conscious of attracting a partner. As we grow and get more settled, we become less concerned about what is hip (to put it mildly!). Yet, being hip communicates a lot more than where we shop. It shows we know what's goin' on, we're living in the world, we're stayin' alive. So, it's time to go shopping again.

Acquire a hip and single twenty-something adult to take you shopping. A teenager might make you look ridiculous, and once an adult gets married, fashion sense can readily decline. Your shopping partner could be your own son or daughter, and boy will they love instructing you for a change! Make sure your consultant is someone who can be honest with you. You don't want to have, as Strother Martin barks out to Paul Newman in *Cool Hand Luke*, "A failure to communicate!" You can go alone, but you might want to read about my experience first (see sidebar).

From the Mouths of Baby Boomers

"I thought it would be easy: One trip to the mall to get an updated pair of jeans. First, they have about 50 choices: boot-cut, tapered, straight leg, flared leg, wide leg, low-rise, at-the-waist, just-below-the-waist, long, regular and ankle length, button-fly (why?), zipper-fly, stone-wash, acid-wash, you get the picture. Then I found that the hip shops now have coed dressing rooms—deep breath. I learned that, to fit in, the secret is to act smug and indifferent, while secretly trying to put out distress signals to a sympathetic clerk. Better yet, take your daughter."

—Class of '79

"After my divorce, I went out dancing. Not to meet a guy, just to have fun. I was thinking, 'when I lose 50 pounds, *then* someone will be attracted to me.' But I connected with a guy that night—I mean *really* connected. He thought I was the most beautiful woman in the world and I was 80 pounds overweight! He told me he loved heavier women, and I realized that a lot of guys do. He gave me my first sense of myself as being beautiful."

—Class of '65

Prepare to enter shops unfamiliar to you. This can be intimidating. When in doubt, just act smug. You may want to just scope things out before making any purchases. Consider it a research trip, and pick up some style magazines—such as *Vanity Fair* or *Esquire*—while you're at it. The point is to get a feel for what is current. In particular, note the leg of the jeans and the style of shoe.

Speaking of the leg of jeans, who ever thought we'd see bell-bottoms again—and hip huggers! Actually, you might find shopping again to be quite a trip—'60s style—as you get that eerie sense that you've been here before. Doesn't it make you feel old to be considered "retro"? But those of us that are packrats may appreciate the opportunity for recycling. Just the other day, my very hip niece was twirling around in my sister's full-length flower-child dress! Check your attic again. Even Candies are back!

Ask your consultant for input on your hairstyle and color, makeup for women, and accessories. If you wear eyeglasses, when was the last time you updated your frames? And male Boomers—haven't you gotten a bit too comfortable with that hairstyle? (If you left off at the mullet, *run*, don't walk to the salon!) An up-to-date cut can make a world of difference. Again, prepare for déjà vu. My teenage godson is wearing a Beatles-style mop-top and does a great impersonation of Mick Jagger. And a recent trip to get my makeup done at a spa gave me a real surprise. The young girl next to me was having false eyelashes put on. Holy 1960's, Catwoman!

On second thought, we may know more about what's hip than we realized! It is rather flattering to know that our generation is setting the tone once again. So, in addition to today's fashion magazines, you may want to pull out your high school yearbook!

Fashion Flashback

Remember…

Short jackets and drainpipe trousers?

The flip?

Winkle pickers?

The pillbox hat?

Mary Quant's "London Look"?

The classic "bob," with hair sweeping to a point at the cheekbone?

Go go or Beatle

Moon boots?

Woven ponchos with fringe?

The baby-doll dress?

The midi and the maxi?

Dolly-bird eyes?

Op (optical) art and pop art fabrics?

Sewing extra denim into your jeans legs to make the "bell" wider?

Fabric, hippie-style purses?

Square-toed lime-green patent-leather pumps with a matching handbag?

Pigtails and long bangs?

Indian-inspired tunics with brocade and embroidery?

Caftans?

Peasant blouses?

    Polyester pantsuits?

    Platform shoes?

Men's screenprint shirts with long, pointed collars, meant to be barely buttoned?

Smocks?

Feathered hair?

Crocheted vests?

Halters?

Macramé chokers?

Afros?

Powder blue leisure suits? (some things are better forgotten)

Getting Your Head Ready

As much as we can do to polish and update how we look on the outside, what's in our heads can make or break the deal. Like it or not, you are selling yourself. In fact, it may be helpful to think of how you'd prepare for a sales presentation.

First of all, you want to know your product inside and out. Think of how you would describe yourself to someone. How would you capture your unique "look?" What personality traits would you emphasize? What books and movies are your favorites? For a helpful exercise, take a piece of paper and quickly jot down words or phrases that describe who you are and what you like. Don't think too much, just write. Try to fill the page. Then read through the list and look for themes. What is your essence? What title would you give to your life story?

Next, you need to know what sets you apart from others. Have you developed a unique area of expertise? What is your professional niche? Do you have a great collection of record singles or beer mugs? Are you well read? Well traveled? Well hung? (sorry, I was free-associating). Are you regarded as wise? What life experience do you bring that is unique? Is there something you can do physically that most people can't (this could come in *very* handy)? Are you a good writer? Musical? Artistic? Funny? Would your talents have better suited *The Ed Sullivan Show* or *Laugh-In*? Are you a compassionate person? A super-achiever? A parent who knows even better than Mr. Anderson in *Father Knows Best*? Just plain smart?

> "*Fashions fade, style is eternal.*"
>
> —*Yves Saint Laurent, from Andy Warhol's Interview*

Finally, think up your pitch. Try to package your best characteristics into a sentence. If you need more material, use the exercise in Appendix A. This is not a time to be humble, yet you need to believe your pitch. You may end up with a phrase such as, "Brilliant architect with a soft spot for animals," simply a word, such as "adventurous," or an all-out brag, such as Muhammad Ali's "I'm the greatest." The pitch is not something you will hand out to your dates—it is for you. Carry it with you to keep you grounded in who you are, in what you love about you.

Now you're ready for a rehearsal.

chapter 10

You *Can* Have a Dress Rehearsal

Drugs and addictions wear many faces,
Helping us run from ourselves to new places,
We use people as booze, causes as crack,
I want to stop, I want myself back.

And I'm letting you
Allowing you to … allowing you to,
Hold me, inspire me
Reignite the fire in me.
Heal me Baby, heal me… heal me.
—From "Heal Me," a dating-again-inspired song, by
Rebecca Aadland-Schoper

Dating again takes initiative and effort, and it may require upsetting a habit or two—like staying home, using the television as your primary source of excitement, or going to bed at the same time every night. In order to fuel this change, you need to warm up to the idea, build up some steam, and get so motivated that nothing will stop you. Let's start the rehearsal.

Seeing It

Remember the days when school was just an interruption to your fantasy life? Although you may have gotten scolded for it back then, daydreaming probably did more to prepare you for life than learning that periodic table. Gazing at your idols in *Flip Magazine*, hanging posters of Fabian or Bobby Sherman, Sandra Dee or Maureen McCormick (a.k.a. Marcia Brady), were ways you began to envision how love felt.

It's time to feed your fantasies again. Don't worry about being practical right now. Imagine the ultimate. Only you can define what is "ultimate" for you. Is it intimate conversation with someone who really gets you? Making passionate love on the beach? Those moments when the sparks just begin and your heart starts to pound? Dating three different people in a week? Your dream wedding? Whatever the fantasy—and nothing says you have to limit it to one—it should stir you up and make you want.

The more specific you can make your fantasy, the better. What does your partner look like? What are you wearing--down to the cologne? What is the setting, background music? What are you talking about (if you're talking!)? Cast someone famous in your fantasy if you want. Watch a romantic comedy or a sexy action flick. Read a book with great love scenes. Be a little dreamy. It got you going back then …

Feeling It

As we will discuss further in Chapter 21, allowing your feelings to get stirred up is a key to getting what you desire. An actor who just goes through the motions and can't feel the feelings will not be very effective. Same with dating. Dig deep. Understand your motivations. Why do you want to date? What are you hoping for?

This is the time to add texture to the fantasy you've been creating—to give it depth and drama. Notice the music that moves you and the stories that make you laugh or cry. Start linking all these elements together in your own story. Include where you came from, the events that shaped you, the needs and desires that arose out of your past. Allow the development of a central conflict or tension, perhaps the tension you are in the midst of, and then, have the story fulfill your deepest longings.

Pay attention to how that fulfillment feels in your body and in your soul. Allow yourself to be moved by desire that goes to the essence of who you are. Chances are, you'll get the part.

From the Mouths of Baby Boomers: Sources of Inspiration

"I loved David Cassidy and Bobby Sherman. Remember *TigerBeat* and their posters? I am mortified to admit that although an older man, I thought Greg Brady was hot, and was sure to wait for me. Unfortunately, I didn't know he liked older women and was seeing Florence Henderson at the time.

During those times I wasn't thrilled with my ex, Cher's *Believe* was great. Lately, I've been listening to of all things ABBA, the *Saturday Night Fever* album (with a lot of disco and Bee Gee's), and Fleetwood Mac—"Don't stop thinking about tomorrow" is so profound when planning a (second) wedding!—and some of the AC/DC headbanger stuff I didn't even much like in high school. Must make me feel immature and irresponsible … kind of fun."

—Class of '78

"Stones, stones, stones."

—Class of '72

"My idols were Davy Jones from the Monkees and Lee Majors (from his Big Valley days). I liked soft rock. Bread was my fav. Now I like all kinds of things but mostly I need to calm down before a date so I listen to New Age yoga music to relax."

—Class of '77

Playing

Kids don't need adults to tell them how to prepare for life. They play their way into adult roles. I'll never forget playing "boyfriend and girlfriend," with an all-girl cast. We pretended to get ready for dates, talked about "the guys," and went out on double dates. Even as we approached dating age, my friends and I would fight over who got Davy Jones as her imaginary boyfriend. (When the Monkees were "the guys," the first pick was always Davy, then Mike, Mickey, and Peter.) We rehearsed flirting, working out conflicts, and the drama of breaking up, and making up.

Humanizing Our Idols

We remember Davy Jones and Maureen McCormick (Marcia Brady) as heart-throbs of the late '60s and early '70s. What we may not know is that both of them had aspirations apart from their sitcom roles. The 5'5" Davy had been seriously training to be a horse jockey when he was cast as one of the Monkees on NBC's hot new series. Maureen's first love was singing. Her child voice sang out in the original Pillsbury Doughboy commercials and was personified in the voice of Chatty Cathy, the twentieth century's first talking doll.

The two idols gave us a vicarious thrill when they got together at Marcia Brady's prom on the December 10, 1971, episode of The Brady Bunch, "Getting Davy Jones."

Although you may not be up to role-playing with friends, there are some elements of dating you can use as you prepare for the real thing:

Picking the Characters

Along with deciding who our boyfriends were, we also spent a great deal of time describing to each other who we were: "I look like Cher, but with blonde hair and I'm a stewardess." Practice being the way you want to be as you date. Maybe you want to be more confident this time—practice confidence. Maybe you want to be more "out there" sexually, or more reserved. What makes this fun, is that you can play it any way you want.

If you're worried that playing will make you less authentic, consider this radical possibility: who you desire to be is who you already are. Remember Narcissus? He pined away for his own reflection, and didn't get that it was him! We do the same thing. We see what we love in others, without realizing that we are seeing a reflection of something deep within. The self you desire may actually be your most authentic self. I was raised in a conservative family, and I learned to suppress any hippie tendencies. I have wanted to be a hippie ever since. What I have realized is that it is my nature to be a free spirit, open-minded, and creative—all characteristics I credited to hippies. The difference is, now I am free to be that desired me.

One huge benefit of deciding who you want to be is that you will attract people who affirm your desired qualities. In her marriage, my sister was always the strong one, and could rarely rely on her husband to be strong for her. It was a role she was familiar with, and she and her husband both reinforced it, even though it didn't serve her well. Through facing her dissatisfaction with her marriage, and with the help of her therapist, friends (and sisters, of course), she began to allow herself to need. She began to long for a partner who could be stronger than her. As she played with her new identity, we saw an amazing transformation. She lost the weight which hid her figure, let her hair grow into curly locks, and allowed the sisters she had mothered to mother her. She is beautiful in her vulnerability and, since her divorce, has attracted men who treat her with care.

As you identify the role you want to play, you can mentally rehearse the interactions your "character" will have. For my sister, she had to watch her tendency to shrug off disappointment and act strong. She is still working with her new role, but she is more and more able to acknowledge feeling hurt or disappointed. Although new to her, this more vulnerable version of herself is actually more real than the role she had been playing. And another irony is, as she's relinquished her façade of strength, she has experienced a new strength that comes with being real. She is no longer hiding, and worried about someone discovering her. She is boldly being who she is. And she's having a great time of it.

Taking on a desired role feels like play, because it is fun to be who you want to be! In fact, fun is a great indicator that you are being you.

> "*All I can do is be me, whoever that is.*"
> —*Bob Dylan*

Find Playmates

I don't mean Hugh Hefner's girls. Identify people you can trust, and let them help you stay consistent in your new role. Relationships with friends and family are a great screen for viewing your relationship style. If you are controlling with friends, you will likely be controlling with your date. If your friends get frustrated with your passivity, your date will, too. And a therapy relationship is a great laboratory for understanding your relationships in general. Therapy as play? Ask my friends why I've spent so much money on it!

Dressing the Part

Time to play dress up! We're already talking about updating your look; you also want to make your look fit your desired character. Red or leather (or red leather!) will help you be more "out there;" a suit lends a sophisticated or professional look; bohemian clothes and jewelry show off your creative side. Many stores now have shopping consultants who can help you put together the look you have in mind.

This is a great time to experiment. Try out different styles, wear a color you "never" wear. And just getting a fresh perspective from someone who doesn't know you can be helpful. Have fun—push the limits a little. If you're a guy who never wears jewelry, try a chain, or even an earring! If you're a woman who never wears nail polish, treat yourself to a manicure. Remember, this is play! Just see how it feels. You may be surprised.

Appreciate the Drama

Besides being fun, playing provides a safe distance to deal with the challenges of dating. When my friends and I played out conflicts, it was good drama, free of the anxiety associated with real-life conflicts.

Dating is one of the best sources of good drama. My sister now frequently entertains me with her stories. While she has her anxious days, the drama is not lost on her. In fact, she refers to the complications along the way as "plot thickener." I have to admit that she wasn't near as fun to talk to when she was married.

Post a reminder for yourself to "enjoy the drama," and sometimes just pretend that none of it is real. (Many of our Boomer gurus would argue that none of it is anyway!) Watch movies and read books that have story lines you can identify with. Tell your story, especially to boring married people who will listen with rapt attention.

Finding People

"So," you may ask, "I'm ready to date, but where are the dates?" You may have noticed that there isn't much left of your social network, or that the people you do hang out with are as set in their ways as Archie Bunker. Part 2 explores a variety of ways to meet new people, including exciting new options such as online dating. You will discover the meeting places that feel right for you, learn how to pursue personal growth and dates at the same time, and find the people looking for you!

chapter 11

"You Too?": Connecting Through Common Interests

Put down the remote, get off the couch, and get out of the house.

—On *"How to Meet a Guy," from* Boomer Babes, *by Linda Stasi and Rosemary Rogers*

Ever get frustrated when people tell you that you'll meet someone when you're not looking? Is that supposed to mean looking is futile, that we should pretend we're not interested in dating in order to find someone?

I don't think so. There's a lot to be said for the simple wisdom of "seek and you shall find." However, when seeking narrows our focus and closes us off to the rest of who we are, it may not work so well. If seeking keeps us from relaxing and enjoying ourselves, we may not come off so well.

A wonderful way to seek without leaving yourself behind is to pursue your own interests.

Knowing Yourself Through Dating

Notice how, when you shop for a major item, such as a car or a residence, you start to get a better sense of who you are? If it's a house or apartment you're looking for, you notice the kind of neighborhood that feels right, the style of architecture that appeals to you, the amenities that are most important to you. Maybe you're willing to trade space for charm; you might discover that privacy is important; maybe a space for a garden is key. As you get closer to a decision, you get a clearer definition of who you are.

The process of finding people to date also provides an opportunity for self-definition. When Smokey Robinson's mama told him to "shop around," she had the right idea. You can start by "window shopping," and just notice people you see and interact with in the course of a day. Pay attention to what you like and don't like. Does somebody at the office always irritate you? Why? Which people do you just like being around? Why? The attitude of a shopper will continue to benefit you as you date. You'll pick up this, toss out that, all the while discovering your own tastes and preferences. That's the paradox: Even as you're shopping around for something (or someone) else, what you are finding is you.

According to the Boomers International website (www.boomersint. com), female baby boomers voted Mel Gibson the sexiest boomer (42%) for the second year in a row. Harrison Ford (33%) and Patrick Swayze (24%) were not far behind.

On Your Turf

The easiest places to start looking for people are the places where we feel at home. Don't take this too literally: unless you have a hot gardener or personal trainer that makes house calls, you probably need to leave the house. Think of establishing a home or two away from home. If you love books, take your reading material to a coffee shop in a bookstore. If you're a runner, try joining a running club. If you're a music lover, become a regular at a club that showcases musicians. Hanging out at places where you feel good increases your chances of "accidentally" meeting someone who shares your passion. And remember your parents telling you to stay in one place if you got lost? The same wisdom applies to dating: Establish a setting, and eventually an eligible date will come along.

There's not really anything that mysterious about finding people to date. They are not members of a club we have to qualify for—they are just people. And the people you want to date are probably *your* people: Men or women who are easy for you to talk to, who share your common values and interests. Romances in books and movies often include lines such as, "It feels like I've always known you." If you think of meeting someone you already know, doesn't it make you feel more relaxed? We broke down barriers in the '60s, as we fought for equal rights and spread messages of love and peace. We didn't have to know the person standing next to us to feel connected. We were sisters and brothers. If we can recapture what we knew then—that none of us are strangers—meeting people might feel like coming home.

> *"80% of success is just showing up."*
> —*Woody Allen*

Getting Involved Again

Meeting people can be a great incentive to get involved in the causes we care about. Volunteering is an easy way to meet people, because you automatically have something to do together. You are also likely to share similar concerns and values. If you want to get involved politically, start attending your party's caucuses, or pick a candidate and get on the campaign. That way you not only meet the people you are door-knocking with, but you may find your love—and a voter—when the door opens! What's really great is that, once you become identified with an organization, you get invited to the *parties*.

Another advantage of volunteering is that we are needed, and our presence is welcomed and appreciated. Coming into a setting with something to offer can feel more comfortable than just coming to look for a date. Whether you're on the board of directors or the construction crew, you can show off your skills and enthusiasm without the pressures of a work setting.

From the Mouths of Baby Boomers

"I volunteered to serve as chair for the American Diabetes Association. It was such a great experience. I organized an art auction and got to meet artists. I met famous people, I must have met over 200 people—of those, at least 30 that I could have dated, but the one I met first was all I needed! These people were intelligent and successful. Think about it—you're not going to volunteer if you're a loser!"

—Class of '79

The Perk of Self-Improvement

The great thing about connecting through common interests is that you get to grow in the meantime! What we often find attractive in other people is *vitality*—the sense that the person is engaged in life. This quality shows on people who are growing. So think about how you want to evolve, how you would like to enrich your life.

Classes are wonderful ways to meet people, as well as ways to expand who you are. Maybe you've always wanted to develop your skill in photography or acting. Or you just think it would be fun to take ballroom dancing or kickboxing. Think of the class you have "always" wanted to take but haven't allowed yourself. Maybe you've been feeling like you missed the boat because you didn't take economics, or wish you'd paid attention in classic literature. Boomers are going back to school for a variety of reasons—career change, completing a degree, self-enrichment, and, of course, to find dates. Join the trend!

Joining a club is another great way to meet people. Name an interest and you will probably be able to find a club to match. I'm a huge fan of roller coasters, and was thrilled to discover the American Coaster Enthusiasts. There are running clubs, jazz appreciation clubs, clubs organized around causes, gourmet cooking clubs, Toastmaster clubs to help develop your speaking skills, writer's groups, and more. Some clubs, such as golf courses and tennis clubs, offer a setting for your use, as well as structured activities and social events.

Clubs You May Not Have Considered

A sampling of clubs in one American city—Cincinnati, Ohio—revealed some interesting options:

Beatles Breakfast Club—for Beatles aficionados

Butler County Chippers—for woodcarvers

Cincinnati Vegetarian Resource Group

Visual Artists Soiree

Extra Terrestrial Experiences Support Group

Citizens Against Censorship

High Cincinnatian's Tall Club—for taller-than-average singles

Martin Luther King Jr. Coalition

Models and Actors Networking Group

Save the Manatee Club

Harley Owners Group

Club-Club, chapter of International Jugglers Association

Greater Cincinnati Blues Society

Bonsai Society

Cincinnati Blade Brigade—In-line skating club

Experimental Aircraft Association

Cincinnati Malt Infusers—for home brewers

Of course, we don't need to take a class or join a club to grow. The more engaged we are in our own development, the more people we will meet. Any new pursuit requires us to make new connections and exposes us to new peers. If you are advocating change in your community, you will meet other advocates—and probably some people to argue with! If you are moving into a new career, people will be there. Even listening to bands we enjoy or viewing art we like will put us in proximity to people there for the same reason. You know how they say, "do what you love, and the money will come?" Let's extend that to "do what you love, and the love will come."

chapter **12**

Meeting of Minds

*The '60s marks the spot when blind faith in
authority went south forever.*
—Steve Deering

It is no wonder that so many couples pair up in a college setting. Beyond the fact that there is a captive population of single adults, it's a wonderful setting for the meeting of minds.
Remember that time of your life when your capacity to think
exploded and you questioned everything? Remember how fun
it was to talk about ideas, to deconstruct and reconstruct the
world in your mind? To come to that "wow, man" insight?
(And if you inhaled, your discoveries seemed all the more
impressive!)

Exploring and discovering truth has always been compelling
to us Boomers. When the exploring happens with a partner,
it's all the more exciting. You bring together your unique points
of view, make connections, enjoy a little aggressive banter, and
feel the intimacy of the moment when your minds meet and
you arrive at the same place—sounds a lot like sex, doesn't it?

Do "Like Minds" or Opposites Attract?

	Turn On	Turn Off	Consider
Like Minds	Soul-mate feeling; You get me!	Boring	Can you light my fire?
Opposites	Good sparring; You challenge me!	Too much work!	Can you respect and hear me?

The Allure of a Good Mind

A good mind is sexy. That may be why we refer to mentally engaging people as *stimulating*. Notice how prominent people with good minds can get by with weird hair or big noses—I must be thinking of Einstein—and still be attractive? Talent and charisma work the same way. We are drawn to people who have something to offer, who can inform and challenge us, make us think and help us grow.

Good minds come in many forms. We admired Joan Baez for her evocative lyrics, Martin Luther King Jr. for his capacity to inspire, Coco Chanel for her ability to capture style, Ralph Nader for his courage to challenge powerful industry. Because these people were prominent, we got a window into their minds. But even us Trekkies can't "mind meld" with someone we see on the street. We may need to seek out stimulating people, while showing off our own attractive minds.

What do you think about when your mind wanders (okay, *besides* sex)? What section of the newspaper are you drawn to? What books are on your bedside table? Because your thoughts are so familiar to you, you probably take for granted how much you know. My friend only recently realized that she has been in lifelong training to be a filmmaker. She has always framed scenes in her mind. She notices how things are laid out, the background, the lighting. Her hobbies include photography, writing, and musical composition, and she has a knack for identifying talent. Now that she has a name for her gift, she has a new focus about her and can expose her genius to those around her. When she does, her mind is very alluring!

Challenging Words from the Minds of Our Times

"… I think that more of our children would grow up happier and more stable if they were acquiring a conviction, all through childhood, that the most important and the most fulfilling thing that human beings can do to serve humanity in some fashion and to live by their ideals …. If you raise a child who has idealism he will have no lack of opportunities to apply it."

—Dr. Benjamin Spock, who influenced the parenting style of our parents

"In the councils of government, we must guard against the acquisition of unwarranted influence, whether sought or unsought, by the military-industrial complex. The potential for the disastrous rise of misplaced power exists and will persist."

—President Eisenhower, farewell address to the nation, Jan. 16, 1961

Food for Conversation

When we get ready to date, it's a good time to sharpen our wits along with our wardrobes. Take the time to tune into your personal genius—the unique perspective or point of view you offer. At the same time, it never hurts to stimulate your thinking by taking on an entirely new area of interest. Notice the excitement in the voice of someone who is learning something new? They seem more alive, animated. Stimulating your mind may be as simple as reading a new section of the paper, or as challenging as learning a new language.

This New Year's Eve, after becoming bored with my own thinking, I resolved to learn more jokes, and learn the intricacies of football. It was fun to be a part of post-game conversations, and even have an opinion to contribute! Although I still need to practice my jokes before I can remember them, it's great fun to make people laugh. Regardless of the topic, when we stimulate our minds, we become more stimulating. And while you're brushing up, check out Appendix E for a Boomer quiz that will stimulate your memories and sharpen your knowledge of our shared past.

More Challenging Words from the Minds of Our Times

"There is a time when the operation of the machine becomes so odious, makes you so sick at heart, that you can't take part; you can't even passively take part, and you've got to put your bodies upon the gears and upon the wheels, upon the levers, upon all the apparatus and you've got to make it stop."

—Mario Savio to students at the Berkeley Free Speech Movement, 1964

"I am convinced that if we are to get on the right side of the world revolution, we as a nation must undergo a radical revolution of values. We must rapidly begin, we must rapidly begin the shift from a thing-oriented society to a person-oriented society. When machines and computers, profit motives and property rights, are considered more important than people, the giant triplets of racism, extreme materialism, and militarism are incapable of being conquered."

—Rev. Martin Luther King Jr., 1967

"The truth will set you free. But first, it will piss you off."

—Gloria Steinem, quote used in her speeches for women's rights

---

Places Where Minds Meet

If your work is interesting to you, the people you work with are probably interesting too. In fact, it is often in the work setting that we reveal our most attractive qualities. Work romances are common, although they have their complications (boss-subordinate issues, awkwardness in the event of a breakup). One way to open up your options beyond the office is to attend conferences and workshops in your field. People are usually more relaxed in these settings, and get to focus on the things that made their work attractive to them in the first place. As you get away and really contemplate your work, you are in a great place to meet others in a more open frame of mind.

If you'd just as soon leave work at work, where else can you find a good mind? It's not too late to check out college again. As we discussed in Chapter 11, classes are great places to meet people. Because more and more Boomers are returning to school, evening and weekend classes are often available. And if you don't want to deal with grades again, you can usually audit a course. The best classes for meeting people are small and emphasize interaction. Classes that encourage self-disclosure, such as writing and psychology seminars, are particularly helpful in breaking down barriers. Want to explore the meaning of life? Try a philosophy course.

In addition to classes, many colleges and communities offer distinguished speaker series, usually followed by a reception which allows for mingling. Bookstores and libraries offer poetry and book readings, and often organize book clubs. Interacting around a shared work of literature is a great way to get a feel for someone else's mind. And, as we discussed in Chapter 11, there are many organizations for minds to meet around a specific cause. As we know from our more involved days, joining together to support a mutual cause is a great way to bond!

Creating Together

If it's the right side of your brain that you're wanting to develop, there are numerous classes that will link you up with others eager to express their creative potential. You can learn to paint or throw pots, write poetry or landscape your garden. Want to show off? Take an acting workshop or a speech class.

Speaking of acting, community theatre is a great way to meet other thespians. And if you get cast opposite a love interest, you could have the entire romance scripted for you! You might even get to practice a passionate kiss—over and over. If you want to connect with theatre people without acting, there are many behind-the-scenes roles available, such as lighting, sound and set design.

Community theatre is just one example of a way to tap into a group with shared interests. Community art galleries have supporting boards and volunteers, and every opera or symphony has its backers. Open mic nights attract musicians and comedians. Collectors gather at swap meets, exhibits and auctions. Whatever your mind is hungry for, there are others wanting to dine with you. Bon Appetit!

From the Mouths of Baby Boomers

He: "This is an example of how a bad situation can turn good. I came into town, had lost my job, knew no one. Since I had the time, I decided to audition with the local theatre company."

She: "It was The Heidi Chronicles. We were cast as Heidi and Scoop. I introduced myself, said 'Hi, I'm Heidi, I have to kiss you.' He said, 'Do you mean in the play?' I said, 'No, I just have to kiss you.'"

He: "A week later, another 'bad-good' thing happened. Her car died. We had to drive to rehearsals together. The kiss was only the beginning. Now we're married."

—Classes of '70 and '76

chapter 13

Partners in Sweat

You hit home runs not by chance but by preparation.
—Roger Maris, who hit 61 in '61

Have you ever noticed how the heroes and heroines of movies keep getting stronger? Back in our day, you were cool if you had a great car or a nice guitar. As we've grown up and watched Olivia get physical and Rocky take those stairs, it's our bodies we're tuning up and showing off. Gyms rival bars as popular pick-up spots, and workout attire has become a major fashion industry. So, let's get physical!

Working on Your Stroke—Together

We never grow out of our need for playmates. Whether your sport is tennis or in-line skating, playing together is not only a benefit to you, it's a great way to start a relationship. You're feeling good about yourself, getting that exercise-induced high, and having fun. And you don't need to make small talk or think of an excuse to be together. You can focus on the activity, and give yourself time to size up your competitor or partner.

Besides, playing together can be quite erotic. For example, could the game of pool be any *more* suggestive? And working up a sweat together on the court can be great foreplay.

People drawn to athletic activity are likely to value fitness, be active in other areas of their life, and be in good shape. By participating in a sport together you can also get insight into how the other person interacts.

Sizing up Your Sports Partner

Competitiveness—Does your partner challenge you? Does he or she take the game too seriously?

Give and take—Does your partner hog the court or the ball?

Having fun yet?—Does your partner make it fun?

Cheating—Does he or she cut corners for an advantage?

Sense of Humor—Can your partner take a mistake in stride and laugh at funny situations?

Sharing the Outdoors

Many Boomers would prefer to meet out in the fresh air rather than in a stuffy bar. People we meet outdoors tend to be active, and are less likely to be depressed (the depressed ones tend to stay in). Outdoor entertainment is often less expensive than indoor options, such as nightclubs and movies. The other difference is that outdoor activities often happen during the day, and allow more time and space for getting to know each other. And romance? What can top barefoot on the beach or lying together in a meadow?

Sharing the outdoors has become easier with the development of trails for hiking and biking, and the Internet can link people up for group excursions and treks. The Sierra Club organizes nature-oriented trips all over the world, and local chapters can plan their own outings. Birders can come together for bird-watching field trips through the Audubon Society. Ecotourism is a rapidly growing trend that emphasizes environmental conservation and attention to the welfare of local people. You can contact the International Ecotourism Society for more information.

From the Mouths of Baby Boomers

"I met a lady on a ski trip to New Zealand in 1988. We flirted a bit and one day after she noticed I wasn't great at skiing (which has changed, by the way), skied with me and gave me some tips. I remember at one point while resting on the slopes, I took out my handkerchief and wiped her nose for her. She was touched by the gesture & we dated on and off for the next 3-4 years."

—Class of '72

"I teach aerobics at my club, and this extremely well-built guy starts coming to my class. The women in the class would just drool over him. I learned that he was a professional football player and he'd just come in to get warmed up before he went to lift weights. But then he started coming to all my classes. And then he started to ask me out! He was so much younger than me, lived such a different lifestyle—I politely declined. And, you know what? He said, 'Well, I'm gonna keep coming 'cuz I want to see you. If you are gonna make me get up early and come here, I will.' His presence was definitely tempting, and made for some wonderful fantasies."

—Class of '69

But you don't have to book a formal trip to get out and meet people. Just getting out on a nice day and going fishing where people fish, hiking where people hike, or even flying a kite in a park, is very likely to provide opportunities for conversation. "Are they biting over there?" "How long to the summit?" "Nice kite." Walking a dog is a great way to meet people, especially if your dog hits it off with the pet of an attractive owner. If you like the wild side, try white water rafting with people you haven't met, or take a rock climbing class. Or try orienteering, a sport that involves competitive cross-country navigation with a map and compass. Who knows—maybe getting good at finding things in the woods will help you sharpen your skills at finding dates!

Where Active People Meet

"The Club": These types of clubs—health club, country club, tennis club—are full-service facilities that are available to paid members. The advantage of being a member of the club is that they provide many opportunities to mix it up—lessons, social events, and tournaments.

The disadvantage is that membership fees can be costly and limit the socioeconomic range of people you meet. Some clubs, such as the YMCA or YWCA, are less expensive and place less of an emphasis on protocol.

Organizations: I've already listed some, such as the Sierra Club, but there are as many organizations as there are sports and outdoor activities. Runners can join running clubs, such as Road Runners. There are clubs for bicyclists, skiers, and Ultimate Frisbee players. Larger cities have fencing clubs, and even the smallest towns have their bowling leagues. And if your area doesn't have a club to fit your needs, think about starting one. National organizations provide guidelines for starting local chapters, and can help you link up with local members of the national club. Or you can create your own club.

Public Grounds and Facilities: Just getting out and using facilities available to the public is an easy and inexpensive way to cross paths with potential dates. Go to the public courts with a friend and look for doubles' partners, or just practice by yourself until a partner comes along. Run on park trails, skate at the local ice rink, join a game of Frisbee or beach volleyball, hike, or bike a popular trail. Just follow this simple rule of thumb for finding dates: Go where the people are.

Super Bowl Trivia for the Sports Bar

Remember those little "super balls" that bounced to the ceiling and annoyed parents everywhere? Apparently it was his daughter's super ball that inspired Lamar Hunt—architect of the AFL and owner of the Kansas City Chiefs—to think up the name "Super Bowl" for the new championship game.

Super Bowl I was played on January 15, 1967, at the Los Angeles Memorial Coliseum. It was a lopsided victory for the Green Bay Packers, who defeated the Kansas City Chiefs 35–10.

You may argue that going where the people are doesn't necessarily mean we will meet people. That is true, but staying by ourselves will guarantee that we don't meet anyone. One way to increase your chances of meeting people is to become a regular. As long as you feel safe, run the same trail every day, or take your lunch break at the park. Swim at a specific time of the day. Becoming a regular will put you in contact with other regulars, and help you feel on your own turf. Seeing someone a few times makes it easier to break the ice. To join up as a partner in sweat, however, you may need to be bold. But the key is to have fun. After all, it's the person who is having fun that we all want to play with.

chapter 14

In the Spirit

A soul mate is someone who has locks that fit our keys, and keys to fit our locks. When we feel safe enough to open the locks, our truest selves step out and we can be completely and honestly who we are; we can be loved for who we are and not for who we're pretending to be.

—Leslie Parrish in The Bridge Across Forever: a Love Story *by Richard Bach (author of Jonathan Livingston Seagull)*

Although the swingin' ways of our generation made for good press, it is our ideals that have made the largest impact—socially, politically and even spiritually. While the cover of *Time Magazine* (April 8, 1966) was asking "Is God Dead?," we were challenging the religious status quo and seeking to bring our spirits to life. The story of Jesus was set in modern times in *Godspell* and put to rock music in *Jesus Christ Superstar*. Jesus did become a superstar, with *Jesus Freaks*, reviving the vigor of the message. Eastern spiritual traditions—from Confucianism to Zen—enriched our Western perspectives and taught us the benefits of spiritual discipline. In Boomer style, we were looking for more, not less.

As a result of our searching, spiritual practices such as meditation, yoga, and spiritual retreats have become mainstream pursuits. We have also built connections between major religions, emphasizing how we are similar over how we are different. This trend toward a more inclusive, experience-based spirituality has been referred to as the "New Age" movement.

Although our culture has been impacted by these developments, Boomers remain a widely diverse group. What we believe is as individual as who we are. Maybe because of this diversity, many of us are seeking to connect with someone on a deeper, more timeless level.

Making Spiritual Connections

"Connecting" is a popular Boomer word. We don't just want to meet someone, we want to connect. And many of us seek to connect spiritually. What that means to you may include any or all of the following:

1. To share the love of a religious tradition. For example, if you were raised in the Jewish tradition, you may feel more connected with someone who grew up celebrating the same holidays, studied the Torah, and feels an intimate historical connection with the Judaic journey. Even if you have just met, you share a frame of reference and an identity.

2. To experience the connectedness of us all. Ever look into someone's eyes and see beyond the individual? Maybe it feels like you are seeing God, or all of humanity. If you believe that, at some level, we are all one, it's not about *making* a connection—it's about *recognizing* the connection that is already there.

3. To share a profound experience with another. Often this kind of experience takes us beyond the limits of our bodies. Whether this happens through praying together or sharing an orgasm, we transcend our individual selves and meet up on another plane.

4. To feel a spiritual affinity with another. This experience is that kind of "wow" that happens when you meet someone who feels familiar and resonates with who you are at a core level.

You are most likely to connect spiritually with others when you are in tune with your own spirit. Each of us needs to find our own path, and when we do, we increase our chances of running into people going in the same direction.

From the Mouths of Baby Boomers

"After my second marriage, the prospect of dating felt terrible. I felt like I had spent all this time trying to be married to someone who didn't want to be married to me. I started attending my sister's church, and I met a woman at the 'Kiss of Peace,' the portion of the service where you greet the people around you. We talked then, met more at church, started talking on the phone, and it grew into love. She is now my wife. We both believe that God brought us together in that Kiss of Peace."

—Class of '63

"My spirituality is very important to me—my sense of self, sense of God, sense of my relationship to others. Before you can connect with anyone spiritually, you have to know yourself. One thing I found helpful was to write down my core values, then prioritize them, 1 through 10. Once you have that, you know what to look for when you date."

—Class of '67

What Is a Soul Mate?

Although "soul mate" defies definition, we usually know when we've found one. You feel cozy together—you share a special intimacy. It's like you've known each other all along. You get your mate in his or her alone spaces because, somehow, you have been there, too. Or your mate fills out your experience, because he or she played out a parallel path and did the things you could only do in your imagination. Maybe you took the safe route, went to school, got a good job, and got ahead. Your mate, on the other, followed her dream of being an actor, lived in a dive in New York, and traded stability for adventure. By coming together, you are able to share what you've lived and move forward as a team.

Whether the path was a wish or reality, the feeling that you've both walked it creates an easy empathy between you. Soul mates fall in love with the growing part of each other—what Carl Jung referred to as the "eternal child." Maybe that's why lovers find themselves using baby talk and pet names. Soul mates often feel the same kind of loyalty and protectiveness toward each other as a parent feels toward a child. If you believe that souls inhabit different bodies over time, you may feel that your souls have journeyed together in the past.

Whether or not you feel like "mates" in a past sense, you share a stake in your futures. Often there is a feeling that you are meant to be together, that your destinies are intertwined. As the much-quoted words of Antoine de Saint-Exupéry advise, "Love does not consist in gazing at each other, but in looking together in the same direction."

If all this has gotten you worried about whether you will find your soul man or soul woman, relax. There is never only one potential soul mate out there, and you can have more than one in a lifetime. One soul mate may come into your life for awhile so the two of you can help each other to the next level; another may be the one you want the whole story to unfold with. Some advisors will tell you not to worry about it, because destiny will unfold regardless—just enjoy the ride. Others will tell you not to worry so much about whether he or she is "right," because it ultimately comes down to making the choice—"you are the one I want to take the trip with"—and then walking the walk.

It is important to note that a relationship between soul mates is not a perfect relationship, but an evolving one. The idea of the process goes to the heart of what soul mates are—partners in the journey. In making yourself suitable to *be* a soul mate, you need to embrace the process of working through conflicts, changing and evolving.

> **What a Soul Mate is Not**
> - Someone who feels familiar because he or she could have been a member of your dysfunctional family
> - A "you and me against the world" partner. Shared hostility narrows your world; shared desire expands it
> - A fairy tale, conflict-free relationship
> - A guarantee

From Church to Yoga: Places to Meet

When it comes to finding a soul mate, the setting is not as important as the intention. One of my favorite pieces of advice in general, but easily applied to finding a soul mate, comes from the movie *Field of Dreams*—"If you build it, they will come." Although Kevin Costner's character cleared his fields to build a baseball stadium, he had no idea who would come and why. If you listen to the direction of the voice within you, build a foundation for your desires, and believe without knowing, what is needed will come.

Spiritual settings and practices are designed to help us clear the clutter of life and tune in. They also can help you meet others who are searching. This is not to say that you need to go to a spiritual sanctuary to find a soul mate. A fair number of soul mates have been known to meet in bars!

The best spiritual settings are the places where you feel understood and loved. For some of us, that setting will be a church, synagogue, or mosque. Many gay and lesbian Boomers have found acceptance and gathering opportunities within churches such as the Unitarian Universalist Fellowship and the Metropolitan Community Churches. While it may be hard to ask someone out during a worship service, organized religions usually offer many ways to gather, including study groups, participation in choirs and athletic teams, social events, retreats, and even singles gatherings. Getting involved as a volunteer will get you in contact with people who prioritize service and religious involvement.

Participating in a spiritual practice in a group setting is another way to make soul connections. Meditation and prayer groups, reiki workshops, and yoga classes are just a few examples. It is also common to find "hybrid" workshops and classes that draw on connections between psychology and spirituality, creativity and spirituality, and so on.

Spiritual retreats offer the opportunity to get away from the distractions of day-to-day life and rejuvenate. Because people are less defensive and more relaxed, retreats can be great places to meet people. On-site workshops are often experiential in nature and create a safe setting for self-disclosure between participants. And retreating is an increasingly popular pastime for Boomers. The website www.findthedivine.com lists over 1,100 spiritual retreat centers in the United States and Canada.

A Sampling of Spiritual Retreat Options

Type	Retreat
Meditation retreat	Vipassana Meditation Centers
12-Step recovery retreats	Matt Talbot Retreats
Church-sponsored camp	Holden Village, WA
Native American retreats	Wind Walker Guest Ranch, UT
Pilgrimage	The Western Wall, Jerusalem
Campus-type retreat	Omega Institute, NY
Zen retreat	Hazy Moon Zen Center of L.A.
Vision quest	Rites of Passage, Inc.
Prayer retreats	Stillpoint Retreats
Yoga retreat	Kripalu Center, MA
Gay/lesbian retreats	Triangle Ministries, VT

chapter 15

Shopping Around

Whoever said money can't buy happiness simply
didn't know where to go shopping.
—Bo Derek

Whatever happened to places like Pops, where you could go out for a Coke and meet someone cute? Or the campus coffeehouse where you could have a bagel and listen to folk music while making eyes at the pre-med student in the corner? Then there were the "meat markets," bars where you knew you were on exhibit, and your fun rested on whether you were having a bad hair day or not. It's been a long time since those days. Where can we find that captive audience of single people now? Where can we shop for a date?

Meet Markets

The good news is that we have gotten more creative about where we can meet dates. Whoever thought up the idea of making laundromats into hip meeting spots was onto something. You can do your laundry in a comfortable atmosphere with music, food, and—of course, other single people who are doing their laundry. So, you might have a washer and dryer at home. Take your oversized comforters and sleeping bags in, or just have a night out with your laundry. The change of pace might do you good.

As dramatized in *Armistead Maupin's Tales Of The City*, the quirky PSB mini-series about the '70s in Haight-Ashbury, markets have become meet markets. After affirming the absence of a wedding ring, just ask the potential date how to know if a pineapple is ripe. The straight (and naïve) heroine of Maupin's series met two gorgeous men through produce discussions. Problem was, they were lovers. So, there are risks, but nothing ventured ....

From the Mouths of Baby Boomers

"After divorce I considered two paths: alienate myself from the male race completely, or jump right back in, use the knowledge gained through divorce, and keep my guard up. I decided on the first path. That is, until I was shopping one day at Home Depot. First, my eye caught this cute guy in the parking lot. Then, while shopping, I looked up to see the same guy standing at the end of the aisle. I smiled, then thought 'why did I just do that?!' He was quite charming, and asked if he could give me his phone number—without asking for mine, said he would like to talk sometime. That quick, within minutes, I actually met someone!

Later, I told a friend about my encounter and handed her the card. She examined it closely, turned it over, and said, 'Did you know he wrote something on the back?' I took the card and read aloud, 'To the most beautiful woman I've ever seen, simply breathtaking.' She demanded that I call him. I called and got his voice mail, panicked, then said, 'Hello, it's the girl from Home Depot (how stupid this all sounded). Thanks for the nice compliment, it was so sweet, hope to hear from you' (where was all this coming from?, oh god, just say goodbye!). That was Tuesday, and we saw each other every night that week until Monday. I haven't smiled so much in several years."

—Class of '77

Actually, shopping by yourself can be a great way to strike up conversations. You can even pick the store that fits your tastes. Look for do-it-yourselfers at home and hardware stores, active people at sports marts, organic food lovers at coops. The key is to be willing to ask someone else's opinion, share a tip, or ask for directions (men who have the courage to ask directions will be justly rewarded). Many times, your contact won't move beyond a brief but friendly conversation. You go your separate ways. But maybe you've made a connection and you both find a need to return to the scene of contact—for more paint or potatoes, of course. Next time, you don't let each other go without a follow-up plan. Or, your conversation about kumquats is so stimulating that you decide to go out to lunch to keep it going.

Any place where people gather can provide opportunities to shop around. Pursue your heritage (or someone else's) and attend an international festival. Take yourself out to the ballgame. Many of your Boomer rock idols are still touring—do the Stones *ever* age?—so you might want to check out a concert. And, watch for more and more Boomer-identified gatherings. Just the number of Boomer websites reveals that we want to get together again. We're ready to play, and, as always, the market will be there to respond.

The Baby Boomer Expo: A New Trend?

The first Baby Boomer Expo was held in Minneapolis in 2002. The sold-out event featured a Hippie Triathlon, which included rapid piling into a VW Beetle; exhibitor booths which featured everything from Boomer toys to "name that tune" contests; speakers, concerts, and, of course, an Elvis impersonator. The annual tradition is continuing with the addition of the Flower Power Playground and a classic car exhibit. Attendees are encouraged to wear their old bell-bottoms (actually you can get them new nowadays!) and happy face buttons. For more information, visit www.101expos.com.

The Boomer's Bar: The Coffee Shop

If you want quiet, go to a library. If you want to be seen as you work, read, or sip a latte, go to a coffee shop. Coffee shops are a great setup for doing semi-serious activities while remaining open to being interrupted. When I got this book contract, I loved taking my writing over to my favorite coffee shop, and having someone interrupt me and ask what I was writing. (Note to editors: I normally work diligently and fend off interruptions.) Because coffee shops are often located in bookstores, you may find the atmosphere more stimulating (especially with an espresso!) than a bar. They also tend to be more intimate. And, a plus for Boomers, entertainment, such as live music or a poetry slam, is offered at more reasonable hours than the bands at clubs—which tend to get started at the hour most of us consider bedtime! Coffee shops also feel like home for us—they have just enough hippie feel to make us nostalgic, yet are upscale enough to appeal to our refined tastes.

Singles Places

Although many places allow for shopping, it's not always apparent who's on the market. There are many meeting places set up for the express purpose of getting singles together. If you are imagining the frightening image of standing around a community hall drinking coffee, eating stale cookies, and looking at people you think really *should* be single, take heart. The options for singles today are vast, and we can be the beneficiaries of the competition. A sampling of singles groups in Arizona (azsinglescene.com), reveals some inviting options:

- Sea and Ski Club
- Back East Singles (for singles from Eastern states)
- Bocce Singles
- Swing and Latin Dance Club
- Arizona Adventurers
- Vegetarian Network
- American Singles Golf Association
- Card Players
- Active Christian Singles
- Desert Sailing Club
- Jewish Baby Boomers
- Lone Rangers (for unattached horse lovers)
- Peace Singles
- Unstrung Racquets
- Single Parents Association
- Desert Sailing Club (no sailboat or experience necessary!)

And this is not a comprehensive list!

If you want to go for the exotic, try a singles vacation. There must be a lot of singles out there to have made Club Med a household name! The idea of meeting other singles by a pool in the Caribbean seems to have caught on. Or, create your own version of the Love Boat and book a singles' cruise. While you may not have Captain Stubing and Julie the Cruise Director to help match you up, you'll avoid those nasty love triangles with married cruisers.

There's Always the Bar

Okay, so as much as people advise you not to look for dates at the bar, there's a good chance you will. Why? Bars are easy, inhibitions are down, and it's part of the social code to flirt. And, let's face it, bars can be fun.

In general meeting settings, gay Boomers have the challenge of trying to guess who's gay and who's straight. Bars designated for gays and lesbians take away that anxiety and make shopping easier. For this reason, such bars attract a broader spectrum of gay prospects, including those that may not otherwise frequent bars.

> "Good girls go to heaven, bad girls go everywhere."
> —Helen Gurley Brown

So how do you avoid the pitfalls of bars while taking advantage of the opportunities? First of all, make sure the bar you visit is a place you feel comfortable. Every bar has it's own character—some attract professionals, some attract young people, others are defined by the entertainment they offer. You may prefer the place that features cutting-edge alternative bands to the jazz club, or vice versa. A sports bar will have a different feel than a wine bar. You might feel most at home at a local bar where everybody knows your name. The diversity of bars today will increase the chances that the people you meet share your tastes.

Secondly, go with a friend or group of friends. Friends help you feel comfortable, can act as scouts, and are great excuses if you need to lose someone. Talk to your friend about the game plan—what happens if you want to go talk to someone? Do you have a plan for meeting up later? Is it okay to go home at different times, or have you agreed to leave together? Talking about it first helps you sort out your boundaries, and helps you avoid misunderstandings with your friend(s).

Be aware of your vulnerabilities. We all know that drinking clouds judgment, so know your limits. If you aren't good at saying no, practice an excuse in advance—or plan a rescue by your friend. Don't put yourself in situations you cannot get out of, like getting a ride with someone you just met.

Finally, have fun! Take advantage of the setting and act silly, dance, flirt. Shake off some stress and celebrate life!

chapter 16

Matchmaker, Matchmaker

He loves her! Love, it's a new starting. On the other hand, our old ways were once new, weren't they? On the other hand, they decided without parents, without the matchmaker! On the other hand, did Adam and Eve have a matchmaker? Oh, yes they did. And it seems these two have the same Matchmaker.

—Tevye, upon the engagement of his daughter in
Fiddler on the Roof

In the 1964 Broadway musical *Fiddler on the Roof*, Tevye has to slowly relinquish the tradition of matchmaking as his daughters find their own mates. While tradition dictates that the town matchmaker make the match, and the father approve it, times are changing. Tevye ultimately acknowledges that love may be the best matchmaker.

To most of us, the idea of arranged marriage seems quite foreign. We pride ourselves on our self-reliance and may not even think to ask for help as we look for dates. It seems there is room for a compromise between Tevye's idea of matchmaking and the idea of going it alone. That's why I prefer to think in terms of "scouts"—people who can help you find people to date. They don't carry the responsibility for finding your match—you do. They just feed you prospects.

Employing Scouts

Your scouts can be anybody—and everybody—you know. Take out a piece of paper and start a list. Friends are great scouts because they know you and what you want. Write down all the friends you can think of—male and female—from your best friend to casual acquaintances. Don't cringe, but family members can be resources, too. List the ones—and include the extended limbs of your family tree—who could serve as scouts. Sometimes family members understand you better than you think! Besides, right now we are going for quantity—you can always edit later.

Next, list people you work with. Then think of people you know through shared activities and community involvement. If you have a book club or a running group, include these contacts. If you go to a church or synagogue, you'll have contacts there, too. Think about a typical week and the people you encounter. Write down as many names as you can. Keep the list handy, because new names are likely to come to mind.

Now just look at the list and appreciate the fact that you have resources. What now? Depending on your personal style, you might prefer to open up a network or just work with selected scouts. Let's look at each of these approaches:

Opening Up a Network

With the feminization of the workplace, Boomers have seen management styles shift in emphasis from authority to relationships. Terms like "team-building" and "networking" have become household words. The logic behind networking is that, when ideas are sent off into the network, energies are applied to them concurrently rather than consecutively.

This wisdom also applies to finding dates. Why limit yourself to your own eyes when you can have a whole network looking for you? And, as businesspeople know, networks can connect you with opportunities you may not have dreamed existed.

How do you develop a network? One word: *Ask.* Take your list of potential scouts, and ask the people on your list to keep their eyes open. Then ask if they might check around with *their* friends. You don't have to act desperate. Simply let your contact know that you're just starting this dating thing and you want to meet as many people as you can.

Feeling shy about asking? I know how you feel. I tend to go into all kinds of contortions to avoid asking. When I finally give in and do it, it's usually embarrassingly simple. I ask, I receive. Sometimes I tell the person I'm asking that I'm feeling a little shy about it, and that makes it easier.

You may be surprised by what the simple act of asking generates. First of all, people generally like to be helpful. We like being able to make a difference in someone else's life. It makes us feel better about ourselves. Secondly, you may get much more than an introduction or two. You will open yourself to support, stories that help you feel less alone, and maybe a tip or two. Whether or not the input helps you, it feels good to know people are in your court.

To get results, you want to make things as simple as possible for your scout. If you have certain parameters for potential dates, such as an age range, smoker or nonsmoker, or if you have a quirky aversion to something, let your scouts know. You can even e-mail them a short ad, describing you and what you're looking for. If you want to look at all the options, just tell your scouts you don't really know what you want right now, so you'd just like to meet a variety of people. That takes any pressure off of them to try to guess your tastes.

If a scout has someone in mind, he or she will probably have ideas about where you can meet the prospect. But have your own ideas ready. If it's someone your scout works with, offer to come in and meet the two of you for lunch. That makes it a low-key, in-the-course-of-business kind of contact. Or you can offer to stop by your scout's place at a time the prospect will be stopping by. You can even find out where the prospect hangs out, get a description and check him or her out yourself. Or, try the mutual "look-see" approach described in Chapter 17.

> **From the Mouths of Baby Boomers**
>
> "Never turn down a blind date. A friend of mine was a waitress, and she met a guy who was eating there. She actually called me at home and told me about him. She said, 'You have to come right now.' I happened to be entertaining another male friend, so I told her I couldn't come. She asked if she could give him my phone number. I said okay. When he called, he said, 'Your friend said I'd be crazy if I didn't ask you out.' So I said, 'Then I'd be crazy if I didn't say yes.' We went out for breakfast. Going out to breakfast is great—try it. We had greasy omelets at Southern Kitchen… and now we're married. My friend saw it immediately, and I'm glad I trusted her."
>
> —Class of '66

The point of networking is to maximize your opportunities. When a scout crosses paths with someone who is out there looking, too, your name comes to mind. After starting my own psychology practice, I called around to my network of therapists and asked them to keep me in mind for referrals. One therapist called later that afternoon and said, "I just got a call from a client I needed to refer. You were fresh in my mind because you called earlier. Thanks!" He had a resource, I got a new client. Remember: You are not only asking for potential dates, you are offering yourself as a potential date for others.

Working with Selected Scouts

If getting the word out feels too overwhelming, you may want to stick with a close friend or two to help you out. The advantage here is that your close friends know what you like and don't like. They also may be in a better position to know what you *need*. They have been with you when things haven't worked so well, and they know your vulnerabilities. Even after time, therapy, and a lot of dating, one of my friends would not agree to marry the man she fell in love with until her friends gave her the go-ahead. We did, and I'm happy to report that she's got a great marriage.

With friends doing the scouting, you may feel more comfortable letting them set up some blind dates for you. We'll talk more about that in Chapter 20.

Old-Time Matchmaking in a New Format?

You really want to maximize your opportunities? It's a long shot, but if you're a woman, see if you can work your way into the reality-dating show *Cupid*. If you get to be the show's heroine, your friends and the viewing public help you narrow the field from thousands of contestants, observe you on dates (through videos) with a selected subset, and, in the old style of matchmaking, recommend a husband! You do get to choose whether to accept the recommendation, but if you do, you'll be married right then and there.

Guys, on the other hand, can "audition" to be contestants. Yes, as in other dating shows, there's money involved. But the guys have to prove their worthiness to some very protective girlfriends!

CBS Network's first reality-dating show, Cupid has joined the growing list of shows in the genre. Time will only tell how long Cupid will be around, but ever since The Dating Game aired in 1965, armchair matchmaking has become an increasingly popular form of entertainment.

Preventing Sticky Situations

When you're working through people you already have a relationship with, there is always the potential for hurt feelings and misunderstandings. For example, you might enlist the services of a scout who loves matchmaking and is good at it, but gets a little too invested. Or your scout may be very close to your potential date. Rejections in either direction are likely to be awkward.

The first helpful rule of thumb, especially with scouts you don't know that well, is to keep things light and casual. Emphasize that you are just wanting to meet people at this stage, and if they can help you with that, you'll be grateful. You might add that you don't feel ready to make any decisions until you get a sense of what's out there. This will take pressure off of you *and* your scout.

With your inner circle, anticipating and talking about potential scenarios can help prevent misunderstandings later. For example, if your best friend takes pride in her matchmaking abilities, talk about how she will feel if you don't hit it off with her pick. Tell her you really want her help, but you also want to be free to say no if things don't feel right.

Chances are your friend already gets this, but talking about it can free you both of any anxieties you are harboring. For example, she might be concerned about how you will feel if her pick doesn't respond to you. Once these concerns are discussed, you can move on to the fun part—talking about your dream date, going through magazines to identify the kind of look you like, and conspiring together.

> *Tzeitel: (About Yente, the matchmaker) "But Mama, the men she finds. The last one was so old and he was bald. He had no hair."*
>
> *Golde: "A poor girl without a dowry can't be so particular. You want hair, marry a monkey."*
>
> —The Fiddler on the Roof

What if your scout keeps sending you duds? Unless it's a close friend you can talk it out with, keep it light. You can say thanks so much, but you're wanting a break (without adding that you want a break from that scout's referrals) or that you're just finding that you're looking for something else. You will need to develop an arsenal of diplomatic letdowns for dating, so it will be good practice.

Another preventative measure you can take is to embrace rejection. If you are a writer or an actor, you know what I'm talking about. The more you really open yourself to the possibilities, the more you open yourself to rejection. You can't have one without the other. That's why successful authors usually have impressive lists of rejections (or would if they bothered to keep track), and successful daters have plenty of stories about the one that got away, and the one they were lucky to get away *from*. As they say, "If you're not being rejected, you are not shooting high enough." And then there's the rejecting *you'll* have do. If you accept the reality of rejection, rather than fighting it, you will free up a lot of energy for the good stuff. Your acceptance of different outcomes will also be evident to your scouts, and free them to join you in the adventure.

The Honesty Contract

A potential sticky situation we haven't covered is the case where a friend is evasive about your request for help. It may just mean that your friend isn't particularly comfortable or skilled in the area of matchmaking. He also could be a little worried about the possibilities we discussed above, and talking it out could clear the air. Or maybe it's more. If you really want help from your friends, open yourself to their concerns—to the kind of information they aren't likely to volunteer. If you solicit their honesty, you may not like what you hear. Maybe your friend doesn't think you are ready to date again. Or, maybe—ouch—there is a reason he is reluctant to refer you. He might think you've let yourself go, or worries about an annoying trait of yours—he accepts it, but is concerned it could get in the way in a new relationship.

If you don't want this kind of honesty, you won't get it. In fact, a really good friend can be counted on to lie to you when that's what you need. The only way you will get the tough feedback is to ask for it. There may not be any bad news, and then you can stop your imagination from running wild. Or you may disagree with the feedback and use your friend's reluctance as incentive to "show him." Or, you may be disturbed by the feedback and be moved to make some changes.

One place that has a built-in honesty contract, without the interpersonal stickiness, is the therapy office. While a therapist isn't likely to tell you if she finds you attractive, she will help you honestly look at yourself. At some level, we all know what's getting in our way. Ironically, the more we try to ignore our less desirable traits, the more power they can take on. My own therapy put me face to face with the ugliest parts of myself, and it hurt. But once I did, my focus was freed so I could notice the beauty others saw in me.

chapter 17

"Date Wanted": Using Ads

... [T]he fresh and untried can carry more infinite appeal than a palpable imitation of the already proved.
—Rod Serling, TV Guide interview,
November 7, 1959

Placing an ad in the personals might be one of those things you said you'd never do. Now you're considering placing an ad, and suddenly Rod Serling appears in the foreground, announcing your entry into the fifth dimension. You are entering the zone of advertising, that place where the distinction between fantasy and reality is not always apparent. Let's exclaim a collective "far out!," and check out the trip. You may be surprised and find yourself back on Earth—with a date!—in no time.

Where to Advertise

Advertising today can literally reach the ends of the earth. Since the Internet arrived on the scene, there are more options than ever. Online personals, which are the subject of the next chapter, are exploding in popularity. Yet, there are many Boomers who still like the feel of paper and ink.

In choosing where to advertise, consider who reads what. Newspapers are great because a lot of people read them. Well, that's the down side, too. If you want to cast a wide net, your city's major newspapers will get you a lot of contacts. On the other hand, you are probably wise to avoid free newspapers and entertainment guides. The net you cast here will include anybody who happens to walk by on the street. Entertainment guides and alternative papers also tend to draw an edgier, younger reader. (Maybe that just sold some of you!)

If you opt for a newspaper, consider the geographical area serviced by the paper, as well as the type of reader that paper draws. For example, my city has just a morning and an afternoon paper, and one is commonly referred to as the "Republican paper" and the other the "Democrat paper."

Another option you may not have considered are specialty periodicals. Magazines titled by the name of your city feature the cultural and entertainment highlights of your town, and often come with a personals section. Just go to your local bookstore and look at the periodicals that interest you. You may be surprised to find a personals section in the back. One woman wanted to date the type of person who reads the *New York Review of Books*, so she placed an ad there. Last I heard, she and her date were still enjoying literary conversations together.

Pick Me! Writing an Effective Ad

This is one place where the exploring you did in Chapters 4 and 10 can bear fruit. The challenge—and it's a big one!—of writing a good ad is to capture *you*. How do you put into words those qualities that make you unique and loveable? Then there's the challenge of describing what you want in a partner. (If this one's got you stumped, you might want to skip ahead to Chapter 21.) Then you have to pack all this into a few lines! Before you sign up for a journalism course, check out the following tips:

- Know commonly used abbreviations, and use them when you have limited space. Looking through the personals will give you a quick sense of information that can be easily coded. For example, SGM55 means single gay male, aged 55, and SAF48 means single Asian female, aged 48. You can add size, as in BB for "big beautiful," and then religion, as in BBJW (for a man, it would be BHJM, "handsome" replacing "beautiful"). Scan the ads before you place yours. Sometimes the standard is to use "S" for all single categories, and sometimes "D" and "W" are also used (to indicate divorced or widowed). The following is an example of a very brief, but bland ad: *"SWF45 129# 5'6" seeking SM45-55 for friendship and possible LTR."* Because abbreviations are standardized, you trade off individuality when you use them, so don't overdue it.

- Use language that is specific and lively. "Nordic looking" is likely to draw more interest than the overused "attractive." Words like leggy, curvy, petite, or muscular help communicate an image of body shape. Use a more specific color name for your skin (almond) or eyes (jade). Rather than saying you like movies, refer to an actor, director, or favorite movie. Speaking of movies, ever notice that it is often the cute quirks of the character that win the heart of another? Share your cute quirk. The following descriptions are specific enough describe real people:

"Emotionally smart, trivia-impaired. Mesmerized by the full moon, neon and attractive men."

"Weekend traveler with improved emotional skills seeks intelligent woman who enjoys politics and can tolerate baseball."

"I can, and have, been quite charming and well-behaved at a business dinner atop the Marriott Marquis, but I'd probably be happier climbing rocks to sit under a waterfall."

- Show who you are through your writing. If you are a "no-nonsense" person, your ad will be pointed and short. My brother is a Major General in the Army, and he writes as if he's rallying troops, using empowering language and capital letters. I get an image of his stature and effectiveness when I read his writing. If you are poetic, write in meter. If you are funny, *be* funny (rather than saying "good sense of humor"!). Rather than saying you are smart, write well. In this newspaper-format example, this woman not only says she's "content with life," her simple, unlabored writing *shows* it:

"Content with Life

SBW58 with carefree spirit, looking for a funny, energetic man to share life and its ironies."

Warmth and idealism, as well as a sense of time, come through in this sample boomer ad:

"Can We Talk Love?

Are you still holding out for love? Me, too. If you're open and intelligent, beautiful inside as well as out, and you want a chance at love, try me. I'm honest and sincere, handsome and in good shape. I'm 50, wear my hair long, and have room in my life for a relationship. If you still believe in love, I have a lot of it to give."

And this response to an essay question on politics demonstrates the writer's wit:

"I had to quickly change my registration once from Republican to Democrat after someone hired me to run a political campaign. I sometimes cry at the National Anthem because I feel so fortunate for the life I have in this country, and once had an erotic dream about Ronald Reagan. So what does that make me? I have no idea. Can someone tell me?"

- Be honest. Don't lie about your age, or claim to be a perfect "10." Why set yourself up to lose rank on your first date? Although you may be trying to make a good impression, ads with lengthy self-descriptions may backfire by coming off as narcissistic. This sample ad demonstrates the tendency to get carried away with adjectives:

"Creative Always

Life-loving, energetic, passionate, enthusiastic, gifted 48-year-old tall, slim, auburn-haired woman experienced in the performance arts seeks an open, spiritually-aware, creative, energetic, and relationship-ready man with whom to share a range of experiences, from nature excursions to cultural feasting to lazy evenings at home."

- Check your spelling and grammar!

You can also use these strategies as you prepare your voice box message and, for online searchers, as you complete your essay.

Shopping the Ads

You don't have to write an ad to take advantage of them. Check out the ads out there and see what you find. If you are attracted to an ad, check it out! Remember, you are in the twilight zone, so you have yet to find out how much of the ad is truth and how much is fiction. When you decide to respond to an ad, you just call the number given, charge your credit card (no, it's not free!), punch in the box number associated with the ad, and listen to a pre-recorded message from your potential date. Here you will get a little better sense of the person from voice tone and an elaborated description. Now you can decide if you want to hang up or leave a message. If you leave a message, *do not leave a last name or a home or work phone number*. If you don't have a cell phone, get one before calling—and use it exclusively for date shopping.

From the Mouths of Baby Boomers

"When I responded to an ad, the man on the message mentioned that he was looking for women between the ages of 45 and 55. I was 56. I left a message anyway, saying: 'Hi, Bill. Too bad for you. I'm 56. Guess I'm too old, but boy did you miss out! If you still want to explore something with an *old* woman, call me.' Mine was the only message he responded to! We enjoyed dating and he was crazy about me, but I eventually moved on."

—Class of '64

"I used voice ads, and had some wild experiences. I met one woman over a cup of coffee. She says, 'I'm not quite divorced yet. My soon-to-be ex-husband is in jail for raping two girls.' I ended up playing counselor. Then there was this other woman. We're just talking on the phone—'blah, blah, blah'—then she says, 'I love you!' But she described herself as very attractive, so I thought, 'What the heck.' We met for lunch. She was, well, ugly, but dumb, too—bad combination. She could tell things were going nowhere, so when we were parting, she asked, 'Can I give you a big hug?' It was brutal."

—Class of '71

When you leave your message, it's your turn to advertise. Being upbeat and pleasant will go a long way. If you can throw in some wit, all the better.

Keeping It Safe

Placing and responding to personals puts you in contact with strangers. As warm as you may feel toward somebody's ad, you don't really know anything about that person until you meet. That's the adventure, but let's keep it a *safe* adventure. Here's how:

- When you place or respond to an ad, never give information that can physically lead to you. That means no last name or address and, as mentioned above, no home or work phone. Use a cell phone with voice mail for receiving messages and for calling. Otherwise, people with caller ID can identify who you are. (If you must call from a home phone, punching in *67 will block the recipient's caller ID.) On the other hand, caller ID can be helpful to you. I have a friend who, after a date from hell, replaced the woman's phone number with the message to himself: "don't call."
- Don't assume your date is single. Confirm this by phone before you meet.
- When you decide to meet, arrange a brief meeting in a public place, and arrive and depart separately. The parameters for this type of "look-see" meeting are described in Chapter 20.
- Never leave your drink or purse unattended.
- Don't wear revealing clothes to the first meeting.
- Offer to pay your share of the expenses. That way, you don't feel any obligations.
- Trust your gut. If it doesn't feel right, it's not right. Don't apologize or make excuses, just say you have to go, and *go*.

You may be surprised at all you learn from this Twilight-Zone experience of using personal ads. You become an advertiser, writer, and buyer all at once. You will probably also develop a very good sense of humor. No doubt you will have an adventure. And, who knows, you might even come home with a real live souvenir!

In her entertaining book, *My 1,000 Americans*, British author Rochelle Morton takes power dating to an extreme. Over a year's time, she met with 1,000 responders to an ad she placed in four U.S. newspapers. And these men were actually a random subset of the men who called! Keep in mind that she only screened out men who seemed threatening or obviously perverted. Here's what she discovered:

1. A substantial percentage of the men she met with were married. They felt entitled to date because the wife had let herself go; stopped cleaning or pleasing him sexually; didn't mind; left on a trip. One of these aspiring fornicators was a pastor!

2. Your imagination cannot cover all the strange turn-ons and weird fantasies some men want you to indulge. It's surprising the number of men who want to pretend they're babies (well, on the other hand…). And, suffice it to say, S&M is alive and well!

3. Inmates respond to personals (she didn't meet with these).

4. There are many men that defy categorization, like the one who was dressed as a robed monarch, complete with crown, and the one who had to reorder his eggs because he prematurely broke a yolk and feared the consequences would be dire.

5. There are good ones out there who aren't taken!

6. She "never had so much fun"!

chapter 18

DateMe.com

My computer dating bureau came up with a perfect
gentleman. Still, I've got another three goes.
—*Sally Poplin*

Do you remember watching *2001: The Space Odyssey* and thinking how far off that seemed? In 1968, the idea of using a computer to find dates may have seemed as weird as the emotional expressions of the movie's HAL9000 computer.

Although you've most likely heard about Internet dating, if you haven't been initiated, you may still think it's a little weird. Welcome to the real 2000's! Internet dating is no longer limited to computer geeks and late-night chat addicts. I just did a Google search using the keywords "online dating service" and came up with 1,130,000 hits! The Internet dating industry has exploded as the demand keeps rising. Why? Because online dating meets our needs. It's accessible, inexpensive, and we can do much of it in pajamas or sweats. Dating via computer is particularly attractive to dating-again Boomers, because our social circles, especially with singles, have diminished. The net gives us almost instant access to a large number of prospects. And, unconstrained by geography, we can literally search the ends of the earth!

Computers and Love

In *2001:The Space Odyssey,* the HAL9000 computer, affectionately known as "HAL," sang the old courtship song, "Daisy, Daisy" as a parting gesture. What you may not know is that this was, in reality, the first song ever sung by a computer. Bell Labs, who experimented with computerized-synthesized speech in the early 1960s, performed the magic. So, the first song ever sung by a computer was a dating song. Prophetic, huh?

Navigating Internet Services

With so many sites, deciding which service to use can feel overwhelming. One way to narrow things down is to focus on a specific group you identify with. You name it, the Internet has it. Just go to a search engine and type in "online dating" and—African American, Hispanic, Jewish, Christian, Hindu, Gay, Lesbian, Baby Boomer—whatever fits you. Even with the narrowed field, expect to get thousands of options.

Another approach is to ask around. You may be surprised to learn that someone in your network has or is using an online service. You may be able to benefit from their experience.

The Internet also offers dating service directories, but often what looks like a directory is actually an ad for a particular service. An example of one that claims to have no affiliate sites is www.singles-online-dating.com. The site offers a list of their "top 10" dating service picks, along with descriptions. The site aLoveLinksPlus.com provides top picks as well as services to avoid, picks by category, and features a "dating service of the week."

Another criteria you can use is cost. There are many free sites available, and others that offer free trials or invite you to stay free as long as you don't write anyone first. But even the for-pay services are a fraction of the cost of offline matchmaking services.

As you shop the various services, use common sense. You want a site that looks good, has easy-to-understand directions, and has an abundance of members. There's also a little matchmaking involved in finding a site—how it's presented will give you a feel for the values the site emphasizes. For example, if you don't want pornographic messages, stay away from sites with "adult" content. As you look, keep in mind that you can, and probably will want to, sign on with a number of sites.

Once you settle on a site, you need to enter the search criteria for potential dates. At minimum, you'll want to specify a gender, age range, and geographical location. Some sites also offer "reverse searches," which find members who are interested in *your* particular set of qualifications. That's one way to indulge your curiosity about who might be interested in you. But, before we continue …

A Word of Warning

Let's face it, there are some weirdos out there. As with other types of ad dating, there will be your married segment, a few fetishes, and the occasional felon. But, as with the general population, most people are just fine. Here's how to protect yourself against the worst of the lot:

- Review and follow the safety precautions for using ads in general (see Chapter 17). Bottom line: do not give any information that can physically lead to you —period.
- Never use your real name as your screen name, and don't use the same screen name that you use for other purposes. Remember the "no specifics rule" that Kathleen and Joe followed in *You've Got Mail*? Good precedent.

Nicknames, Photographs, and Surveys

Although photos are optional, you need a nickname (screen name) to identify you. Because your screen name is the first clue you give to who you are, pick a good one. As in paper ads, online screen names often use acronyms to communicate basic information, as in SWF50 for "single white female, aged fifty." Beyond that, see if you can capture the key to your attractiveness. Some advisors say to stick with physical descriptors and others suggest capturing an interest that communicates something essential about you. So, it's up to you whether you go with BlueEyez52 or Monet49, or something witty like Catch44. Unfortunately, as much as words like "fun" and "playful" can describe many of us, they can be interpreted as a readiness for sexual involvement. Not everyone uses age as a part of their screen name; sometimes numbers are just used to personalize the name. To get a feel for what's out there, browse around.

Jargon for the Uninitiated

Blocking: An online feature that prevents others from knowing you're online. If you don't want your prospects to know you're home on a Saturday night, this can come in handy.

Chat Room: An online site set up for, well, chatting. Discussions take place in real time, meaning you punch in a message and it gets posted with your screen name, then others can respond, and so on. You can come and go as you please.

Cybersex: What it sounds like.

Emoticon: An attempt to fill in the emotional void in cyberspace (HAL would have loved this!). Because your email partner can't see you smile, you send a ☺ You can find whole directories of emoticons online, but I wouldn't work too hard at it. Many people find them annoying ☹.

Exclusive: Online version of "going steady."

Instant Messages (IM): Some of us would define these as a pain in the—you know what. It's a way for someone to jump into the corner of your online computer screen with a message, and try to engage you in a chat. IMs cannot come in if you're blocked. Or, if you don't want a particular person to jump in, you can go to your "buddy list" and block that person.

Finally, be honest. Don't use "Cruiselook" unless you have had more than one stranger mistake you for Tom Cruise. Why set the stage for a potential date to be disappointed later?

Now for the topic of photos. Although providing a photo is optional, most people do it and most people want it. High-profile daters sometimes worry about being recognized, but many still opt to provide a photo. People with photos get more responses, and some people limit their searches to "show only members with photos." Whether warranted or not, the absence of a photo tends to raise suspicions.

On the other hand, I have talked to people who feel strongly about not leading with the physical impression. They don't want to display a photo, and aren't really interested in seeing photos. Just goes to show, there's enough room in this world for all of us!

From the Mouths of Baby Boomers

"People present themselves in the absolute best light when Internet dating. You have to realize that most people do not have a very realistic view of themselves. And, let's face it, we search the Internet because we're very much in need of a connection. It's easy to jump at a small connection and forgive the big stuff until you meet and then it's … Ick! Just don't let your wishes get ahead of reality."

—Class of '71

"I met people through the Internet, but I refused to provide photos. So many guys would go right from 'How are you?' to 'Got a pic?' I'd respond, 'I'm fine. Sorry I don't have a pic, but I'm intelligent, hard working, and when I've met people in the past, I haven't had anyone run away screaming.' I'm still dating a guy I met through the Internet."

—Class of '75

"When we finally decided to meet, I was very concerned that we wouldn't be attracted to one another. So I asked him to send me a picture and he sent one via email. When I opened it I realized he had sent me a picture of Mr. Potato Head! When I asked him how I would recognize him when we met, he said he'd be the one wearing the white gloves (like Mr. Potato Head). I fell for his sense of humor."

—Class of '80

As with your identifying information, make sure the picture looks like you. Of course you want to use a good shot, but just as casting directors get angry when an actor doesn't look like her head shot, your date won't appreciate false advertising (nor will you!). Get someone with a digital camera and some photography skills to get a good photo of your whole face and upper body, or scan in a *recent* photo you like. Avoid using a web cam, as they are known to produce unflattering results. The photo may actually be the best place to put your energies, because, like it or not, they are what get looked at. And remember, a good smile goes a long way!

In addition to submitting a screen name and the optional photo, you will need to fill out a profile form. Most advisors will tell you not to agonize over this, and to cast a wide net by endorsing more items rather than less. Of course, be prudent about the criteria you really care about, such as gender, smoking vs. non-smoking, religion, children or no children, age preference. And, no, it does not go without saying that you require an unmarried date—say it! The profile usually includes a personal essay, and together, they make up your ad. See Chapter 17 for tips on effective ads. Even though you have more room online than you do in a print ad, don't do a dissertation—you will come off as overzealous and run the risk of boring your prospects.

Getting hooked up with an online service is typically as easy as signing on, providing your data, and paying a fee (if any). But as the online dating industry becomes increasingly competitive, some services have begun to do a little selecting of their own. In their report, "Sorry, You're Nobody's Type" (7/30/03), *The Wall Street Journal* cites some dating services that claim to offer better prospects by being selective. For example, eHarmony.com, which was founded by a clinical psychologist, attempts to weed out liars and losers through personality testing. Other services target an exclusive group, such as those with a degree from an elite college (TheSquare.com) or people with salaries over $100,000 (highlighted as the "millionaires" on MillionaireMatch.com).

Taking It to the Next Level

There are four levels to online dating. The first is to make email contact, the second is the phone call, the third is the "look-see" meeting (see Chapter 20), and the fourth is an actual date.

Once you submit your personal information, you will get to view information on your matches. If you want to get to know someone better, you follow-up with an e-mail. A note to women out there: Some advisors will tell you not to initiate contact with men, and there is some evidence that women do better when they wait and respond. As much as our technologies have evolved, seems a lot of men still enjoy the chase. Other advisors say the "don't initiate" rule is hogwash and note the irony of going to the trouble of signing up with a service, then playing hard to get. Use this conflicting advice as an asset, and decide for yourself. After all, the best way to find a match is to be who you are. If you happen to like the feminine mystique, kick your feet up and wait. If you like going after what you want, you go girl! Those men who are kicking back will appreciate it.

I am also impressed with how polarized the advice is about how quickly to move to level three. Some say to move as quickly as possible to phone contact and then meet in person ASAP. The reasoning here is that it is only through the actual contact that you get a real feel for each other, so why waste your time gabbing online? Check it out and move on.

The other, more common school of thought is to take your time. Ask and answer a lot of questions by email before you step it up. That way you will narrow down the field and get a sense for who you click with. Ironically, the same argument about wasting time can be used here: Why bother to make actual contact with many when you can narrow things down online, and then even further via the phone?

Keep in mind, however, that until you meet, you are still in the twilight zone. Some people lie, and some of us see what we want to see. A woman who describes herself as a "tall blonde with blue eyes" will have hopeful men picturing Cheryl Tiegs—compete with bikini, regardless of what the photo looks like. Just mention the blue eyes, and us Boomer women will be thinking Paul Newman. Like the Rorschach test, as long as the information is ambiguous—and it always is—there is room for us to project our own images. Which means, there's always room for disappointment.

Usually, there is a middle ground between lingering in an online fantasy relationship and rushing to the first drink. And, again, it comes down to your personal style. If you are an action-oriented, "seeing is believing" type, you may want to step things up more quickly. Just be careful. Chapter 20 will tell you what you need to know about setting up your meeting.

On the other hand, if you need time, take the time and enjoy each phase. Besides, a little mystery can be fun! And, whatever your style, don't do anything before you're ready. After all, this is supposed to be about *you*.

chapter 19

Professional Matchmaking

You come to love not by finding the perfect person,
but by seeing an imperfect person perfectly.
—*Sam Keen, Boomer author and lecturer*

With the popularity of online dating, you may wonder: "Is anybody using traditional dating services anymore?" Yes— Boomers are. In early 2003, an Associated Press headline ran: "Dating services attract baby boomers: Short cut to romance ideal for some." The article stated that Boomers make up the bulk of those using professional matchmaking, because we have more money than younger daters, we may prefer to keep our privacy, and we like using experts. If you have a personal trainer and a shopping consultant, why not add a professional matchmaker? Let's look at which Boomers are making this choice.

Who Uses a Service?

First of all, offline dating services are expensive, so people using them usually have money. Private matchmakers can charge between $4,000 and $25,000, and services ask up to $4,000 for a year's membership. (Compare this to a max of about $600 a year for online services!) So, if you're targeting the jet set, you may have found your home.

Boomers who use a professional service also may be concerned about privacy issues. As we discussed earlier, a high-profile individual may be reluctant to post his or her photo on the Internet. Boomers may also be willing to pay for the additional screening an offline service can provide. One of these services, Great Expectations, attracts clients by publicizing that one-third of online contacts are married. Some services conduct criminal and credit checks on their clients.

Finally, some Boomers feel they spend enough time on the computer already and don't want to find dates there. As easy as online dating is, it can be time-consuming to keep up with the responses (maybe not the *worst* problem to have).

So, as much as the online services expand, some Boomers will opt for tradition (at least our version of it!) and hire a matchmaker. If you're one of these Boomers, let's look at what options are available for you.

Approaches to Matchmaking

Depending on the particular service or matchmaker, the following approaches may be used alone or in combination:

Computerized Dating Services

While the "computerized" part is not so impressive anymore with online options right at hand, many services rely primarily on computer profile matching. With these services, you fill out a survey, answer essay questions, and get your photo taken. Although you probably have a personal interview, it is the computer that does the matching. Matches are provided to you on a regular basis, while other clients receive your profile. You do the follow up. Sound familiar?

"Hand Matching" Services

These services are more expensive than ones that provide computerized matching, but appeal because of the personal attention provided. Clients meet with an agent, who conducts an extensive personal interview and uses the information gathered to make matches. Surprisingly, you can't assume that the person doing the interview is the one who will be making the match. In her book, *Single No More*, Dr. Ellen Kreidman tells of a case where a (straight) man was matched with another man, because his interviewer passed off his profile without bothering to clarify the gender!

Video Dating Services

These services offer the opportunity to view videos of a variety of clients. It's kind of like going to the library and pulling out books to page through. The advantage of videos over photos is that they allow you to see how the whole package works together—voice, looks, and nonverbal communication. It's also easier to rule out liars. Clients can get nervous sitting in front of a video camera, so take that into account. The down side of using a video service is that, like going to the library, it takes time.

From the Mouths of Baby Boomers

"I'm not a big 'sit uptown in the bar' kinda guy. So I looked up a service called 'It's Just Lunch.' I went in, they interviewed me and took a picture. I immediately started getting phone calls. We'd meet for lunch, then agree on whether to follow-up or not. It was a little spendy—$1,200 for a 2-year time frame. They guarantee 16 dates. They make the reservations, deliver the person there. I met some very interesting people. Like one women—she was not terribly attractive, but very scholarly. We ended up in a fascinating discussion. I met about 12 women, most were quite attractive, and there were two or three I was interested in. One of them was on a vice squad, and had some great stories. I really liked her, but before things could get going, I met Angie through a friend. She turned out to be the best fit of all."

—Class of '71

"After my divorce, I used the services of a self-proclaimed 'matchmaker.' It was not an unpleasant experience, though obviously I didn't meet Ms. Right (I told them: 'You may not be Ms. Right; but you can be Ms. Right Now!'). This lady personally interviewed all candidates, male and female, and just used her intuition to make matches. I met some nice ladies-probably gave up too soon on some, and some probably gave up too soon on me."

—Class of '73

Independent Matchmakers

This category is the most like the old idea of the village matchmaker, except that these practitioners are more likely to be found in the most populated cities than in small villages, and they charge big bucks! The good news is that you get to work exclusively with an experienced (hopefully!) matchmaker throughout the process. Like an agent working to get you a contract, the matchmaker works to make you a match.

Colorful Matches

Television has given us some entertaining, yet inspiring, reminders that there is someone out there for everyone:

Remember the *Andy Griffith* episode where Andy plays image consultant to Ernest T. Bass? Ernest, the scruffy country bumpkin, gets cleaned up and coached on his introduction, "How do you do, Mrs. Riley?" By getting out and being social, Ernest found the woman of his dreams: An equally unpolished bumpkinette.

A one-of-a kind '60s icon named Tiny Tim, know for his wavy, dyed-red hair, flashy clothing, companion ukulele, and curious hit "Tiptoe Through the Tulips," showed off a match made in Hollywood when he got married on *The Tonight Show*. His bride was 17-year-old "Miss Vicki" (Victoria May Budinger), the night was December 17, 1969, and over 45 millions viewers witnessed the ceremony. According to johnnycarson.com, not only did the evening mark the most attended wedding in television history, but it also polled the highest rating in television history for a talk show.

Innovative Approaches

Creative approaches to matchmaking keep popping up. One that has taken off is SpeedDating, a service that trains you to evaluate a potential date in 7 minutes. Once you're trained, the service has you meet with seven different prospect for 7 minutes each, all in the same evening! It works sort of like "musical chairs," but with tables. This one involves less mediation, but also costs much less than standard services. Another interesting approach called "Eight at Eight" brings four men and four women together for dinner and provides a comfortable way for them to get to know each other. A host sits with the singles and helps make introductions and initiate conversation. Meeting while eating seems to be catching on, as new services arrange dinner gatherings and services like "It's Just Lunch" expand. At the same time, more services are catering to religious preference or specific interests—from athletes and adventure-seekers to vegetarians. For a state-by-state directory of dating services, see Appendix D.

Questions to Ask

Before you pull out your wallet, check out the following:

- How exactly do you make matches? Do you rely entirely on computerized matching, or is there a human element? Don't be pacified by catchwords like "quality assurance." Use the old "help me understand," and have them walk you through the process. Their attention to your questions will also give you a sense of how individualized their approach really is.

- Do you do the searching or do I? Profile-type services provide files or videos for you to look through, but it may be your fingers that do most of the walking.

- Is the person interviewing me the one who does the matching? If the answer is no, insist on meeting personally with the real matchmaker.

- How many *active* members do you have, and what percentage of them are in my preferred age range? As talented as a matchmaker is, if she only has two other active clients, you're pretty limited.

- What kinds of background checks do you conduct? Of course, whatever others go through, you'll have to go through, too, but find out up front.

- What membership options do you offer? Some services offer short-term (i.e., six month) memberships, others do not.

- What else do I have to pay for? Don't assume the membership fee covers everything.

- If I meet someone, can I put my membership on hold or get a pro-rated refund?

- Do you have counselors on hand, and what is their training and background? Some services have counselors on board to help answer relationship questions as they come along.
- Especially with independent matchmakers, check out how long they have been in business, and get references.

Matchmaking is big business—a $917 million business according to Marketdata Enterprise. Keep that in mind as you listen to the sales pitches. Be clear that if you're going to pay more, you expect more.

What to Expect

Expect to reveal a lot about yourself. If you want someone else to do the matchmaking, you need to leave them with a good sense of who you are.

Expect paperwork. It's not likely you will get out of completing surveys and questionnaires.

Expect your service to be accountable. Dr. Kreidman recommends documenting your dates, so that you can let the service know if they've sent you a mismatch. Mix-ups can happen, and any good service will offer a way to rectify such a situation.

Mostly, expect good things. Having someone in your court that you really trust makes life a whole lot easier.

chapter 20

The Blind Date

My friends have been trying to set me up on dates.
They mean well, but it's always the same thing.
They would say, "We found someone perfect for you."
I meet the person and I ask myself, "What do my
friends think of me?"
—*Mike Dugan*

What comes to mind when you think "blind date?" A good joke? Images of boredom so acute that the recipient opts for physical pain? (Remember the parody *Airplane*, where a man's relentless talking is so intolerable that the lady next to him hangs herself and he keeps talking?)

No, blind dating has not gotten good press. Well, until now. Back when we were dating the first time around, blind dates were full-fledged dates where you were stuck with someone for the evening and had to endure the awkwardness of a bad match to the bitter end. With the increased use of personals and the onset of Internet dating, we have developed easier formats for blind dates, we're doing it more, and the success stories are following.

So you've done your prescreening. It's time to make it real.

The "Look-See"

Boomers like to see results. We go "power shopping," do "power work-outs," eat "power bars," and take "power naps." We are busy and want to get as much as we can out of our efforts. This approach has made its way to the blind date and resulted in what I call the "look-see."

The look-see is an abbreviated version of the blind date. It offers what both daters are needing—to get a quick sense of the other person and see how you feel together. It is a safe, low-pressure way to meet, move on, and be free to decide what to do next. Here's how to do a look-see:

1. Arrange to meet in a very public place, during the daytime or right after work. Easy options include meeting for ice-cream, coffee, a light lunch, or a quick drink.
2. Set parameters for the meeting, such as a time frame, or use natural parameters, such as "I'll have to get back to work by 1 p.m.," or "I'm meeting my friends afterwards." (They can always come over, interrupt, and hold you to it!).
3. Arrive and depart separately. This strategy keeps it no-obligation, and keeps it safe.

In a way, the look-see is more like a pre-date, which helps the two of you—independently—decide whether you want to give a date a go. If you do, you follow up. If you don't, you don't.

Double Dates and Group Dates

Double dates are a common approach to blind dating, often with a match-making couple hosting two people they want to get together. Advantages of double dates include: The established couple can provide a common frame of reference for the just-met couple and help promote conversation. With the four of you together, things are likely to stay light and fun. Having your girlfriend or your best buddy along can be a lifesaver. For example, you take a powder room break with your girlfriend and let her know if things are not going well. Later, she deftly looks at her watch and says she needs to get home to take the dog out, and you all agree to call it a night. There is also safety in numbers.

Opening the Blinds

When you are being set up, you can get a feel for what's ahead—and get some material for conversation—by asking your contact the right questions:

- How well do you know him/her?
- What do you like about him/her?
- What do you dislike about him/her?
- How do you see us getting along?
- What does he/she do for a living?
- What does he/she do for fun?
- Do you have a photo/description of him/her?

Double dating can be a problem when the established couple indulges in intimate exchanges, such as kissing or making references to their sexual relationship. This can leave the other couple feeling awkward and uncomfortable, especially if the chemistry isn't there. The host couple may also want to draw out the evening because, of course, they like being together and with their friends. Other pitfalls can stem from the multiple relationships involved. If you double-date with your sister, her husband, and his boss, you may be concerned that a mismatch could threaten your brother-in-law's relationship with his boss.

As we discussed in Chapter 16, anticipating and talking about potential scenarios can help a great deal. It should be clear that the purpose of the double date is to help *you*, and things need to be set up with that in mind. Express your concerns and anxieties, and work out in advance how to deal with them. This can result in working out comfortable seating arrangements at the restaurant, having the host couple agree to save intimate exchanges for another time, and establishing codes or check-in strategies to communicate how it's going (although it may be obvious!) and when to cut it short.

By the way, the parameters for a look-see are just as relevant here. By arriving and departing separately or with your friend, and having a set time frame, you avoid awkward partings. You are then free to evaluate for yourself whether you want to initiate further contact.

Double dates can also be "double blind" where you and a friend are both meeting new potentials at the same time. For example, you and an online prospect agree to both bring a friend to your look-see. I always think this could get a bit hairy: What if your online date likes your friend better? Of course, your friend's date could like *you* better … Again, there's no substitute for talking it out—in advance.

Bringing a friend or a group of friends is becoming a popular way to engage with a new contact. It really takes the pressure off, and can be a lot of fun. Some dating services are capitalizing on this approach and arrange group dates (see Chapter 19). If you're open to a mix-and-match approach, this is a way to access and assess a number of options at once. The icing on the cake is that when groups come together, you can expand your network of friends as well as dates.

From the Mouths of Baby Boomers

"My good friend, who knew me well had always admired her pharmacist. She talked about his patience, his friendly face, and his sincere desire to help people especially in times of need. She found out that he was a former triathlete and that he like to be involved in fitness. She said she wanted me to meet him. I went down and had a prescription filled (well almost … after the divorce my insurance card was a problem and so it turned out a bit embarrassing) and that gave us a reason to talk. We went to dinner after he finished work that evening on my invitation … and then the next day was our first official date, Valentine's Day. He asked me out and it has been pretty darn good ever since. So my blind date was in a pharmacy! Even though I didn't get my prescription, meeting him was definitely healing."

—Class of '70

"Bill and I met through my cousin who was a friend of his. Bill thought I was rather bold on our blind date, but that is only because I had all that prior experience with the one-liners. He withstood the interrogation and eventually asked me to marry him. I said yes."

—Class of '63

Keeping Your Sense of Humor

If there's any topic that has gotten skewered by comics, it's the blind date. You can either see this as a reason to avoid the experience or to join the fun. I've always thought it would be fun to be a comedian, because every stupid situation you get into becomes material. The telling of a joke or a good story transforms something embarrassing into something attractive. Laughter is a wonderful way to break the tension, release our anxieties, and lighten up. When you and your date can share in the humor of the situation, all the better.

Misery Is ...

Remember the heartwarming "Happiness is.." books that featured *Peanuts* characters and the simple things that made them happy? In 1963, two of these Charles Schultz creations—*Happiness is a Warm Puppy and Security is a Thumb and a Blanket,* topped the nonfiction bestseller lists.

But lest anything get too cute and sentimental, a good comic is always ready to balance things out. Mad magazine spoofed the series with the July '63 cover cartoon, "Misery is a Cold Hot Dog." By 1967, Johnny Carson came out with a collection of "Misery is ..." jokes, the title revealing a favorite subject of comics: Misery is a Blind Date.

Rather than thinking about your blind date as a test that you and your date pass or fail, think of the experience as an adventure. Imagine you are a crew member on the U.S.S. *Enterprise*, exploring the vast territory of civilization, including the strange and new. What an opportunity you have!

With this spirit of exploration, your attentions aren't exclusively on the question of yes or no. You are an observer. You are getting to know another human being, seeing what it's like. In addition to finding dates, you are learning, making friends and contacts, and expanding your world.

"... [T]o explore strange new worlds, to seek out new life and new civilizations. To boldly go where no man has gone before."

—Star Trek *mission statement*

As you go into this new territory, leave your expectations at the door. If you hit it off, great! If it bombs, it's experience. Consider keeping a journal of your dating experiences. Writing it down will help you appreciate the richness of your experience, what you are learning, and most of all, how wildly entertaining life is.

Embracing the Adventure

Here goes! It's time to date. Part 3 is your guide as you
explore your attractions, test the waters with looks and lines,
make a date, go out, and feel the heat of close encounters.
Now is your chance to recapture the excitement of being with
someone new! By approaching dating as an adventure, you
can transform anxiety into excitement, mistakes into experience, and fears into an attitude of discovery.

chapter 21

Chemistry 101: The Secrets of Attraction

The meeting of two personalities is like the contact of two chemical substances; If there is any reaction, both are transformed.
—Carl Jung

What is that elusive feeling, that magnetic pull that makes us want to be around a person? We call it attraction, but we often can't explain why we feel it. We just do. When two people are mutually attracted, we say there is "chemistry." Ah, chemistry. We think of Maria and Tony in *West Side Story*, Oliver and Jenny in *Love Story,* Elvis and—women. Is there anything better? Like a chemical reaction, things start to sizzle, energy is emitted, and new and wonderful feelings are generated. Although elusive, the components of attraction are well worth exploring. So, get back into the '60s mode and get ready to experiment. The chemistry we're about to explore is completely legal and not only can produce the high of a lifetime, but quite possibly a lifetime of highs!

What Excites You?

Da da da da da da da da ... It's *The Dating Game*! Enter Jim Lange in his velvet suit, accompanied by the contestant. You are behind the partition with two other potential dates, sweating to come up with the right answers so you get picked. If this is what the prospect of dating feels like, maybe it's time to get out of your chair, look around, and ask your own questions.

Chemistry Defined (sort of): Chemistry is that charged feeling you both experience when you look into each other's eyes. You are turned on, not just sexually, but your whole being—your history, your hurts, your desire—is drawn to this other person. What is amazing is that, at the same time, the person you want desires you just as much. When you are together, you feel energized and enlarged.

As we start to date, we tend to focus on our ability to attract someone else. Like the bachelors on *The Dating Game*, we often work to meet the imagined criteria of the potential date. Problem is, this one-down attitude keeps us from evaluating what *we* want, and can also make us less attractive. So, for a moment, let's forget about how you look and act, and explore what turns you on. We'll get back to your magnetism at the end of the chapter.

Ask yourself, "What excites me in another person?" If you respond "a body like Raquel Welch" or "eyes like Paul Newman," that's great, but not complete. We run the best chance of discovering chemistry when we fill out the vision of what we want. This vision includes a combination of body, personality, mind, and spirit. It's how the person relates to you, a look, a touch. Or the way he makes you laugh or inspires you. One of the most exciting opportunities of dating is the chance to experiment with different combinations of these factors. Yes, it's a complex mix, and one that we can never fully grasp. But the more we sort out what we want and don't want, and the closer we get to the winning formula, the more likely we will find it—and have chemistry!

Name that formula. The way you begin to identify what you want in a person is to start paying attention. Pick up a magazine, go to a movie, sit in a coffee shop or bar, and look around. Take notes—mentally or literally. What makes your heartbeat accelerate (and other body parts wake up), and why? Really try to identify the magical elements. Compare the different people you are attracted to and notice traits that keep coming up. Consider the four "P's":

Physical: Are you drawn to dark—skin, hair, attitude? Is it a fresh, fair look that works for you? Are you turned on by muscles and tone? Blue jeans or tailored threads? Do you check out the butt first or the eyes? How would you construct and dress your ideal partner?

Professional: Is it the professional presence or charisma of a person that you are drawn to? Wanting to be examined by a doctor, or cross-examined by a lawyer? Is it the person in that exercise video that does it for you? The parent playing with his kids at the park? The artist with a sketch book? Is wealth an aphrodisiac? Since talking about work will be part of what you do, what do you like to talk about? Do you enjoy intellectual debate, or would you rather compare your favorite episodes of *Gilligan's Island*?

Personality: Are you drawn to the ringleader of the group or the more quiet and thoughtful member? Do comedians turn you on, or do you prefer actors in serious, dramatic roles? Does the object of your attraction seem gentle and smooth, or someone who would challenge you? How would this person be in bed? Be specific.

Philosophical: What worldview does your fantasy love hold? Is she deeply religious? Is he an activist for social causes? What about political leanings? Does it comfort you to know you both voted for McGovern, or would you like to mix it up and find a hippie to your Young Republican? Do you want someone who is open to new ideas or strong in their convictions? A vegetarian or a meat-eater?

As you review these areas, you may find one that stands out as particularly powerful. This may give you a clue about where to look for your date. For example, if artists drive you wild, get on the mailing lists of all the galleries in your area, and you'll get invited to artist receptions.

If you are using a personal ad or dating service, your clarity about what you want will come through in your ad or survey.

From the Mouths of Baby Boomers

"I answered a personal ad and this guy sounded really interesting—witty, bright and articulate. He had a nice voice. We talked awhile on the phone, decided to meet for dinner. When I reached the restaurant, I walked in, saw him from 20 feet away and said to myself, 'What a waste of a good evening.' The thing was, he was not ugly—he was a good looking businessman. I couldn't pinpoint it. He even greeted me with flowers. But I knew in a split second that there was no chemistry.

I think you know when it's *not* there, but when it's like, maybe, the personality can take over. When I first met Dave, I thought he looked like a homeless person. But now he makes my heart pound!"

—Class of '73

"Her reactions to me were exactly what I wanted them to be, what I had imagined."

—Class of '72

"As I explored what I was looking for, I realize that it's a combination of Sean Connery, Andrew Weil, Deepak Chopra, and Jesus! Not someone you run into everyday."

—Class of '65

Allowing Excitement

When we begin noticing what excites us, we start to feel things we may not have felt in awhile. You may ask, "Why should I get all turned on if I can't get satisfaction?" Even if you loved singing it with the Rolling Stones, don't assume you can't get satisfaction. Desire is a great motivator and automatically moves us toward our goals. Secondly, being aware of our desires helps us notice when fulfillment is standing right in front of us. Finally, desire is sexy. I've been amazed by the transformation in therapy clients—including myself!—when they learn to express their desires. Plastic surgery could not do as much for their attractiveness. And, not surprisingly, they start to get dates. Ever thought of what it means when you say someone is "hot"? Hot is turned on, alive, ready to engage. A hot person is about to create chemistry.

So allow your excitement to build. In fact, go ahead and add fuel to the fire. Fantasize, regularly. Self-help guides repeatedly tell us to envision our desired outcome, because it works. Don't be afraid of becoming preoccupied or regressing to an adolescent state. Revel in the fact that you get another shot at one of the most compelling experiences in life. Ah, chemistry.

An Attitude of Experimentation

As any scientist learns early in the game, an experiment that refutes the hypothesis is as valuable as one that comes out as expected. The same applies to dating. If we base success on liking everyone we date and having every date like us, we are not only setting ourselves up, we are limiting our experience and learning. My friend's therapist asked his clients to bring back stories of five date rejections to assure they were getting out there and experimenting. Remember the potential of kissing toads. Your image of what works will evolve and grow as you date. In experimentation, there is no failure, only discovery.

frogs

> "*Let me say at the risk of seeming ridiculous, that the true revolutionary is guided by great feelings of love.*"
>
> —*Che Guevara*

Unleashing Your Magnetism

In Chapters 9 and 10, we discussed your part in the chemistry equation—what makes you unique and special. In order to draw others to us, we need to make these qualities visible. If you have great eyes, accentuate them and use them for flirting. If you are witty, tell jokes where you can be overheard. If you have a toned figure, wear something tight. If you are smart, know how sexy that can be. Read *War and Peace* at a coffee shop rather than alone in your bedroom. Take your exceptional qualities into the world, and allow them to spark a reaction.

> "*That's it, baby, if you've got it, flaunt it!*"
>
> —*Mel Brooks, in his film,*
> The Producers (1968)

chapter 22

First Contact

Good things happen to those who hustle.
—Anais Nin

Okay, let's say you see someone you find attractive. Now what? Give him or her your phone number? Run the other way? Making contact with a new person can feel like trying to engage someone at the cantina in *Star Wars*. We're not quite sure if the person is friendly or hostile, and may not know what the rules are anymore. Here are some ways we can make the first contact easier.

Making Eyes, and Other Signals

Fortunately words are not the only way we can communicate. Body language helps us test the waters without having to say a word.

The great thing about body language is that much of it happens without thinking. We look at someone we're attracted to, we smile. An interested woman may unconsciously touch her hair, a man may slightly puff out his chest. (At our age, many of us pull in the gut!)

When we become conscious of our body language, we can use it more deliberately. Posing is a way we enhance our attractiveness and invite the admiration of the person looking our way. By posing, we give the looker what he or she wants, and may draw that person our way. However, if we work too hard at it, posing can undermine the sense of confidence we project. This is likely to happen if we put ourselves into a position that is uncomfortable—like those after-the-diet photos at the back of magazines where it looks like someone needs to give the model oxygen!

Another way we work body language is to play the aloof, hard-to-get angle. If you're engaging someone who loves the chase, this might be just the ticket. Hard-to-get postures work best when accompanied by some contradictory cues. A great example of this is Ann-Margret's approach to Elvis in *Viva Las Vegas*. Remember how she smiles and widens her eyes at the same time that she brushes him off? On the other hand, faking hard-to-get may be transparent—betraying the fact that we're really working too hard—and backfire. There are also some people who don't want to work so hard, and blow off someone playing this game. The difference between fun hard-to-get and just plain hard-to-get may come down to the element of play. Ann-Margret and Elvis were clearly having fun as she stepped back and he stepped forward. Notice how babies smile and look away when you get close, and grow to love games like peek-a-boo and hide-and-seek? These are natural ways we playfully regulate the intensity of relationships.

The easiest way to work your body language is to make it congruent with how you're feeling. If you're feeling shy, a shy smile can be very alluring. If you're in a great mood, show it. If you approve of how another person looks, give a slight nod. If you're feeling playful, engage the other person in a nonverbal game. If you just want to meet somebody, it's hard to beat a look and a smile.

But what about that "look"? Making eyes can be one of the most enjoyable activities of predating. This is often when we feel the first charges of chemistry. But when does looking become staring? Here are some tips for making eyes:

- Stick with occasional glances until you catch the other person's eye.
- If the person you look at looks back, give a smile, hold briefly and look elsewhere. How did it go?

- If the object of your attraction sees you and works to keep his or her glance out of your field of vision, take the hint. There are plenty of fish in the sea.
- If the other person's response is unclear (which is often the case), wait it out and play detective. What is the other person communicating?
- If you lock gazes and feel the chemistry, savor it!

What Are You Waiting For?

So, you see somebody you'd like to meet, maybe exchange that look and smile. What's keeping you from saying something? It's not hard to come up with excuses: "I'll look stupid." "I probably won't see the person again." "Maybe the other person will be offended."

Let's take these concerns in reverse order. Unless we make comments like "oh, baby" or hang around after we've been dismissed, we are unlikely to offend someone with our attention. Most people feel good when given the compliment of attention, whether or not they reciprocate our attraction. And many of us are turned on by people who have the confidence to initiate contact. On the other hand, people have bad days—and bad views of relationships—and can respond rudely. For these situations, keep this reminder in your back pocket: "It's not about me."

The idea that you might not see the person again is actually a wonderful excuse *to* make contact. Now's your chance! If you blow it, you probably won't see each other again anyway. We can waste a lot of our lives wondering "what if?" and later asking "why didn't I?" Let's get out there and quench our curiosity, find out how it turns out, and move closer or move on.

The idea that we might look stupid is only one of a list of thoughts that can mess us up. It's actually quite self-centered of us to think that others are tracking our every move and really care that much if we look stupid. So, we run the risk of looking stupid. We also risk looking friendly, confident, fun, witty, or just plain hot.

If I Had My Life to Live Over

I'd dare to make more mistakes next time. I'd relax. I would limber up. I would be sillier than I have been this trip. I would take fewer things seriously. I would take more chances. I would take more trips. I would climb more mountains and swim more rivers. I would eat more ice cream and less beans. I would perhaps have more actual troubles but I'd have fewer imaginary ones. You see, I'm one of those people who live sensibly and sanely hour after hour, day after day. Oh, I've had my moments and if I had it to do over again, I'd have more of them. In fact, I'd try to have nothing else. Just moments. One after another, instead of living so many years ahead of each day. I've been one of those people who never go anywhere without a thermometer, a hot water bottle, a raincoat and a parachute. If I had my life to live over, I would start barefoot earlier in the spring and stay that way later in the fall. If I had it to do again, I would travel lighter next time. I would go to more dances. I would ride more merry-go-rounds. I would pick more daisies.

—Written by Nadine Stair at age 85 and first published in *The Association for Humanistic Psychology Newsletter* in 1975.

What's My Line?

Hi.

As we work to be clever and come up with winning lines that will charm a potential date, we overlook the simplest and most effective greeting: "Hi." A University of Chicago study found that a simple "hi" worked better than any other opening line, followed by "how do you like the band?" (assuming a band is playing!). Forget suggesting that God is missing an angel, or trying to mimic Marilyn Monroe. The best and easiest lines are simple conversation starters. Here are some ways to get things going:

- If we want to be approached, it helps to bring along a conversation piece. Wear a T-shirt with a clever slogan or carry a cigar-box purse. I once had a guy reading French off of a screen print shirt I was wearing. He started to get embarrassed as he realized he was reading off my chest, but I was charmed. If it fits the setting, bring a book or a sketch pad, or just pick up a unique magazine.

- Comment on what's happening in the current setting. We can always generalize "how do you like the band?" to "how do you like—that book, your latte, or this artist? If someone in the room is obnoxious, it's a great opportunity to share puzzled looks and say, "What's up with *her*?" If there's a raging thunderstorm outside, we can comment, "It's getting bad out there," and ask about the forecast.

- Give a compliment. "Nice body" might be a bit out there, but "I like your earrings" or "nice tie" are good openers. But then again, an outrageous compliment that comes from the heart can be quite moving. If the words "wow, you're beautiful" or "I'm sorry, but I can't stop looking at you" are pushed out in the passion of the moment, let it happen. You are probably under the spell of chemistry.

- Remember "hi"? When we say "hi" and leave it out there, the other person often responds "hi, how are you doing?" and so on. Allowing space in a conversation is a sign of self-assurance, and leaves room for things to build naturally.

- Build a framework. Those of us who are regulars at the gym or a coffee shop can gradually build conversations with other regulars. One strategy recommended on www.pick-up-woman.com is the "goodbye introduction" which involves making a first-name introduction on the way out. i.e., "I was impressed with your form on the court and wanted to introduce myself before I leave." Next time, you can greet the person by name. Regulars are also often known by employees of the setting, who can sometimes be drawn on to provide an introduction. Once you have a name, remember it. Addressing someone by name is a sign of social savvy.

- Play yourself. Think of the great first lines in movies. These lines are usually good because they could only happen in those particular situations with those particular people. For example, in *Viva, Las Vegas,* when Ann-Margret stops at the auto mechanic shop and complains that her motor whistles, Elvis seizes the moment and responds, "I don't blame it." You've probably heard the saying, "Luck is what happens when preparation meets opportunity." Elvis' character was prepared to flirt, her line gave him an opening, and he seized it.

In Chapter 10 we talked about rehearsing who you want to be in a dating relationship. Cary Grant himself said, "There was no Cary Grant until I invented him and then became him." Once you invent yourself, imagine that person in different situations, and rehearse who you are, the rest will flow. For you, the moment may provide the opportunity to physically bump into somebody (by accident, of course) and smile and say "nice running into you." Or it may feel more like you to pass a cute note, or to walk right up to a special someone and say, "I'd like to date you." When we use our characteristic charm, humor, coyness or candor in the present, we can create our own movie moments.

From the Mouths of Baby Boomers

"After I was divorced, another gal and I often went to this bar and on one occasion I met a guy who told me he was a pilot and on another occasion another one told me he was a professional golfer. I believed both of them. I didn't date them, just had a good night of flirting and feeling really good about myself and my ability to pick up some good looking guys—and ones with some money! Later that year I was at one of my class reunions and I was visiting with a classmate who I had a crush on in high school and he asked me if I had been meeting guys. I told him the above story of meeting those two guys and both were interested. He looked at me in disbelief and said (while hooting) 'You are so naïve. I can't believe you bought that story. Don't you know that those two lines are told by all guys to pick up dates?!!' I was so crushed …"

—Class of '64

The Art of the Flirt

One easy way to think about flirting is that it is a way of "working around the edges" of a relationship. When we flirt, we don't directly display our feelings or intentions, we play with them. The playing allows both parties to test out their own feelings as well as the reactions of the other. So, rather than saying, "I want to see how it feels to touch you," I punch you on the arm when you tease me. I may feel an exciting spark or I may feel nothing. Either way, it's good information.

Flirting also involves playing with closeness and distance, as in the contradictory interchanges between Regina Lambert and Peter Joshua in *Charade*. You may deliberately talk to the *friend* of the person you are interested in for awhile, moving your way into the desired circle and flashing looks toward the one you really want to talk to. A compliment may be packaged in a tease, an invitation in a racy joke. If you observe people flirting, you'll start to notice a rhythm to it, a quite lovely pattern of dipping closer and stepping back, blushing shyness interspersed with peacock-feather displays. And, as in dancing, it's much easier to flirt when you just let the rhythm move you.

Not everyone could pull off the challenging repartee between Regina Lambert (Audrey Hepburn) and Peter Joshua (Cary Grant) in the movie *Charade*, but it is so them:

Peter: (stopping by Regina's table) "Do we know each other?"

Regina: "Why, do you think we're going to?"

Peter: "I don't know, how would I know?"

Regina: "… Because I already know an awful lot of people, and until one of them dies, I couldn't possibly meet anyone else."

Peter: "Hmmm, well, if anyone goes on the critical list, let me know." (He starts to walk away.)

Regina: "Quitter."

Peter: (turning) "Huh?"

Regina: (laughing) "You give up very easily, don't you?"

---

chapter 23

Making a Date

So on canteen night we could get out on the cafeteria floor in our tight white Levi's that ended about three inches above our shoes (everybody wore this look) and, with serious, purposeful expressions, we would swivel mechanically back and forth on the balls of our feet with all the relaxed spontaneity of motorized Christmas lawn ornaments. But we were fast-dancing! With girls! How cool was that?
—*Dave Barry, on the liberating effects of the Twist from* Dave Barry Turns 50.

"Okay, now things are getting real. I want to see this person again, and that means D-A-T-E! I don't know if I'm more afraid of getting turned down or actually going through with it. Help!"

Although this might sound like the neurotic rambling of a sixteen-year-old, dating angst is just as real (or unreal) for us as we start dating again. If you're the one suggesting the date, you may feel that a lot is at stake. After all, "date" defines the relationship a certain way. A date also implies the possibility of physical intimacy, or at least the ritual goodnight kiss. So here we are, asking someone to do this thing called a date.

What if he or she says no?—or yes? Asking someone out on a date holds the potential of success or failure.

After all these years, we've earned the right to ease up. As far as I'm concerned, the act of asking someone is a success regardless of outcome! After all, it's only in the doing that we discover. And, remember, we aren't asking someone to prom—thank God *that* pressure is off! Now that we're out of high school and living on our own, dating is less public. When it comes right down to it, we don't even have to ask someone to go on a date as in, "Will you go on a date with me?" You are more likely to ask someone to join you for a drink, or dinner, or to just stay around so you can talk some more. Unless you are nostalgic and like the retro version of dating, you can think of dating today as a whole new game.

The Art of Asking Someone Out

I remember in college having to attempt to define beauty. While it was an exercise in futility, one theme stood out for me: The idea that beauty holds a combination of soothing familiarity and exciting novelty. Without familiarity, the vision is too uncomfortable. Without novelty, it loses life. I think this idea applies well to the art of asking someone out.

Familiarity is built from the connections we make in our initial conversations. You meet at a place you both choose to enter, even if that place is cyberspace. You are both unattached at this point in your lives. As you talk, you make other connections and this new person feels less of a stranger. Unless the other person takes it up a level, you can approach the relationship as a friendship and build that sense of familiarity. This can happen quite naturally if you both frequent the same places, or meet through a class or club. You can also invite your "friend" along to activities that involve other people—like "why don't you come to my book club?" As you spend time together, you eliminate more and more of the unknown. This approach can feel soothing and comfortable, which may be just what you need after all you've been through.

However, if you start supporting your date through other romances, that's a clue that you've been a little too subtle about your own romantic desires. The big screen best friends Harry and Sally still pulled off a romance, but a friend of mine didn't fare so well. He befriended a single

Mom he hoped to date. She had become pretty isolated, and he encouraged her to take more chances and get out more. To make it easy on her, he said he'd just come over Friday night and they could watch TV together. She liked the idea, and when he arrived, she was all dressed up. Flattered, he commented that she didn't need to do that and she replied, "I've been thinking about what you said about taking chances, and I've got a date! Would you mind watching Kari while we're out?" So much for being the accommodating friend!

At the other extreme, we walk up to someone we find attractive and step it up right away. This heightens the risk—we have no idea how the person will respond—and the potential for excitement. The asking out itself is charged with the energy of spontaneity and the power of directness, and it can just work. Then there's the date. We get to experience the thrill of novelty—to cozy up to someone with a different texture, voice, smell, and personality. If you've spent most of your adult life in one relationship, this might be just what you're craving. Downside: We're operating with very little information, and risk disappointment or, worse, walking into an unsafe situation. If you go right to the date, just use the safety guidelines described in Chapter 17. Or wait on the date, and opt for the immediate thrill of a slow dance or intimate conversation.

How you ask someone out will have to do with your own preferred mix of familiarity and novelty. There are as many different combinations of these elements as there are artists. The cool thing is, we get to decide. We can suggest anything from a casual game of tennis to dinner at an elegant restaurant.

Asking someone out need not be a one-sided event. We can take cues from the other person as well. If the person you are interested in talks in general about how she's been burned and is a little gun-shy about relationships, you might want to hold off on evening plans. Many times, the next meeting is a mutual decision that evolves from the conversation. You may realize that you both love film, and agree to attend the upcoming film festival together. Even when the other person is doing the asking, you still have a say in how it's set up. Mostly, the other person just wants to see you again. If you suggest an alternative plan, he may be relieved not to carry all the responsibility for the pacing.

From the Mouths of Baby Boomers

"I knew I needed to start dating after the divorce when my 7-year old son looked at me with big eyes one day and said, 'Mom, you don't really have anyone to help you except Leo.' Unfortunately, Leo is our cat! The hardest part for me was learning things about men that I never really had known when I was younger. I was very proud of myself when I found the courage to get the e-mail address of a guy I wanted to go out with. We have a date in a couple of weeks!"

—Class of '78

"I saw a very attractive woman at a dance class I participate in. I was in the DJ booth, and came down and positioned myself and said, 'Wanna dance?' We hit it off. After the lesson, I told her, 'Some of us are coming back Sunday evening. If you want to come, I'll be here.' She came, and we danced most of the evening, talked—we both were divorced and had kids. We were the last ones out. I called her and invited her to a dance. We started dating and dancing. She even wanted to practice between dance lessons!"

—Class of '72

Is the Guy Still in Charge?

The answer to this question depends on who you ask. Traditions die hard, and some of us feel safer when we follow the "boy asks girl" rule. Yet, ours was the generation that fought for liberation from restrictive roles. A couple of years back, when I was a mentor at a "Love, Marriage and Sex" retreat for teens, I had the chance to talk with other mentors—male and female—about what dating was like in our day. The female mentors, including myself, complained about the powerlessness we felt as boys freely expressed their desires, called the shots, and we responded. And even as Erica Jong was writing about wild women, most of us felt restricted in how much we could express our own desires. The male mentors opened up about the weight of the responsibility they felt as they had to set the pace, to try to guess what the girl wanted, and felt they had to keep things moving even when they weren't ready. Being the carrier of desire restricted them as well.

So, have things changed? Again, the answer will depend on who you ask. Read *The Rules: Time Tested Secrets for Capturing the Heart of Mr.*

Right by Ellen Fein and Sherrie Schneider, and you'll think you're back in the '50s. Read Franklin Parlamis' book, *The Passive Man's Guide to Seduction*, and you'll be convinced that women are the new aggressors and men will do well to sit back and respond.

Rules for Women: To Make or Break?

"Don't Talk to a Man First (And Don't Ask Him to Dance)."

—Rule 2 from *The Rules* by Ellen Fein and Sherrie Schneider.

"Boy meets girl. Boy likes girl but thinks girl doesn't like him. Actually, girl likes boy a lot, but she plays by the rules, pretending that she doesn't like him by playing hard to get. Boy gives up and looks elsewhere."

—Introduction to *Get a Life, Then a Man* by Jennifer Bawden.

You won't find "for men only" and "for women only" sections in this guide. Boomers have learned—through the shifting of gender roles and the more vocal presence of gay, lesbian and bisexual people—that sexuality and gender roles are more complex than we've been taught to believe. Maybe some of us are looking for "rules" to anchor us again. Yet, the best rules are the ones that come out of your definition of who you want to be—what you value and what you desire. In fact, you may want to draw up your own set of rules. You could even get them published!

Beyond "Wanna Do Something?": Having a Plan

Doesn't it bug you when someone says, "Let's do lunch," and leaves it out there, while you know full well that it's not going to happen? Open-ended suggestions are problematic for a number of reasons. They send a mixed message: "I'd like to do something with you, but I'm not ready to make a plan." They can also leave the other person feeling responsible to pick up where you left off. Ultimately, they leave a question mark as to who will follow up and when.

Open-ended invitations don't necessarily reflect insincerity. It just may feel too risky to propose something specific. If you both agree, "Wouldn't it be nice … someday?" then you get the comfort of a shared wish without the risk of proposing something specific and getting turned down.

Then again, if we want to move from wish to reality, it helps to be specific. Even if you negotiate a completely different plan, starting with a specific suggestion gives you something to work from. Building in a choice takes the focus away from "yes or no" to "when and where." Here's an example: "I'd like to continue our conversation over dinner at Luigi's. Would Friday or Saturday work better for you?" With the pace of our lifestyles today, don't be surprised if you need to do a little schedule volleying before your plans are confirmed.

Even though it may feel risky, proposing a specific date idea is a sign of confidence. It is a way of communicating that you know what you like, and that you are confident enough to expect someone else to want to share in the experience.

Creative Dates

We've come a long way since a movie and a bite to eat was the stock format for a date. If we think of a date as simply a way for two interested people to see each other again, the sky's the limit. Speaking of the sky, outdoor dates can be a refreshing alternative to a smoke-filled bar. Suggest a walk in the park, or if you share the interest, run, hike, or skate together. You can add a little romance and have a picnic (guys will score points on this one, especially if you bring the food!). Playing a sport like golf, tennis, or bowling are fun options as well. And remember, being an amateur adds to the fun. Risk a little humiliation and enjoy yourself. And who doesn't feel great at a baseball game? Go early to catch home runs at batting practice (women will score big points here!). Or try a NASCAR race—and rent the headsets so you can talk. If it's winter, try snowshoeing or ice skating.

Lunch and dinner are popular choices because they are conducive to conversation. Sitting across the table from one another promotes eye contact and mutual attention. If you'd like to share an activity other than eating, challenge your date to a game of cards or chess. Coffeehouses often supply board games for the use of customers.

If there's something you've been wanting to do, try making a date of it. Explore your tastes together by gallery-hopping or attending a wine-and-cheese tasting. Check out your community's listing of events—festivals and outdoor concerts make great dates. Or go anywhere you can dance, dance, dance!

Good first dates provide opportunities for easy interaction and laughter. Unless you are both regulars, settings that place a lot of emphasis on protocol, like the opera or an exclusive restaurant, are probably not good first date options. We feel enough pressure on the first date—we don't need to add the worry about evening attire or which fork to use.

If you opt for a performance, go with ones that allow you to talk while you're enjoying the talent. An outdoor festival featuring musicians will allow more interaction than an indoor symphony concert. Sports events leave plenty of room for conversation. The traditional movie is actually not optimal—you're in a dark theatre, looking at a screen… Okay, the dark theatre can be an advantage. But if you're just getting to know each other, create a date that allows you to get to know each other. For more date ideas, check out the A to Z list in Appendix C. Look for options that give you a vision of pleasant interaction and fun, then make it real!

chapter 24

The First Date Primer

I base most of my fashion taste on what doesn't itch.
—Gilda Radner

It's a date! Congratulations—you are officially "dating again!" You've gotten out there, made a connection, and booked a date. You probably already have some stories to tell. Let's continue the adventure!

Get Ready

Getting ready—as in a jazzed, psyched kind of ready—has more to do with what we do in our heads than how we dress. As we've discussed, seeing dating as an adventure helps us value every aspect of the experience. Here you are, getting ready for your first date—again! Isn't that wild? Observe yourself in this drama, take notes if you like. Appreciate the irony of the situation as you ask your daughter or son for advice on what you're wearing, as you feel the kind of butterflies you haven't experienced since your youth.

Speaking of what you're wearing, make sure you're comfortable and confident in your choice. No need to add to our normal level of gut-sucking by wearing something too clingy. If you want to get a new outfit to mark the occasion, go on and have fun with it! On the other hand, whatever you wear is probably new to your date, so you might do well with that shirt that always draws compliments. It is a good idea to bring in a fresh eye on what you're wearing, as others are often better able to tell what flatters you most. One more thing— don't overdo the perfume or after-shave (you may reek of trying too hard!).

As you get ready, crank your stereo with tunes that inspire you. You may want to pull out an old favorite like "Light My Fire" or "Joy to the World." Dance in front of the mirror, sing out loud, get excited. You are going on a date!

Relating While Dating

The skills of dating really come down to some very basic elements. Take social skills. Thankfully, we have shed a lot of the narcissism of our youth, and we've learned that people enjoy being acknowledged and listened to. A simple greeting like, "Hi, Grace. You look great! How's your day been going?" communicates: (a) I'm glad to see you, (b) I'm attracted to you, and (c) I'm interested in your life. A step up from the honk of the horn, huh?

Recalling elements of previous conversations helps us to build relationships. If you know that your date helped his son move into his college dorm since you last talked, asking about how it went shows that you are tuned in. It's also a great way to get the conversation going, because it is something your date already let you in on. As the date goes on, open-ended questions such as: "Where did you grow up?" "How did you get into (your line of work)?" and "Where do you like to travel?" encourage conversation.

A friend of mine hit on a great approach to conversing with dates: Get them to teach you about something they are interested in.

From the Mouths of Baby Boomers

"Let's say your date mentions an interest in modern art. You express your igno-rance about it, which to the uninitiated would be a conversation-stopper. But instead, you ask them to tell you something about it. That does four things: First, it shows them you are willing to confess your ignorance, signifying a healthy lack of ego. Second, it shows you are interested enough in them to try to share their pas-sions. Third, it puts them in a comfortable, impersonal content area which allows them to reveal their expertise. Fourth, it builds a base of shared knowledge that can serve as common ground later.

Everyone wants to feel that they are expert at something, or at least moderately knowledgeable. This builds confidence in a way that does not threaten too much self-disclosure. If, on the other hand, learning from your date leaves you hope-lessly bored or even disgusted, well then, you probably don't want to spend a lot of time with this person anyway. Their passion is something you can neither share nor appreciate. And even that is a lesson well learned. This applies even to women and football. If he's a fanatic and you can't stand to listen to him explain the rules or the political intricacies and implications of Trade Day, you are both going to be spending a lot of frustrated time down the road.

Which leads us to my favorite motto: NYKMO: Now You Know, Move On. This is a great motto. But that is another story."

—Class of '76

Keep in mind what feelings you want to take away from the date. Although the element of chemistry will make a difference, what you talk about also influences the feelings you and your date take away. When we've been through a lot, and there's a good listener sitting across the table, it may be tempting to vent and complain. Check that temptation. Disclosing too much too soon can leave us feeling out there and vulnera-ble tomorrow. In addition, it can be a downer for both of you. You know how, once we start getting into our woes, we can suddenly become depressed and self-preoccupied? That's okay for therapy, we're *supposed* to be self-preoccupied there. But let your time with your date be a break from your troubles.

So, what if you've had a rotten day and that's what's on your mind? A simple, "I've had a tough day and I'm ready to relax and have fun," will do. Creating good feelings isn't about telling lies, it's about shifting our focus. If I get into a discussion about favorite movies, I know I'll be feeling good in no time! See "The Best and Worst Date Topics" for topics that induce good—or potentially nauseating—feelings.

As always, there are exceptions. There are some people who are so entertaining about their complaints that they ironically make you feel good. These people are called comedians. If you have this skill, complain away! And if something very immediate is troubling you, the sharing could foster a special bond with your date. It's never all or nothing. A little bit of the negative can add depth to a conversation—just avoid falling in!

The Best and Worst Date Topics

Worst:

- Anything that starts with "my ex"
- Recent surgeries
- The pain of childbirth
- My rehab experience
- Euthanasia
- An imaginary area of expertise (you always get caught!)

Best:

- Favorites: Movies, bands, restaurants
- Travels
- Where you've lived
- Pets
- Funny stories
- Anything that starts with "I like" or "I want"

"Who Pays?"

Let's start with the question of who pays. If we go with traditional gender-oriented rules, it's easy. As Ellen Fein and Sherrie Schneider instruct women in *The Rules*, "Don't meet him halfway or go Dutch on a date." So guys, a "Rules girl" is going to expect you to pay.

If we take out the gender element, simple etiquette says that if you do the inviting, you do the paying. There is a simple logic to this approach—the person inviting can assess what he or she can afford. It is particularly rude to invite someone to an expensive restaurant without being willing to pay.

But because this area has become so fuzzy, always have money along. Being prepared to pay or split expenses will save you potential embarrassment. And when your date insists on paying, say "thank you" and enjoy the gift.

Assessing the Date

As with asking someone out, date outcomes don't need to be defined in terms of success or failure. Remember Chapter 11, where we discussed the value of all dates, and the opportunity they give us to discover what we do, and don't want? The real success is in having "gone out," out of your house or apartment, into a real and wonderful world that offers the chance to know someone new, and discover what feelings the relationship generates. Pay attention to what you're feeling as you spend time with this new person. If your emotions shift, notice when and why. Enjoy the excitement of discovery.

Let's say that the relationship pretty quickly generates feelings of boredom or worse. What do you do? As long as you feel safe, you can wait out the date as an observer, noting what makes this date so bad. Remember, you are shopping at this point, and learning what you don't like is a part of the process. But *never* feel like you have to provide a sympathy *anything*—conversation, kiss, explanation. And if you feel threatened in any way, just say you have to go and leave. If it's just a matter of a personality clash—or the discovery that your date *has* no personality, all you need to do is politely exit. If you want, say you're tired and need to leave (you certainly are tired of the person you're with!). Beyond this, trying to explain just opens up the conversation and keeps things going.

Let's say you experience the scenario we all hope for: You feel great with this new person, your heart is pumping, and you want to spend as much time as possible in his or her presence. In shopping terms, you've made a find! Chances are, your great feelings will attract some other emotions as well, like fear and vulnerability. The real challenge for us is to stay in the present and revel in our good feelings. In fact, this can be so challenging that we've dedicated Chapter 29 to the subject. For now, you may find it useful to memorize some wise advice from a sixteenth Century blessing, "Take joy." Don't let the pleasure pass you by as you worry about the future—take it! And speaking of the future, feeling great can only make you more attractive.

Unlike the above scenarios, a date often generates a mix of feelings. A part of you really likes the person, and another part is skeptical. These mixed feelings provide a wonderful opportunity to clarify what you want. Take mental notes of what makes you feel good and what triggers negative feelings. Do the negative feelings reflect a particular vulnerability of yours? For example, if you overreact to a good-natured tease, maybe it reminds you of a hurtful way your ex treated you. On the other hand, maybe the tease isn't so good-natured after all. Once the date is over, you can step back from your own reactions and get a more objective perspective. But usually, it is time together that helps us really see who the person is.

chapter 25

Dating Widely

Develop interest in life as you see it; in people, things, literature, music—the world is so rich, simply throbbing with rich treasures, beautiful souls and interesting people. Forget yourself.
—Henry Miller

Between the idealized images of dating in the late '50s and early '60s, and the publicized lovefests of the late '60s and early '70s, you'd think that all Boomers have extensive dating bios. The reality is, many of us didn't do much dating at all. Some of us had childhood sweethearts that became life partners, some of us chose marriage because of a pregnancy, and some of us were just too shy to date very much. Now that we've come into our own as adults, it's a great time to explore a variety of relationships, both for the fun of it and for the opportunity to make a find of a lifetime!

From the Mouths of Baby Boomers

"I'm actually enjoying meeting all kinds of people and appreciate having a variety of relationships. I am much more confident about what I want and not looking for 'the one' all the time. If I meet a person with whom I have a big connection (and I do now and then) I am more patient and enjoy it for what it is instead of trying to make it something it isn't."

—Class of '75

"The first person you date after the divorce can be idealized. If your marriage sucked, the first one out is like heaven. Dating more is helpful, because you find out it can be even better. Even when you date people who you like less, it helps you get really clear about what you want."

—Class of '72

The Benefits (and Fun!) of Tasting

Too often we think of dating as just a means to an end. We have spent much of our lives in a long-term relationship and hope to find another committed relationship for the rest of the journey. So, we have this relatively short break called dating. Why rush it?

Rather than getting it over with it, let's get into it. Each person we meet and date brings out something different in us. As we engage in different conversations, each one expands our world. We can learn about different professions, hobbies, and points of view. We might even learn a new skill or sport, or be inspired to change in an important way. People who date widely report getting more courageous about being real and better at setting boundaries. The better we get at loving ourselves in the context of relationships, the better our chances of experiencing that love from others. Dating can also help us feel a special camaraderie with the people we date, whether or not a relationship comes of it. After all, all daters share a similar mission. This kind of empathy makes dating easier on all of us.

Then there's the obvious: Dating more gives us more to choose from. In a special show on dating, *Oprah* featured a woman named Ann Marsh who, in search of a life partner, approached dating like a business. She dated over 100 men in less than six months! An online dating service fed her prospects, and to prevent herself from getting prematurely attached, she established a no-kissing rule. She arranged the type of look-see dates described in Chapter 20, and started meeting with several men a week. After a few stings, she became very good at accepting signs of disinterest and moving on. As she put it in a companion article in *O Magazine* (Feb, 2003), "… he was simply another woman's catch. I got out of her way." She also learned to be honest with those she knew weren't "the one." She accomplished what she set out to do—she found and eventually married the man she was sure was the one.

But no kissing?! Ms. Marsh had experienced physical passion; this time, she wanted time to get to know her dates first. Like many Boomers, she had burned out on the movie version of love, where couples front-load the physical intimacy and fall in love later (if at all). For other Boomers, dating provides the chance to taste in a very literal sense—to revel in the newness of intimate exchanges again, to feel the charge of touch, the excitement of first kisses, and the wonderful feeling of desiring someone new. Either way, dating again can provide a refreshing contrast to life as usual.

> "You can't do anything about the length of your life, but you can do something about its width and depth."
>
> —Evan Esar

Analyzing the (Date) Data

The more we date, the more *data* we collect about what we like and don't like. If you're a researcher, you know that the larger your sample, the more confidence you will have in your findings. As we collect impressions from our dates, we start to get an increasingly refined idea of who we like to spend time with.

Let's say you are drawn to someone because of her depth and thoughtfulness. When you met, she was the one in the group who seemed to be observing and processing things. When you're together, you love talking with her and hearing her insights. Yet, she often expresses a preference to be alone, and this is becoming frustrating. You love her mind, but want someone who has more of a desire to be with people, particularly you.

Maybe you date another woman who loves people, but has an annoying habit of looking beyond you when you are together. While she really likes being with you, she seems to stay on the surface of topics and become easily distracted. Through these experiences you clarify how important it is for you to have someone who craves intimate conversation. The first woman had the capacity for that kind of conversation; the second had the social interest. You want someone who has both the capacity and the interest.

As we clarify what we want, the voices in our heads may say we are too picky, nobody's perfect, and—my favorite: "Who do you think you are?" Although we addressed old voices in Chapter 2, they are likely to pop in throughout the dating process—especially when we're getting what we want!

Often, the best response is let the voices be and move on. But, for now, let's respond:

"You're too picky." This voice comes with the idea that we expect too much and flows easily into "who do you think you are (to expect more)?" Sources of this voice include unhappy people who didn't dare to pursue what they wanted. They settled; why shouldn't you?

Sorting out what we want and don't is not about being picky, it's about being honest with ourselves and expecting good things. People who expect more tend to get it.

"Nobody's perfect." Using your own experience to clarify what you want is different than signing up for some agreed-upon image of perfection. Models of perfection are as lifeless as Barbie and Ken; the vision you create is unique and alive, because it is yours and it is evolving. And while you identify your priorities, you also learn where you can flex.

"Who do you think you are?" Each one of us is worthy of joy and love, and there's enough for everybody.

By staying truthful with ourselves, we not only increase our chances of finding great relationships, we also do better once we're in those relationships. Partners who say what they want are better able to negotiate and fulfill each other's desires.

Love is All Around

The producers of the *Mary Tyler Moore Show* managed to keep Mary Richards supplied with dates for seven seasons (1970–1977). The series begins after Mary breaks up with a man she dated for several years. She moves into a studio in Minneapolis, joins the team at WJM-TV, and embarks on a new adventure in dating. She dates men who are too short, too young, too old (Murray's father!), too attentive or inattentive, and too evasive. She dates her journalism instructor, a politician, an architect, a newspaper columnist, the comedy writer for Chuckles the Clown, an anchorman (not Ted, although he starts rumors …), and a father of an obnoxious 12-year-old boy. She inadvertently gets into love triangles with friends, dates a married man, and gives second chances to various ex-boyfriends who arrive on the scene. In the second-to-last episode, Mary dates a man she has taken for granted—Lou Grant. Although we had to endure some frustration with all her unfulfilled romances, it's hard to imagine the show being near as entertaining if Mary had gotten married!

Expanding the Menu

If you'd like to gather more data, but aren't getting a lot of dates, it's time to expand the menu. You can do this by reviewing Part 2, and adding a supplemental strategy or two for finding dates. Another way we can broaden the menu is to avoid the tendency to wait by the phone or computer. Instead of waiting on contacts you've made, make new ones.

Waiting time is actually the best time to open up our options. As in a job search, the tendency can be to wait for certainty on one opportunity before pursuing another. The problem with this approach is that we wait on someone else's choice rather than enhancing our own options. Even when the person you're waiting on is someone you really like, it might be the one you haven't met yet that you will love. You may be hungry, but still make a point to check out the range of menu options. After all, how many times have you ordered in haste only to find yourself drooling over what you see on someone else's plate?

chapter 26

Enjoying the "Almost"

Sex without love is a meaningless experience, but as far as meaningless experiences go it's pretty damn good.
—*Woody Allen*

I've heard it said that the power in Michelangelo's famous fresco is in the space between the two reaching figures, in the "almost." In human relationships as well, as long as the gap isn't filled, we are energized and enlivened. The space that separates also compels, and once it has been filled we often wish we could have it back.

So, it's a bit of a paradox that we long to recapture the almost, yet we have a hard time staying there for very long. Let's look at how we can make the most of almost.

Savoring Sexual Anticipation

Boomers have become very good at reducing the space between desire and fulfillment. We lived through the ease of eating TV dinners in our dens, then topped that by "zapping" food in the microwave oven. We also became less patient with slow-cooking our sexual relationships. As the Jetsons flipped switches to serve up meals, we wanted to be "turned on" sexually. Why waste all that time on romance?

But what happened? We discovered that TV dinners taste as synthetic as the trays they come in; we got tired of trying to figure out how to "brown" in a microwave oven; and even sex lost a little of its flavor. Time is in vogue again. We've traded our space-age furniture for antiques. Some of us are not only cooking our own meals—we're growing the herbs to flavor them! We've discovered the sensual pleasures of chopping the vegetables, breathing the aroma, and tasting the sauce as the meal is prepared. And many of us are also ready to slow down and savor the touches, looks and longings that come with a new relationship.

But how do we *do* that? How do we slow down as our heartbeats speed up? Actually, you don't have to *do* anything. Just *feel the desire*. It won't hurt you. (Sorry, guys, the "blue balls" myth has been exposed!) Desires are as flexible as the stretch pants we wore in the sixties—they feel good now and lead to what we want later.

Still, feeling the intensity of desire can mean exploring new territory. If you've come out of an unsatisfying relationship, your desires may have become so buried you no longer recognize them. If the sex was good, maybe you became accustomed to having a regular diet of it. But either scenario can lead to the same outcome—the cooling of desire. Chances are, though, as you've read this book and started to date, things are heating up. For those of you pulsing with desire right now and wondering if you can stand it, read on. Learning to savor desire has many benefits.

As we've discussed, unfulfilled desire is energizing. In fact, desiring creates a chemical high. The brain is bathed in hormones and natural amphetamines that produce euphoria. (Makes you wonder if it was all that sexual indulgence in the sixties that left us with the need to create new artificial highs!)

Desire also feeds creativity. Great works of art, poetry, and music have been inspired by people in the throws of desire. Freud taught us that channeling the sex drive is a great way of getting work done. Enjoy the spring in your step, the alive feeling in your body, and the inspiration to expand and create.

Finally, desire naturally leads us toward fulfillment. If we trust desire, we don't need to push it—we can ride! I recently was feeling a bit overwhelmed as I saw my desires working themselves out—in one week I had writing deadlines to meet, was performing a play with an attractive actor, and would be flying to Minneapolis to get together with my favorite people. Here I was, looking at my fantasy week, and I was feeling oppressed. It was a roller coaster week, but as I've mentioned, I love roller coasters! So what was the problem? What I realized is that I was trying to drive the coaster—to anticipate and worry about everything in advance, to stay in control. Then I remembered that the fun of roller coasters is that I get to ride, and that changed everything. I let go, put up my hands and enjoyed the crazy ride of late nights, performance highs, time changes, and intimate conversations.

Here are some tips for savoring desire:

- Practice. When you get excited about something or someone, just notice how it feels. Pay attention to what is happening in your body. Just allow it.

- Make room. When we want something, the fear of not getting it is often close by. Fears cause us to either stuff it or push it. Tell yourself, "There is room for all of what I want," or "There is time." Successful desiring requires the ability to keep the wanting alive even as it is unfulfilled. When you start to feel calm and excited at the same time, you'll know you're mastering the art of desiring.

- Allow competing desires. So part of you wants sex NOW and another part of you wants to give it more time. When you allow the awareness of both feelings, you have the best chance of getting what you want, regret-free. The conflict between desires is often the source of creative solutions. For example, you may decide to talk it out with your partner, and in doing so, reach a whole new level of intimacy—and clarity.

Staying on the Hot Tin Roof

Maggie, the heroine of Tennessee Williams' *Cat on a Hot Tin Roof*, knew how to keep desire alive. In the 1958 film version, the beautiful Maggie (Elizabeth Taylor) expresses her desire for Brick, her embittered husband (Paul Newman), even as he responds with apathy, hatred, and revulsion. At times, his rejecting behavior is betrayed by the way he looks at her with his piercing eyes. Through it all, she seems to know that her desire can be trusted. At one point in the dialogue he asks, "What is the victory of a cat on a hot tin roof?" She responds, "Just staying on it, I guess, as long as I can."

Stay on it she does, and as Brick's defenses chip away, she finally reaches him. As family members scowl with doubt, Paul Newman's character stands at the top of the steps and declares with a smile, "Truth is something desperate, and Maggie's got it. Believe me, it is desperate and she has got it." Brick's brother silences his slandering wife while expressing his respect for Maggie, "Yep, that girl's got life in her all right." As Maggie joins Brick in the bedroom, he stares at her with those blue eyes and utters the sexiest three words in the history of film: "Lock the door."

The Electric Charge of First Touches

So, as you're out there encountering new people, savor that look that is charged with chemistry, the "accidental" brush of an arm, the friendly nudge that you know is more than friendly, the arm at your waist or neck as you come together to dance. These first touches remind us of the very sense of touch—of what it means to reach across the gulf of separateness and make contact. There is a charge that comes with these touches, a "wow—I feel!" kind of charge. People describe the feeling as tingly, warm, intense—hmm, similar to descriptions of orgasm! Now, we wouldn't want to miss *that*.

And touches can happen without any body contact. The most intense touches can be the ones made with the eyes. Remember the chess game between Faye Dunaway and Steve McQueen in *The Thomas Crown Affair*? Chess was never so interesting. There were few words, but much communication. She touches her arm, pulls in the satin folds of her backless dress to gently expose the flesh near her breast, pouts her lips. He studies her, and unconsciously mirrors her as she runs her finger across her lower lip. After she lightly strokes her bishop, he is moved to action. He stands up and approaches her, saying, "Let's play something else."

From the Mouths of Baby Boomers

"After spending decades going to bed with the same man, being just touched by a new man is better than sex."

—Class of '69

"We were at a conference for work. A group of us went to the bar after our sessions. A man I was attracted to casually put his hand behind me and started massaging my back. Then he took my hand and studied my palm. Oh My God!"

—Class of '74

"The first time I kissed her I was a bit tentative. But she turned it into a very passionate kiss. This was just after going through a Christmas season when I didn't really have anybody. It was very powerful."

—Class of '72

It's in the Kiss

It is amazing how much meaning a simple kiss can hold. Yet, we often don't feel sure of the chemistry until we've experienced the first kiss. We judge the chemistry in romantic performances the same way. After the chess game, Dunaway and McQueen rose to the occasion with one of the longest kissing sessions on the big screen. Their lips just seemed to fit, and the film captured the way the contours came together over and over.

It has been said that a kiss surpasses sex as the most intimate form of expression. You can fake your way through sex, but a kiss tells all.

> "... [T]hen I did the simplest thing in the world. I leaned down ... and kissed him. And the world cracked open."
>
> —Agnes de Mille

Sexy Talk

One great way to mediate the space between desire and fulfillment is to put our desires into words. While this may have seemed like an appalling option when we were teenagers, we know better now. Back then, we thought romance meant being as unconscious of our desires as possible, that it helped to be a little buzzed and to keep the lights off. At this stage in our lives, we no longer need to hide the fact that we are sexual beings. We've become more comfortable with our desires, and we're better at communicating them. And nothing makes for more stimulating conversation!

When desire is in the air, sexy talk can come quite naturally. Common statements become filled with innuendo, and we make playful references to desires as we flirt. At more intense moments, honest statements of desire can be an incredible turn-on. A good way to ease into this kind of talk is to say it in your mind first. Just be honest with yourself about what you feel and what you desire. Pay attention to your fantasies. The moment will come when your passion meets opportunity and your words flow into the space between you. Charged words are as exciting to speak as they are to hear.

Besides providing a pleasure of its own, talking about desires opens the way for fulfilling them. As we'll discuss in the next chapter, you and your date bring different sexual experiences and hopes to the relationship. Talking about your desires, as well as concerns or conflicts, will go a long way to making it good for both of you.

chapter 27

Before You Unzip

Sex is identical to comedy in that it involves timing.
—Phyllis Diller

Just because you've spent a lot of time married or in a long-term relationship does not mean you have been sexually satisfied. In fact, living in a lifeless relationship can leave us famished for real contact and sexual pleasure. That is why the advice to "take a break" seems so ludicrous to many divorced individuals, who feel they've had a long enough break from intimacy. A "break" from the usual may really mean to get to experience passion again!

On the other hand, if you fell into a bad relationship because of the good sex, you may be more cautious about following your hormones. Or maybe you've felt used sexually, or are just tired of playing around. In 1980, Gabrielle Brown responded to rising concern about STDs and the sexual burnout of the 60's with her book *The New Celibacy*. Brown challenged us to remember that being sexual is a *choice*, not a biological imperative.

Whether dating again feels like your chance to indulge in sexual pleasure, or your chance to slow it down and focus on the relationship, it is *your* chance. The clearer you are about what you want and don't want, the better your chance of having it your way.

What Do I Need to Feel Good About This?

When a married client of mine shared her dilemma about whether to have an affair, my question to her was why she could only get pleasure on a part-time basis. Expecting me to criticize her for her desire for pleasure, she was taken by surprise by the suggestion that she was not treating her desire well enough!

When sex causes harm, either to ourselves or someone else, it undermines our pleasure. My client had the belief that she was not really entitled to pleasure, so she could only get it in a devious manner. By having an affair, she would have only reinforced the idea that pleasure was bad. Instead, we explored how pleasure could be a more conscious, full-time aspect of her life. As she expressed her desires more openly with her husband, she no longer needed a secret plan—she got what she needed at home.

It is good for all of us to think about how we can get what we want without morning-after guilt or regret. Here are some questions to consider:

- Safety. Do I know this person well enough to be assured that he or she will be respectful? Is my partner disease-free (see Chapter 5)? Do we have a condom? (If not, just say no, or later!) Will I emerge from this encounter healthy and whole?
- Personal values. Will having sex now put me in conflict with who I am and what I believe? What are my values about sex now anyway?
- Desire. Do I *want* it? Am I having sex to hold onto the relationship, because I can't think of a reason to say no—or because I want to? If I'm ready, what flavor of sex am I craving?

Remember, you deserve to have sex that not only feels great while it's happening, but can also be savored afterward.

The STD talk

If you've been in a monogamous relationship for most of your adult life, the prospect of talking about STDs and protection may feel daunting.

It helps to remember that anybody approaching a sexual relationship is in the same boat: wanting to be safe while keeping it pleasurable. Thankfully, couples today assume they need to talk about these issues, and doing so has become much more benign. The attitude is, "we're adults, we can talk about this." Talking about each others' sexual history may also help open up conversation about what has worked for you and what hasn't, and can help the two of you make it better. What is important to remember is that you both have a right to know what you are getting into.

From the Mouths of Baby Boomers

"There just comes a point where it comes up. We talk about what kind of protection we need. I say 'let me know a little bit more, like the last time you had sex, your last physical.' At my age, it's a lot easier to come out with the questions. Sometimes I joke about it and say, 'I'm a reporter, it's my job.' It's never been a problem."

—Class of '74

"One thing that made me know he was a cool guy was that he was absolutely insistent that we get tested before we got really involved. We went together."

—Class of '70

"When my friends and I were younger, we didn't use condoms. Then we were married forever. After a divorce, we'd find ourselves looking in the drug store, trying to figure out what kind of condoms to buy. Oh, and you've got to practice putting them on. I mean, use a banana or something."

—Class of '65

Asking about STDs may seem awkward, but telling a partner that you have an STD may feel terrifying. Questions run through your mind, such as: "Will she run?" "Will he think I'm promiscuous?" "Will she see me differently?" What you may not know is that STDs in general, especially herpes, are extremely common. Medical association statistics indicate that one out of every four or five individuals is carrying genital herpes, and most do not know it. The fact that you know you have it is actually a gift to your partner, and simple precautions can prepare you both for a satisfying and healthy sexual relationship.

If you have an STD, you need to come to terms with it yourself first. You're probably angry, ashamed, and would love to deny the whole thing. Get support. Talk to your doctor about your symptoms and ways to prevent transmission. Support groups and hotlines—such as the National Herpes Hotline (919-361-8488), can help you deal with the feelings, fears, and identity distortions that can come with having an STD. The American Social Health Association (ASHA) provides helpful online information at ashastd.org.

Once you accept that you have an STD, it will be much easier to talk to your partner. You will be able to approach it calmly, provide accurate information, and feel worthy of a loving response. You can acknowledge that it's hard to talk about, but that you want a relationship based in honesty and trust. This will set an important precedent, and your partner may disclose difficult information as well. The strength of your character will overshadow the weaknesses you may feel.

Values, Now?

If you thought you had your values regarding sex all worked out, dating again can throw everything off. Maybe you associated sex with marriage only, but are now single and you're not so sure you want to marry again just for the (bedroom) door prize. On the other hand, maybe you've had sex in the past without much thought about what your boundaries and values are, and are now looking inward for answers. The fact that there are fewer roadmaps for the sex life of a dating-again Boomer makes it a highly personal, and sometimes perplexing journey.

For you to have the best experience possible, make sure that it's *your* values you're following this time. It is so easy to look around for cues, when the best ones are inside you. Here are some places to look for answers:

1. Your gut: There's a reason we talk about "gut feelings." When you feel queasy or tight in the stomach, this may be a helpful signal that you're experiencing conflict.
2. Your intuition/small voice/knowing: Called by many names, this is the part of you that calmly and quietly knows the answer. It is usually accessed through meditation and reflection.

3. Your sense of who you are: From the journals and photo albums you've kept to the explorations you've done in this book, this is about how you see yourself. It's about where you've come from, who you are, and how you see yourself evolving.

Discovering Good Sex

Clearing away the potential for guilt and hurt leaves the coast clear for really good, savorable sex. Good sex is loving and honest, not perfect. Good sex leaves a sweet impression that makes partners smile to themselves throughout the next day. Each of you carries a body-sense, a touch memory that provides a sense of connectedness even in the absence of the other. As many times as we've done it, and as many friends as we tell, we can still feel like we're carrying around a little secret the morning after.

chapter 28

Sex, This Time Around

Healthy, lusty sex is wonderful.
—John Wayne

Sex is no longer a mystery. Unless you've been living in a monastery, you've done it. Chances are, you've done it quite a bit. And so has your date.

When it comes to sex, Boomers have the advantage of experience. This chapter will help you use that experience to clarify what you want now, and to make sex this time around the best it can be. Because you and your date have taken different paths to get here, we'll also discuss how to negotiate differences in what you want.

> ### Boomer Sexpertise
>
> If any generation can claim to be informed about sex, it's ours. The research team William Masters and Virginia Johnson went where no lab had gone before when they brought the bedroom to the laboratory. Equipped with instruments to measure sexual response, they observed over 700 men and women during masturbation and intercourse. Their findings were published in 1966, in the book, *Human Sexual Response*. Even though the book was intended for the medical community, it caught the attention of the public, and became a bestseller. The work of Masters and Johnson made a tremendous impact on the treatment of sexual dysfunction and dissatisfaction. In 1970, the publication of their second book, *Human Sexual Inadequacy*, and the opening of their clinic in St. Louis, launched the field of sex therapy.
>
> Yet, it may have been the clever title and user-friendly format of David Reuben's book that made it the most famous and successful book ever written on human sexuality. *Everything You Always Wanted To Know About Sex* (*But Were Afraid to Ask)*, published in 1969, became a #1 bestseller in 51 countries, and has sold over 100 million copies.

The Benefits of Being a Grown-Up

One of the best things about being a grown up is that we wear our sexuality so much more comfortably. We can talk about our sexual desires without feeling guilty, we know our bodies and what makes them feel good, we have relinquished myths that used to make us feel bad. Once we know that women need more time and stimulation, that mutual orgasms are a rarity, and that nobody looks like a model when naked, we are free to be really present and enjoy sex for what it is. And, ironically, we are more free to play. What is more fun than talking about sex with someone you want to have sex with? Sure, the unconscious sex of youth has it's place—and has surely gotten idealized over time. But conscious sex—sex that can be talked, seen and relished—is one of the best rewards of maturity. We can be there and acknowledge being there at the same time. We are freer to indulge fantasies and experiment with positions, places and props.

We also know that sex is much more than intercourse. A sensual foot massage can be a wonderful form of lovemaking, sleeping together with your body contours aligned can be exquisitely intimate, and there are an abundance of ways to stimulate pleasure and orgasm. In fact, if you left a marriage that involved regular intercourse, you may be more excited about new touches and foreplay than the traditional punch line.

From the Mouths of Baby Boomers

"This was a surprising discovery for me. I've dated men who have felt used for sex by women! I'm dating a very attractive guy, and I have to reassure him that I'm not using him for his body. When I think about it, I don't know why I'm so surprised. Nobody wants to be used."

—Class of '73

"Even dating the second time around, I still find you have to second-guess what a woman wants. Sometimes you get cues, sometimes you don't, and sometimes you can't trust the cues. And, let me emphasize this: I'm a guy who really believe 'no' means 'no'."

—Class of '71

"Morning sex? What's up with that? I guess they're bigger and firmer in the morning. But here I am all dolled up for the date, we have all this foreplay, and then he rolls over. Then he wants it in the morning! Especially for us baby boomers, if you don't feel that confident in your body, we're going to be less inhibited with lower light."

—Class of '65

"I was catching up on the adolescence I had missed. It got to the point where I asked my counselor if I was a nymphomaniac! I was, like, *insatiable*. Then it ran its course. I also remember a friend suggesting I could pick up the guy sitting next to me. That had never occurred to me. It was a whole new adventure!"

—Class of '68

Negotiating Sexual Styles

What if you're hungry and your partner is on a diet? How do you get what you need without feeling that you've spoiled things for your partner? Or how do you tell your partner that it's important to you to wait? More and more, I'm talking to women who are ready to sow their oats and find themselves dating men who want to purify their systems and renounce sex for awhile. So, if you're expecting things to go according to old gender norms, forget it.

Negotiating desires in relationships can feel risky. You may worry about losing your partner, or just looking stupid. Yet, if there's any time to practice this skill, it's now. Playing it safe can buy us a little time, but it won't make a relationship.

The best way I have found to negotiate differences in relationships is what I call "the good fight." Good fighting happens when we negotiate with our desires. Rather than saying, "Do you know how long it's been since I've had sex?," you say "I really want you—all of you." (Think about which sounds sexier!) Since childhood, we have learned to leverage our arguments with tales of our deprivation rather than just expressing our desires. ("Everyone has a Twister game but me!") When you are in a relationship, good fighting means going after what you want *and* going after the relationship. So you might say, "I want to wait on sex and I hope you'll wait with me, because I'm crazy about you." Speaking from your desires empowers your partner to speak from his or her desires as well. The more forthcoming you both are, the more likely you are to come up with creative solutions.

Once you're both ready, you can take your negotiation skills into the bedroom. As Masters and Johnson discovered, sex is best when each partner takes responsibility for making his or her desires known. This can be as simple as saying "mmm" or "yes" when your partner is doing something you like. When you want more, let your partner know! When desires go underground, they sap energy away from the sexual encounter. For example, if you're preoccupied with the thought, "I really wish he'd touch me there," you are applying energy to the thought and are not available for the lovemaking. Saying it out loud or saying it with your body, by placing his hand there, moves the desire into the relationship. Your action will most likely be exciting to your partner, as desire inspires desire.

But let's say your partner doesn't respond. You have a choice here: you can see your partner's lack of response as a cue to close down and feel ashamed of your desire, or you can stay confident about what you want. This may mean pushing harder, checking in on what's up with him (pun not intended, but convenient), touching *yourself* there, or engaging in some playful sexual sparring. In all of these scenarios, intimacy is enhanced and the sexual relationship becomes more honest, alive, and satisfying.

Keep in mind that it is our differences that energize relationships. While you might fantasize about having someone with the exact same needs as you, that person would in fact *be* you. I don't know about you, but for me, that is a frightening thought.

Variations in Arousal

This is something we didn't think much about as young adults. But add a Boomer's sexual experience together with the effects of age, fluctuating hormones and increased use of medication, and arousal may be an issue. While one woman going through the stages of menopause may feel insatiable, another may be looking for the female version of Viagra. In her book, *The Wisdom of Menopause*, Dr. Christiane Northrup notes some of the contradictory symptoms that have been associated with perimenopause, including "decreased clitoral sensitivity, increased clitoral sensitivity, decreased responsiveness, [and] increased responsiveness."

Boomer men have the bad news of being at increased risk for erectile dysfunction (ED), but the good news of having a the pharmaceutical industry clamoring to help, providing treatment options such as the popular Viagra. Findings from the first large-scale study assessing age and erectile function, reported in the August 5, 2003, issue of *Annals of Internal Medicine*, noted that only 4 percent of men between the ages of 40 and 49 reported ED, whereas 26 percent of the men between the ages of 50 to 59—and 40 percent between the ages of 60 and 69—had experienced erectile problems. It is interesting to note that the men who stayed lean and physically active had a lower prevalence of ED.

If you are experiencing concerns about arousal, you are certainly not alone. First, look at whether your concerns come out of some idea of what "normal" *should* be. Sexuality is a very individual thing, and it all really comes down to what *you* want. If *you* are not satisfied with your sexual response, talk to your doctor about treatment options. There is so much help available, there's no reason to sit home and feel helpless.

Psychological issues can also get in the way of sexual responsiveness. Memories of sexual mistreatment, long past or recent, create a mental association between sex and pain. Internalized voices telling us we are unattractive make it hard to feel confident in our sexuality, which can either drive us to sex to get affirmed or away from sex out of shame. Anxiety can interfere with our ability to relax and open up sexually. Then we all have our sexual scripts we are working out. But this needn't be a problem. Nobody comes to this stage in the dating game with an empty slate—how boring would that be, anyway? Again, you need to decide if there's a discrepancy between what you want and what you have. Just talking it out with a therapist may relieve a great deal of tension and free you up sexually. Or you may decide that it's time to face some issues you've been avoiding in order to really get what you want.

It is always heartwarming to hear stories of when couples work through their sexual worries and longings together. These stories remind us that sex is not something that we each have to have all worked out individually, but that couples can work into (or *play* into) sex together by developing a base of intimacy and understanding. So what if we're high-maintenance—*life* is high-maintenance. Embrace it!

Morning and Evening Lovers

Back then, time of day did not have much influence over our sex lives. What mattered was how we looked and who we were with. Today, time of day matters as much as size. We care about routines, lighting, and whether the room has feng shui. So what happens when our routines clash? When we're both accustomed to sleeping on the same side of the bed, or making love at opposing times of the day? Many women associate sex with the evening date, while men often feel more aroused in the morning.

Again, while these differences can feel disruptive, they also can infuse new energy into our lives. You don't have to choose between familiarity and novelty—if beauty is defined by the combination of these elements why not have both? And the mixing it up itself, is what gives a relationship form and identity. Maybe you'll end up with some exotic morning dates and lazy evenings in bed. The two of you will develop your own unique sexual style, and it will work for you.

Making It Better

We are in a great place in our lives to have great sex—*however* we define it. We have some experience, so we can ease up on the performance anxiety. We've learned a few things about what works, and may have even hit on a personal specialty.

Most of all, we have lived enough to discover what doesn't work. We know life is short, and we're ready to shed old defenses and imposed expectations and to risk getting what we want. Most of us know what will make it better this time around. Now is the time to allow it to happen!

chapter 29

Saying It

Life is about not knowing, having to change, taking the moment and making the best of it, without knowing what's going to happen next. Delicious ambiguity.
—*Gilda Radner*

So, you're dating someone you like—a lot. Or someone you really think you could like, but you just don't know each other well enough yet. You want to be closer, to share more, but you're scared. Much of what you feel and want is staying up in your head—to the point where you may seem distracted and distant.

If this sounds familiar, you aren't alone. It seems as we start to develop wishes for a relationship, we can just as quickly click into a kind of safety mode. We become self-conscious, watch our words and hold back. Let's look at how we can buck this trend and risk getting close.

Expressing Ourselves, '60s Style

- Righteous!
- You are so fine.
- Bitchin'!
- That shirt *rules.*
- Right on!
- I am so stoked about tonight!
- Solid!
- That dress is *bad.*

- You are one cool cat.
- Neat!
- Your car is really *boss.*
- You are outta sight!
- I really dig you.
- Groovy!
- I am so gone over you.
- Everything is copacetic between us.

What's Holding You Back?

Whether your reason for holding back is "I'm afraid of losing her," or "I might look stupid," the source is the same: fear. Our desires are the most intimate expressions of who we are, and sharing them can leave us feeling vulnerable. It makes some sense to be cautious when you're just starting a relationship. Yet, some of the most cautious people I see are the ones who have been married for years. What happens, it seems, is that partners confuse commitment with constancy. The thinking is, "This is who he *thinks* I am; I don't want to mess that up."

So, when things are going well, we want to freeze the moment, and freeze ourselves. Our fear of losing the relationship causes us to lose contact with ourselves. No wonder so many marriages dry up (or so many people dry up in marriages)!

Operating out of fear makes the world smaller. Fear comes out of the attitude: "There's not enough to go around, so I have to cling, hold, constrict." Acting out of fear keeps things small, and reinforces the belief in scarcity. If you really believe that your date is happy with you because you haven't shared your desire for more, how likely are you to open up? Maybe you're thinking, "Better to wait and see if that's what she wants." But what if she's holding back, too?

Expressing ourselves is a risk, but so is *not* expressing ourselves. As far as risks go, I highly recommend the risk of desiring openly.

The Risk and Excitement of Desiring

Expressing our desires can feel risky because it means standing alone. If you say "I can't stop thinking about you," you run the risk that your feeling is not shared. And if your date doesn't repeat the same words back to you, fear will assume the worst. Of course, if he repeats the same words back, fear will have you believe that he's just appeasing you. The joy of expression is lost if we are trying to secure a particular response. *The pleasure of expression is in the act of expressing.*

My favorite photograph captures a 5-year-old boy just after he threw a ball up into the air. His hands are wide, his head is lifted to the sky, and his expression is of pure joy. He doesn't seem to have any concern about whether he will catch the ball as gravity pulls it down. His pleasure is in throwing it up there and letting go. That's what we can feel when we express ourselves—when we share our childhood dreams and fantasies of the future, when we show how giddy we are about something that just happened, when we dance around like Maria in *West Side Story* singing "I Feel Pretty."

From the Mouths of Baby Boomers

"He walked me to the car and I said 'kiss me.' It felt so good to do that. I would have never done that 20 years ago."

—Class of '72

"We'd been going out a lot, but I was tired of neglecting my other needs. What I really wanted was a clean house. So, this time, I told him. He stayed with me and helped me clean. I was so driven, and by the time the house was clean, I was a mess. Just when I'd finished vacuuming, he tapped me the shoulder. I turned around and he smiled and said, 'The place looks great!' Then he pulled me into an extremely deep kiss. Here I was, looking like crap, feeling like a bitch, and he's turned on! Definitely a reward for asking for what I wanted!"

—Class of '79

When we have the courage to express our desires, and we are loved in response, that's heaven on earth. There is nothing like being really seen and really loved at the same time. As we discussed in Chapter 4, we are the most likely to get loving responses when we love ourselves. Here are some tips on putting that love into action:

- As you express your desires, think to yourself, "… and I love this about myself!" If you can't honestly say that to yourself, you may be unsure and looking for validation. You might need a little more time to get clear with yourself before putting it out there. When I told my dad I was thinking about going into psychology, the uncertainty came through in my voice. He picked that up and suggested I stay in premed. After becoming absolutely clear with myself that I hated chemistry and loved studying relationships, that this was *me*, I came back to him. This time I told him, "I'm going into psychology!" I was confident and clear, and he was pleased for me. We unconsciously give people cues about how to respond—if the cue is "you're gonna love this!" the responder probably will.

- Carry the attitude, "I am good for you." I am so impressed with my friend's ability to do this. She recently expressed to her boyfriend her desire to spend more time with him. He had been under a lot of pressure, and became defensive. She calmly responded, "Listen to me. I'm just telling you that I love to be with you." He did listen, and he got it. She had the wisdom to know that her desire was not an offense to him, but that he had heard criticism rather than love.

- The preceding example leads to another point: Your partner's response is not always about you. If you're excited about a new prospect of yours and your girlfriend just lost her job, she may have a hard time sharing your enthusiasm. Even these situations can offer opportunities for intimacy. By saying "what's wrong?" you can understand the source of her feelings, while separating them from your own reality.

- Trust the truth. If your desires are consistently rejected by your date, you have learned something important. Your date doesn't love what you love, and it's time to say goodbye. Stay strong in who you are, and look for a better match.

Secrets of Intimacy

Intimacy simply means closeness. Whether the channel is physical, spiritual, or emotional, the way you touch each other is by making real contact. Real contact requires reaching to the place where the other person is alone, understanding in a way that is completely specific to that person, taking the time to really "get it." It is so easy to project our own reality onto one another that intimacy can require some work. As a therapist, my job was to get intimate with the thoughts of my clients, to go into them and really try to see things as they did. Intimacy is a journey that is never completed, but when two people share in it, they walk in the world with a sense of being known. Just as you can sense when two people have made love, couples radiate something different when they share what they once carried alone.

"Fill each other's cup but drink not from one cup.
Give one another of your bread but eat not from the same loaf.
Sing and dance together and be joyous,
but let each one of you be alone,
Even as the strings of a lute are alone
though they quiver with the same music."

—*Kahlil Gibran, from*
The Prophet

Having Fun Yet?

*The kingdom of heaven, blessedness, moksha,
nirvana waits here and now.*
—*Yrjö Kallinen, Finnish Minister of Defense, who
publicly promoted the idea of Finland's unilateral
disarmament to set the world an example*

Doesn't it seem, when people ask you how the dating's going, that they're expecting to hear about an *outcome*? We seem to be programmed that way. Without thinking, we aim our questions toward a resolution: "So, do you *like* him?" "Is she the one?" And when we're the ones responding, we may feel like we don't have much to say. What if someone asked you, "What is it like for you?" or "What are you learning?" These questions focus on the *process*, the adventure, and make for much more interesting conversation.

The way we converse about our lives reveals much about how we live. We tend to live with resolution in mind. We *think* the outcome questions: "Is this the right person for me?" "Will I marry again?" While these musings are normal, they can distract us from the fascinating process we're in. Much of the fun of dating lies in the uncertainty and the gradual unfolding of the story. If you're not having fun yet, try shifting your focus.

Life According to Zippy

If you're one of the people who skips over the "Zippy the Pinhead" comic strip in the newspaper, you may not have a full appreciation of the impact Zippy has had on our culture. Zippy, the pinheaded brainchild of Bill Griffith, made his debut in his polka-dotted mumu in 1970. Zippy has been credited as the inspiration for the recurring Conehead skit on Saturday Night Live, and was the first Boomer to use the phrase "Are we having fun yet?"

Zippy is a microcephalic—which technically means "small head"—whose illogical outlook takes us out of our heads. Griffith describes his microcephalic this way: "Their scrambled attention spans struck me as a metaphor for the way we get our doses of reality these days, Zippy is living in the moment, He's at peace with himself because he's out of step with everyone; he doesn't know it, and he doesn't care. … Zippy has no problem with the irrationality of the universe, whereas most of us are desperately trying to make order out of the universe, and our lives. Zippy accepts chaos as what it is, which is the real order of everything."

Staying in the Present

The present was where we lived in the '60s. We valued living for today and forgetting tomorrow. Spiritual and psychology gurus helped us tune in to the present moment. Fritz and Laura Perls challenged therapy patients to get off the couch and bring issues into the "here and now" through the role-playing techniques of Gestalt Therapy. Places like California's Esalen Institute offered experiential therapies along with hot tubs and a party atmosphere.

While it might have been easy to be present at a resort setting, it's more of a challenge to savor the "here and now" when we're balancing all the pulls of adult life. With jobs and children and aging parents, the future grabs our attention. College savings and 401Ks can take the focus away from what's happening now. And even if we're enjoying dating, it can feel like a major interruption in our efforts to get ahead. But see, that's the beauty of it.

Dating takes time, and in so doing, gives time. If you weren't dating, how else would you justify indulging in so much entertainment? How else would you meet the people you've met? What is so wonderful about dating, and so often lost when we're "done" dating (why do we quit when love comes?) is that our date time is devoted exclusively to the relationship. I suspect that the conflict we have about taking time to date is based on guilt. Our culture still places a higher value on individual pursuits than on relationships. Taking time just to enjoy each other seems frivolous rather than essential.

Let's embrace the inconvenience of dating. Be present for it. Trust the flow of life and, for awhile, forget about where the relationship is going—just notice where it is right now. If you're confused about the relationship, allow a part of you to step back and observe. Whenever I do this, I encounter surprises. It's so easy to miss the subtleties of experience and the delightful nuances of relationships. And whether the date you're on sucks or soars, it all makes for wonderful drama.

Enjoying the Drama

Would you enjoy a book or a movie if there was no crisis, no tension, no problem to work out? Probably not. Yet, we so often bemoan the twists and turns in our own lives. Why the difference? First of all, in movies and books, we generally assume things will work out in the end, or at least something of value will come out of the story. We may not have the same confidence about our own lives.

Secondly, we have no control over what happens in books and movies. We're there to watch, to go for a ride. In fact, we don't *want* to know how things turn out. That would spoil it!

Finally, the stories in books and movies are about other peoples' lives. We can participate without consequences.

If we want to experience dating more as we would a great drama, we can treat it the same way. Try posting a note on your mirror to remind you to observe. Use background music. Step outside yourself and watch. Try to guess what's going to happen next, but let go of the outcome. Think about who might play you if your story is made into a movie, and then decide who would play your date. If you're experiencing emotion, get into it! You may even want to take some risks to make things more interesting. The thing is, with drama, you can't lose. Whether you play it like James Bond or Jerry Lewis, it's entertainment!

You can also try this exercise to free you to enjoy the now. If you are hoping to "end up" with someone you're dating, assume your wedding is set for a specific date, like a week from today or a month from today. Now, what do you want to do before then? Assuming a happy ending takes the focus away from the future and helps you fully participate in the drama. Another way to approach this exercise is to assume the best possible ending, without having any idea what that ending will be. I prefer this approach, because it leaves room for discovery and for outcomes beyond the scope of my imagination.

Collecting Funny Stories

A sense of humor will go a long way as you date. Comedy gives us even more latitude than drama. The worst dates can make the best stories, and your own embarrassing moments become great material. Write down your memories. You don't need to keep a journal (although you may enjoy that), just jot down some notes in a computer file or in a little notepad. Take a look at it once in while to keep yourself grounded and to relive the humor that comes with enjoying a full and adventurous life. You may have died of embarrassment the night you walked all the way across the dance floor with three feet of toilet paper stuck to your heel, but laughing at yourself is healthy. If you can laugh at yourself at the time you make you a mistake, even better. Occasional self-deprecation makes others feel you are approachable, and helps them ease up, too.

Serious Wisdom from a Comic

Dave Barry has a way of exposing the humanity of us all. Here are five of his "25 Things I Have Learned in 50 Years" (from *Dave Barry Turns 50*):

- Nobody is normal.
- A person who is nice to you, but rude to the waiter, is not a nice person.
- No matter what happens, somebody will find a way to take it too seriously.
- Your friends love you anyway.
- Nobody cares if you can't dance well. Just get up and dance.

And tell your stories. A woman I know meets regularly with a group of other dating women, and they get to share their stories. Sometimes it's the people in your life who are *not* dating that will appreciate your stories the most, because your experiences provide a refreshing contrast to their own lives. Go ahead and exaggerate a little. You've put a lot of energy into this—milk it!

From the Mouths of Baby Boomers

"There was a gorgeous guy at the pool and I was trying to figure out how to meet him without putting myself on the spot. When he went into the changing room to get ready to leave, I saw my chance. My bike was by the men's door. I ambled over there and put on my helmet, turned around and promptly slammed into him with my bicycle."

—Class of '78

"I call this one 'Flaming Idiot':

Sometimes the universe has powerful ways to tell you you're somewhere you shouldn't be. It's my first venture into a hotel room with a man, post my divorce. Our evening of a single overnight road trip was, to put it mildly, less than satisfactory. Next morning I rose while IT was still sleeping. Put on my lush terry cloth 'well-known label' robe, a gift from my ex-husband, and lit a cigarette (there was no smoking the night before, if you get my drift). I look in the dresser mirror to see small flames racing up my lapels. I run to the bathroom sink for water. In the bigger mirror there, I see flames on my sleeves and back. Into the shower I go … no harm done other than a few slightly singed tresses. My date, Satan, slept through the entire incident. The fire was the most exciting part of our time together. There were no more dates."

—Class of '77

chapter 31

From Date to Relationship

Never go to bed mad. Stay up and fight.
—Phyllis Diller

So you and your date went shopping the other day—for toothpaste and light bulbs? When you find yourselves sharing more than the entertaining side of life, you have probably moved beyond just dating. You are entering that wonderfully entangled experience we call couplehood.

Becoming a Couple

How do we distinguish a couple from two people who are just going out? Maybe it's the comfort couples radiate, or the fact that they don't need to fill every space with conversation. When we see a couple, we see more than two people together, we see a unit, a partnership.

The simple difference that distinguishes people who are just dating from a couple is the time spent together. You know you're becoming a couple when you want to share more and more of your experiences with each other. Somehow, events in your life don't feel complete until your partner knows about them. You want to share news, family, and friends. You might take each other to your favorite places, and begin to introduce your partner to who you were as a child through stories or photos.

You Might be a Couple if...
- You have purchased an extra set of toiletries for his place
- You are starting to count trips to Target and Home Depot as dates
- You find yourselves staying in more
- You feel compelled to tell each other about your day—*every* day
- You have met each other's parents
- You *like* each other's parents
- You talk on the phone—even when you're going out that night
- You have your own drawer in her bedroom
- You've seen each other without a lot of things, including makeup

---

Although you enjoy dating, you also want to share the mundane aspects of life, which brings us back to shopping for toothpaste. When couples can turn such a task into play, all the better! The ability to be playful together is a key ingredient in good relationships. Couples often develop a secret language composed of pet names, baby talk, and inside jokes referring to experiences they have shared. Early in the coupling process, the two of you may become rather exclusive, and feel less of a need for other relationships. Although this is a natural tendency, it's worth the effort to stay in touch with friends, or at least to let them know you are temporarily obsessed and please stand by. Most of us need people of all sorts, so think more rather than less.

"What, You're Not Perfect?": Making It Real

Along with the pleasures of sharing, couples can also experience disillusionment. In the beginning, you only saw the dressed-up, best-behavior versions of each other. Now you are beginning to see the real thing, complete with uneven skin tone and emotional baggage.

We can react to imperfections with both relief and disappointment. The relief comes with the realization that both of you are human and fallible. You aren't the only one who has a weird family and some silly habits. Disappointment comes when you start to realize that the person you are with is not who you thought he or she was. If you find your date is increasingly rude and disrespectful, you will rightly question the relationship.

Sometimes, however, our disappointment is primarily based on fear. After divorce, for example, we tend to have sensors up for any problems that might put us back into an unsatisfying situation. My friend has a very healthy post-divorce relationship, yet tends to react to even minor conflicts with fear, "Now I'll probably have to break up with him." She doesn't, of course, and they get past those times, but it's just taking some time for her to trust her choice. If you're concerned that you're repeating an old relationship, check out Chapter 37.

Finally, it can just be hard to replace the fantasy for reality. As long as you are not in a relationship, you can invent someone who makes up for all your past hurts and never disappoints you. Reality is less certain, but it's also far more interesting.

From the Mouths of Baby Boomers

"It's how we started introducing each other that made me know we were a couple. Now I say, 'This is my girlfriend, my girl,' rather than just telling people her name, or saying she's my friend. Also, we don't ask *if* the other wants to do something on the weekend—we ask, '*What* are we going to do?'"

—Class of '80

"Yeah, it's hard when you see the differences. On the other hand, if my partner thought exactly like me and agreed with everything I said, he would *be* me! That's a scary thought! A little conflict helps you know there's two of you."

—Class of '76

First Fights: Getting Out or Working It Out?

As you become a couple, you naturally close off other options. It's important to check in with yourself about whether this is what you want. Deciding whether to stay a couple isn't always easy. You've made an investment in each other, so there's a pull to make it work. On the other hand, you're learning the good, bad, and the ugly about your partner—can you handle the whole package? First fights put us directly in touch with this dilemma. Let's look at how to assess the fight, and the relationship.

Fighting by itself is not a problem. As you've probably gathered by now, I enjoy a good fight—as in a fight based in desire rather than destruction. Of the couples I've worked with, it was often the ones who never fought that I worried the most about. As Ernesto Che Guevara put it, "Silence is a fight carried out by other means." These couples had withdrawn their desires from the relationship.

What happens when you fight can help you know how the relationship will go. While arguments don't typically end in one round with a pat "I'm sorry," good fights cause each of you to take the other in, to ponder the other person's points, and to move in your partner's direction. If you are having a hard time letting your partner in, and tend to stay on the defensive, you may be the one who isn't ready to be a couple. If your partner consistently seems unmoved by your desires, you might need to consider moving on. If both of you are struggling, but really want it to work, get yourselves to a couple's therapist. The therapist can often quickly identify what gets in your way, and help you develop conflict-resolution skills. And the earlier you do it, the less likely you are to pile up baggage between you.

You've probably heard people say that all relationships are "hard work." I don't agree. Good relationships are "easy work," because the work comes out of a passion for the relationship, a desire to bridge differences, and a sincere interest in really knowing each other. Similar to loving your job, you work hard, but it doesn't feel like it. The energy flows out of you. If you both consistently come to the table and work through what needs to be worked through, just because that's what you do, you're a couple. Celebrate what you have together.

If you're confused about what you want, give it time. Allow yourself the room to experience different situations together, and to know each other more fully. Most things become clear over time. We make the best decisions when we operate out of abundance. Say this to yourself: "There are plenty of options, and there is plenty of time." And practice believing it.

Troubleshooting

As with any adventure, dating presents its challenges. Part 4 addresses common dating dilemmas, such as whether to play games, concerns about love on the rebound, how to cope with rejection, and whether to settle in or move on. As much as we wish we could leave dating angst behind with our record singles and mood rings, it's likely to surface. But we don't have to stay there. These chapters help you to transform dating troubles into opportunities for more, rather than less. We even tackle the question that drives us dizzy: "Is this love?"

chapter **32**

Nothing's Happening!

To every thing there is a season, and a time to every purpose under the heaven:
A time to be born, and a time to die; a time to plant, and a time to pluck up that which is planted;
A time to kill, and a time to heal; a time to break down, and a time to build up;
A time to weep, and a time to laugh; a time to mourn, and a time to dance;
A time to cast away stones, and a time to gather stones together; a time to embrace, and a time to refrain from embracing;
A time to get, and a time to lose; a time to keep, and a time to cast away;
A time to rend, and a time to sew; a time to keep silence, and a time to speak;
A time to love, and a time to hate; a time of war, and a time of peace.

—Ecclesiastes 3: 1–8, *the inspiration for Pete Seeger's song* Turn, Turn, Turn.

"She's not calling back. He's not giving me the time of day. Why no 'You've Got Mail' message? Why do I keep attracting losers? Why do the guys I like ignore me? I'm not getting any younger. I want to find somebody while I still can remember her name! I don't know how much longer these moisturizers will hold off the wrinkles. Will anyone need me when I'm 64? What's wrong? I've done everything I'm supposed to do—why isn't anything happening? Why do I even bother? I can't take this—I quit!"

Calming Yourself

Stop! If you're having the kind of escalating thoughts listed above, take a deep breath and read this chapter. I know these panicky thoughts— I've had them myself, and I expect they'll pop up at the next lull in the action of my life. As Boomers, we are known for our ability to make things happen. We are good at activism, and many of us have protested *and* pursued the American Dream, both with equal fervor. Whatever our cause, we like to see the effect. It's never been easy for us to wait.

When you've gone into dating with confidence and optimism, it can be particularly confusing when nothing happens. You may find yourself searching for an answer, and starting to question what you have to offer. When we don't see activity, at least we want an explanation.

Yet Boomers are beginning to recognize the value of waiting. As we tune into the rhythms of nature, we are compelled to wait. Organic farming has arisen out of our awareness of the consequences of pushing nature with quick-fix chemicals. Maybe it's time to relax our dating style as well and consider waiting an important part of the process. Here are some ways to calm down and appreciate the ebb as well as the flow:

- Let go of what you can't control. This means recognizing the limits of your own vision. The trickiest thing for us humans to comprehend is that just because nothing is happening, it doesn't mean nothing is happening. We never know when the seeds we have planted will sprout. A friend of mine just got a call from a guy she gave her business card to—almost a year ago! Seems he was in a relationship at the time, but is now free *and interested*.

We can't see what is going on in someone else's mind and in someone else's plans. Don't assume something is wrong just because you don't control the whole story.

- Keep your own mind. While letting go of what you can't know, attend to what you can. Use the waiting time to become clear about what you feel, what you want, and what is really important to you. Often this clarity will give you a new boost of energy to go for what you want.

- Remember this: The world can change in a day. I've seen it happen over and over. We hold onto this awareness of what we want, show up, don't have a clue how it's all going to work out, then— bam!—it's all there for the taking. Transitions such as the beginning of an intense relationship, take a lot of energy, so now may be a good time to rest. Waiting gives us time to gear up for change.

The Day Bonnie Met Clyde

In the 1967 film, *Bonnie and Clyde,* nothing was happening for Bonnie, the Texas beauty played by Faye Dunaway. That is, until Clyde stopped by to steal her mama's car. When Bonnie joined him for a ride, a quick robbery and lunch, Clyde, played by Warren Beatty, recited her life to her:

"… So then you got your job in the café, and now you wake up every morning and you hate it. You just hate it. You get on down there and put on your white uniform (Bonnie: 'pink—it's pink') and them truck drivers come in there to eat your greasy burgers and they kid you and you kid them back but they're stupid and dumb boys with the big ol' tattoos on 'em and you don't like it. And they ask you for dates and sometimes you go, but mostly you don't because all they ever tryin' to do is get in your pants whether you like it or not. So you go on home and you sit in your room and you think now 'when and how am I ever going to get away from this.' And now you know."

Bonnie was in for the wildest ride of her life. Be careful what you wish for.

- Ask what you need to attend to before the wait is over. Think of what you need to take care of before your schedule gets filled with social engagements. Use this time as an opportunity to get your house and head in order. Maybe you've been avoiding taking care of some old business or just taking care of you. What is time waiting for you to attend to?

- Get away from the phone! Often a change in environment will help shift your mood. If I find myself compulsively checking my e-mail and phone messages, I know it's time to get out of the house—without the cell phone! Leave behind the cues that remind you of what's not happening. Give some time to a friend, take a short trip, or go for a vigorous workout. If someone wants to get in touch with you, let *them* wait a little.

- Practice being in-between. Take a bus or a train so you can peer out the window. Daydream. Wait with a friend. Ask a friend to wait with you.

- Create more to wait for. Put in a call, send an e-mail, ask for help, meet another person, send another signal, make another introduction. Get the world busier working for you.

The Waiting Checklist

We tend to see waiting time as an *absence of something* rather than time with a purpose of its own. Let's look at what you might reap from your wait:

- Time to Feel. As long as we're scurrying about, our feelings can get pushed aside. When nothing is happening, they surface. Let them come and bring their message. You may acknowledge that you're exhausted and finally give yourself some rest. Maybe you need some time to grieve the changes you've been through. Maybe you need some help. Keep in mind that feelings are like a wave that fills you, then diminishes. The intensity is only temporary, and you are likely to feel cleansed once you allow them to rush over. What you are left with is a part of yourself you have been neglecting.

- Time to Expand. Sometimes it is the absence of action that forces us to take a crucial step. It may be that step we take out of sheer frustration—placing an ad, going someplace new, calling someone on a whim—that ends up making all the difference. Getting angry can empower us to push beyond our perceived limits and surprise ourselves. I can credit becoming an author with the fact that nothing else was happening. I wasn't getting any of the practical but boring jobs I was applying for. I finally decided that the time I had was a gift, and I started the book proposal that got me my agent—and here I am!

Think of the opportunity this "nothing time" is offering you. You have no excuse, there's literally nothing in your way. Take the next big step.

- Time to Let Go. On the other hand, sometimes when we feel like giving up, that's exactly what we need to do. We need to give up some control, stop working so hard, and let go of the outcome. Notice how hard it is to remember something when you are focused on remembering (especially at our age!)? Then you relax your mind, and there it is? The same is often true when we are looking for something—or someone. Too sharp of a focus can narrow our range. So, relax your mind, open your heart, and prepare to be surprised!

Feeling Good *Now*

Focusing on what *isn't* can make it hard to recognize what *is*. This might be a good time to give yourself credit for what you've done to get to this point in your life, to look around and notice what is there. It can be especially helpful to look back at times when we couldn't imagine having what we have now. Maybe you felt trapped in an empty marriage, and couldn't imagine how you would get out. But you did. Maybe there was a time when you looked at people in a certain professional position with envy—and now you're there! Or maybe what is right in front of you is a marvelous human being that you feel proud to call your child.

Give yourself credit for how far you've come. Take inventory of what you've learned. Look at photos of your life, jot down a timeline of your experiences. Do what you need to do to get centered in yourself, and to celebrate who you are *today*.

From the Mouths of Baby Boomers

"When I left my husband and faced the reality of being alone, I made a point to write an affirmation about all the people in my life who loved me. I felt such gratitude for my brothers and sisters, my father, and all my dear friends. I'm extremely fortunate to be loved by all these people. I started my day with those affirmations. That had a huge impact on my approach to life … and I bought a good vibrator."

—Class of '65

"After dating a lot, I faced a weekend with nobody. This may sound weird, but it kinda scared me. But, you know, it turned out to be an amazing weekend. I had this incredible time with my kids. They're older, so we just hung out, laughed— they included me in all their activities, they seemed proud to have me with them! And my son and I had this amazing talk. I would have missed all that if I had been out with a date."

—Class of '78

---

chapter 33

The Games We Play

What is in other people's minds is not in my mind.
I just do my thing.
—Audrey Hepburn

As much as we claim to hate games, we find ourselves playing them. We look away from a tempting glance, wait awhile before returning calls, and happen to mention other people who hit on us. Let's look into why we play, when playing becomes work, and whether there's a better way.

Should I Call?

You may recognize this dilemma: "I want to talk, but I don't want to call this time. I need you to make an effort, too. If I don't call, am I playing a game?"

Before we get too much into the subject of whether to call, it's important to distinguish if you are responding to a pattern—i.e., the person you're dating consistently neglects to call, or an isolated event. Just because you don't hear from your date when you're supposed to doesn't mean she hates you or he's a jerk. We often build up all kinds of negative fantasies, only to find that there's a benign explanation. If you find yourself making things up, just call and save yourself the head trip.

Good Call

This excerpt from Jacqueline Susann's 1966 pop classic, *Valley of the Dolls,* illustrates the heroine's emancipation from her hometown rules as well as the welcome response of her sleepy lover. It's also a good reminder that a missed call can have a very simple explanation:

> "Ten-forty-five. Lyon hadn't called. Three times she had started for the phone to call him, but decided against it. She lit a cigarette and stood staring at the wintry sunlight from the window. The minutes ticked by. ... Somewhere a steeple bell chimed. Well, now what? Was she going to stand around in the room all day? Or go to the theatre alone? No, that wouldn't look right. If he was there and hadn't called her, it would look as if she were running after him. Ridiculous! This wasn't Lawrenceville, and Lyon wasn't just a date. There were no silly rules now. She marched resolutely to the phone and asked for his room.

His voice was muffled at first. Then he shot into action. 'Good God, darling! Is it really five of eleven? I thought I left a call for ten o'clock! ... Come on down and keep me company while I shave.'"

When it's time for your date to make the call, your dilemma reveals the fine line between games and truth. Not calling could be a game: "I'll pretend not to be interested to get you worried, then you'll call." But not calling could also be an expression of your honest desire for more: "I want to talk to you, but I'll risk giving that up, because I need more from you than I'm getting." In both of these cases, you don't call, but the intention is different. In the hard-to-get game, you are attempting to manipulate the behavior of your date. In the second case, you are operating out of what you value, while letting go of the outcome.

The difference, while subtle, is important. When you are playing a game, you are putting out a lot of energy to control someone else's behavior. That's why game playing can be so exhausting and unrewarding.

But when you act out of your own truth, all you control is you, and you win either way. If your date doesn't make the effort, you have eliminated someone who doesn't give you what you need. If your date calls, you get what you want.

Another, often overlooked approach is to share your dilemma with your date. Can't you just see Audrey Hepburn calling and saying, "I don't want to call you, but I want to talk to you. What am I supposed to do?" Audrey's way of relating was so refreshing because she had a way of putting her vulnerability on the line without apology—and who could resist? Audrey is a great example of how attractive honesty can be.

If the imbalance in who calls who has become a problem in an otherwise good relationship, talking it out can help you understand each other better and make some changes. Maybe you'll discover that your date doesn't really like the phone, and prefers saving conversation until you're together. This may still be a conflict, but now you know what's behind it.

I Want to Make You Jealous

The "make you" in this subtitle is a clue that we're entering a game. Again, what makes a game is the attempt to manipulate. The Jealousy Game is a way of showing your date, "See, she appreciates me. Why don't you?" This can work, but if you're cozying up to someone else, it can also backfire. Even if your date works harder to lure you back, she can lose trust in the meantime.

Why not talk directly about what you are wanting? Usually what you really want is to stay with the person you're dating, while adding a little of what the potential rival offers. You can honestly tell your date, "I'm attracted to the attention Sarah gives me, but I really want it from you." It may not have occurred to your date that you need more attention, and your feedback could improve communication between you. Your willingness to bring your desires to the relationship is a complement: You are expressing your interest in having more *together*, rather than going to someone else to get it.

> "I was born with an enormous need for affection, and a terrible need to give it."
>
> —*Audrey Hepburn*

But My Date Is Playing!

What do you do when your date is playing games? First of all, be complimented by the fact that your date is expending so much energy to keep you interested. Then, rise above it. Let's say your date likes to play Chase. When you're busy, he gives you all kinds of attention, but when you're attentive, he backs away. He's attracted to the chase, and puts you into a situation where *you're* playing games.

The most straightforward way to deal with this game is to call it. You can say something like, "I know you get hot for me when I'm less available, but this isn't fun for me. I like it when a man can be hot *with* me." By calling the game, you avoid the set-up of looking desperate by just being affectionate. Keep in mind Audrey's magic formula of *unapologetic* honesty.

From the Mouths of Baby Boomers

"I think there's a difference between playing games out of insecurity and just having self-respect. There's power in loving yourself enough to not act desperate. And that has taken a long time to learn. I don't want anyone to be with me because I've guilted them into being there, or they're afraid I'm not going to be okay, or because they think they need to rescue me. Because that will never sustain itself."

—Class of '70

"Some people seem to think it's a turn-on to go to a party with your date and then separate and flirt with other people. I don't actually find it all that exciting. If I'm on a date, I'd just as soon be with the person I'm dating."

—Class of '68

"Guys really have to second-guess. A lot of times, we really can't tell what women want. Sometimes you get cues, sometimes you don't, and sometimes you can't trust the cues!"

—Class of '72

This approach can be applied to the Jealousy Game, as well as Hard to Get. Just let your date know it's not working for you, and that the games are turning you off rather than luring you in. Open up an opportunity for your date to let you know what he or she is trying to get out of the deal. For example, you can ask her why she's distancing, or what's up with the flirting. Your date may not fess up about the game, but knowing you're not playing takes away the incentive to keep it going.

Making Your Own Rules

The great thing about dating this time around is that we know ourselves well enough to make our own rules. If you like being the initiator, it might not faze you to be the one doing most of the calling. And maybe you'd rather have a date who flirts a little than one who is socially withdrawn. You are the best judge of where you draw the line. If you find yourself taking on a role in your relationship that you don't like, stop playing it. It is better to risk losing the relationship than to lose our self-respect. We usually get what we expect from relationships. If you expect your date to make advanced plans with you, don't participate in his last-minute plans. If you find her flirting offensive, tell her. If she continues, leave her to flirt away.

Fortunately, getting what we want out of relationships isn't just about setting boundaries. It's about saying what we want. Tell each other about your fantasy date. Let each other know what gifts excite you. Notice the little things that make you feel loved. And when it's working, say so! The words "thank you" are often underutilized in relationships, yet they carry more power than a whole list of criticisms.

chapter 34

I Need You (For Now): Healing Relationships

A woman called up the police department and said,
"I have a sex maniac in my apartment. Pick him
up in the morning."
—Henny Youngman

Sometimes a relationship seems to fill you in a way you've never experienced. Then, at some point, that same relationship loses it's power. What happened? You may have experienced a "transitional relationship," or a relationship that helps you heal and move on. Let's look at the nature of transitional relationships, and how we can see them as a gift rather than a mistake.

Rebounds and Transitional Partners

When we leave a significant relationship, it is common to receive warnings about finding love "on the rebound." The concern, of course, is that we are particularly vulnerable after a break-up, and could get hurt. This is a possibility, and we need to consider whether we are ready for that risk. There is

223

another possibility, however. Your rebound relationship may be a part of your *healing*.

After spending a good portion of your life in one relationship—especially if that relationship wasn't working, you are likely to have desires and needs that have been neglected. A new relationship offers the exciting potential of filling that void. Often, that void is a sexual one, and the affirmation of both your own desire and your appeal to someone else is incredibly nourishing. So, if you initially find yourself drawn to a Don or Donna Juan, there may be some method to your madness. As long as you see the relationship for what it is—and take precautions for what you could catch!—it can be wonderful to have someone bring you to life again.

However, the function of a transitional relationship will vary depending on the individual. I knew a woman who suffered a great deal of guilt for past sins, and was drawn to an extremely religious man. Although she seemed to carry a wish to be blessed by such a man, the real gift to her was her discovery that this man had his sins as well. She ultimately was turned off by his restrictive approach to life and moved on, taking with her a less restrictive view of herself.

Many of us go through a series of transitional relationships, each one resolving a different area of need. In fact, every date is a kind of transitional relationship, because different people tend to activate different parts of ourselves.

But how do we avoid the fallout of moving on? First of all, it helps to acknowledge to yourself that your initial relationships might be transitional. Unless you're dating someone rich just to get wined and dined, or going out just to get laid, transitional relationship are not usually planned. We typically come to understand the relationship's meaning to us as we are *in* it. But if you just want some overdue fun, be open about it. All you have to say is, "I'd really like to be with you tonight, but I really don't know what I want beyond that." Or you can acknowledge that you're pretty fresh out of a long-term relationship, and you just want to get to know different people right now.

From the Mouths of Baby Boomers

"There was this young woman who used to intern where I worked. She would give me these cues, like standing very close to me. I was divorced, but she was in her '20s! We stayed in contact after her internship. She really liked the Beatles and, of course, I was into the Beatles. One day, she showed me this place where she loved to go to watch the planes. We sat on a blanket. She got very close, so I kissed her. I'm thinking, 'She's almost half my age … but it's fun.' So I went with it, and we dated for awhile. Then, sure enough, as I predicted, she was ready to move on. I'm like 'okay, it was fun.' I was *really* flattered, and I really enjoyed it, but I didn't get emotionally involved."

—Class of '72

"It was my relationship with my therapist that really healed me. In a gentle way, she showed me what my role was in creating problems in relationships. She was like a test case, allowing me to work out those problems in my relationship to her. But it was always safe—she didn't retaliate or get angry. It changed my life."

—Class of '79

Unless you deceive your partner, you don't have to worry about your transitional needs. In every relationship, you both come together for a reason, whether you know the reason or not. And in every relationship, you both are vulnerable, whether you want to be or not. The religious man who dated the woman I mentioned earlier was challenged to face his own demons, and came out of the relationship more grounded and open. And, somehow, they both seemed to know when it was time to move on.

"Finally, Someone Who …": Welcome Contrasts

When we start dating again, we are likely to be drawn to someone who compensates for the weaknesses of the prior partner. The problem is, we can initially *overcorrect* for these weaknesses. After living with a reserved and introverted person, you may find your date's gregariousness wonderfully refreshing—that is, until it starts annoying you. Or it might just feel great to have a date who really listens, or who isn't cheap, or who dresses well. The gift of dating is to get the chance to check out the extremes, as well as the many variations on the theme, and to find what really works for you.

Healing Relationships on Screen

In *Annie Hall*, Alvy (Woody Allen) encourages Michigan-native Annie (Diane Keaton) as she pursues her singing career, while challenging her to broaden her knowledge. While she doesn't get too excited about his books on death, she starts taking classes and gains confidence and sophistication. Her worldliness eventually takes her away from him. On the other hand, his desire to find her gets the New Yorker behind the wheel for the first time.

Harold and Maude pairs the car-stealing, life-loving, soon-to-be 80 Maude (Ruth Gordon) with the young death-obsessed Harold (Bud Cort). As Maude joins Harold in his fascination with a demolition, she asks him, "Is this enough?" She gets him to sing and smell and touch, to play the banjo, to laugh and cry, to dance and do somersaults, to make love, to give up his suicidal preoccupation and live. As she is dying, he utters above his sobs, "I love you!" She responds, "Oh, Harold. That's wonderful! Go and love some more."

In *Breakfast at Tiffany's,* Holly Golightly's (Audrey Hepburn) neighbor Paul (George Peppard) becomes her loyal friend and protector. But as she drops off "cat" in an alley and snubs Paul's love with her philosophy that "nobody belongs to nobody," Paul confronts and breaks through Holly's fear of loving. As "Moon River" plays in the background, Holly tearfully recovers the cat as well as Paul.

Hiring a Healer

It could be said that we go into any relationship with a desire to be healed. In a good relationship, partners can serve as mutual therapists, using their empathy and their differences to challenge each other's growth. While every relationship has this potential, if partners are too needy, the relationship can become overwhelmed. When this happens, couples are more likely to repeat old patterns than repair them (see Chapter 37). For example, if you enter a relationship with a strong fear of abandonment, you want that person to be there for you, yet you may find yourself looking for evidence that he's not. When we keep testing a relationship, we can set it up to fail. These are times when it's wise to enter a relationship that is designed for healing: a relationship with a therapist.

Choosing a therapist is not unlike choosing a partner. You want someone you feel safe with, who you believe will both understand and challenge you. The difference is, the therapist is not bringing her needs (other than to get paid!) into the relationship. The therapist learns from his interactions with you, but uses that understanding to help you grow.

If you are attached to a partner and you both are feeling overwhelmed, another option is to make your relationship into a healing one by seeing a couple's counselor. In this case, the interactions are still between you and your partner, but the counselor is there to help you work things through and to develop skills you can take with you.

chapter 35

"Ouch!": Dealing with Rejection

The hardest thing about getting out of a relationship is listening to the radio. Because every song is about being in love, or being heartbroken. And I found that the only song I was comfortable with is that Peter, Paul, and Mary song, "If I had a Hammer."
—Ellen DeGeneres

We had to get to this sooner or later. Let's face it, rejection sucks. How much it sucks, however, has a lot to do with how we deal with it. Let's look at how to make the best out of the worst part of dating.

Avoiding Rejection Traps

A mutual break-up can be hard, but being rejected is particularly difficult because it's not in our control. We feel cut off, powerless, vulnerable. And often, rather than acknowledging this reality, we fight it. The problem is, our attempts to recover a sense of control over rejection tend to keep us focused on the rejection. That's how we get trapped.

The rejections that come passively, through the lack of a response or follow-up, can hook us into the "why?" trap. We have no information, and expend all kinds of energy trying to fill the void. We usually fill it with our own defects, or mistakes in the way we approached things. If you're doing this now, *stop*. If you need to, invent an exotic explanation, that he has been drafted into the CIA and had to cut-off all personal associations. Whatever it was that caused your date to go away is tied up in his life and his personality, all of which are as mysterious as the CIA explanation. You may look like someone who betrayed him once. He may think you're great, but you're not right for him. He may not even really know why he's not wanting to continue. So it's futile and self-destructive to try to pin it on something that's wrong with you. Let it go.

On the other end of the continuum is the victim trap. Here, we don't focus on what we could have done better, but rather on the rejection itself. Along with the lament about the current rejection, you may pull up all kinds of evidence about how this "always" happens. You suddenly forget about relationships that went well, or people *you've* rejected. You load past hurts onto the present, regardless of how much life has changed for you since then. Sometimes we create patterns as a way of making our lives more predictable, and assuming a sense of control. Then we can say, "See? I knew this would happen." The antidote for this thinking might be to develop a little amnesia about the past. Past rejections don't have to mean anything about today, and today's rejection says nothing about tomorrow. Rejection is a fact of life for everyone—you have no special claim on it. Risk moving forward with a little less certainty.

When "Let's Just Be Friends" Doesn't Fly

- No. Let's just not.
- No. My friendships don't come with a sexual history.
- No. I don't like guzzling beer and watching ESPN classic.
- No. I prefer sex to pajama parties.
- No. I wouldn't want to cut into the therapy sessions you'll be scheduling soon.

It's tempting to look for answers in ourselves, to blame fate or to overanalyze what went wrong. We've all heard it, either directly or in the movies: "It's not about you, it's me." The statement rings false, because rejection does reflect some kind of dissatisfaction with the other person. But as lame as the phrase is, it's true. Rejections reflect the psychology of the person rejecting. The rejecter could have issues with commitment, or might have issues with you that go beyond who you are. For example, someone who likes order and predictability in his life may have a problem with your more spontaneous style. Does it mean your style is bad? No! That very same quality will excite someone else. Why not save yourself a lot of grief and find that someone else?

Staying on Your Own Side

When we suffer a separation, it is natural to fight it. In order to deny separation, we often take on the thinking of the rejecter. If your date told you that you were just too "intense," you might find yourself aligning with her criticism and feeling ashamed of who you are. Certainly there are times when rejection can help us face something we *want* to change. But many times, rejection simply reflects a poor fit. We can all probably think of jobs that we are now relieved we didn't get.

When you suffer a rejection, even if it's a subtle one, like a brush-off when you flirt, try to stay on your own side. Say to yourself, "that didn't work for him" rather than "wrong move." Feel the power of staying with who you are and attracting the people that it does work for. These are the people you want anyway! As you practice staying aligned with yourself, you will feel stronger and radiate a confidence that makes others want to know you.

The Positive Side (Yes!) of Rejection

We can become so busy fighting the reality of rejection that we forget some of its benefits. Despite what Woody Allen and Groucho Marx said, you deserve to be in a club where you are accepted. You deserve someone who is crazy about you, and someone who can weather the challenges of a relationship. Rejections usually come from one (or both) of two sources: Your date is not crazy enough about you, or your date is afraid of getting too close. Either way, it's good to eliminate these reluctant lovers from your pool.

From the Mouths of Baby Boomers

"Rejection? It sucks."

—Class of '71

"I can't date him. What if I have to break up with him? I can't stand the thought of breaking up with him, so I'll have to date him a long time!"

—Class of '82

"Once you've been divorced, you have this belief system that you're bad at relationships. So, if things don't work out, you think it's you. But look at the other person. Have they chosen anyone else? If so, is it going any better? A lot of times, the answer is 'no.'"

—Class of '66

"Everything was going so well. I thought, 'This is the one I want to spend the rest of my life with.' Just when it was getting right where I wanted it to be, she does a 180. She said those fatal words, 'We need to talk,' and she told me she wasn't really ready for a relationship. It was very tough. My friends helped me get through. It was especially helpful to talk to my female friends. Some of them told me they had seen a problem in the relationship well before this. They saw signs that I hadn't. But it's still puzzling to me. She had said, 'You did everything right.' That made it even more confusing! I guess, even when you do everything right, it can still come out wrong. That's the illogic of love."

—Class of '72

If you stay strong in yourself, as well as in your desire for a good relationship, rejections are a gift. They move along the natural selection process that leads you to the really great relationships. This may sound odd, but try trusting rejection. The sooner you do, the sooner you will see new doors opening for you. Life is too short to spend looking backward.

It's no accident that the most successful people are usually the ones who have endured the most rejection. Successful people are not controlled by the possibility of rejection. They may not like rejection, but they don't focus on it. Their experience with rejection becomes increasingly benign, and they become stronger in their ability to believe in themselves even when all the external evidence says not to. And, one day, the world comes to believe as well. So try viewing your rejections as both an affirmation that you are risking and as strength training.

Just as a muscle gets stronger by being torn down and built back up, you are working your dating muscles. And as you've probably discovered, the game called dating requires strength!

When You Are Doing the Rejecting

This is one area where we may believe it is better to give than to receive. However, rejecting can be very hard to do, especially when you really care about the other person. And, of course, we know what it's like to be on the receiving end.

The thing that can be hardest to do is to be clear. Just as we can focus too much on being rejected, we can drag out the rejection process in ways that do more harm than good. Very early on, the clearest communication might be no communication. Don't engage in flirting or allow someone to buy you a drink if you don't want to encourage that person. Don't go on a second date if you know you're only doing it because there are no other options. Allow better for yourself *and* your date. When you have to turn someone down, you can let him or her know that you just don't feel that special something that makes you want to continue. It's honest and it doesn't indict the other person. Engaging in a prolonged discussion about it just keeps you involved. Even when you've been in relationship for awhile, you need to know when to end the conversation. Chances are, you and your partner have already talked about what isn't working. If you've moved from discussing it to ending it, say so.

Yes, rejection hurts. Unfortunately, once you decide to leave a relationship, you are no longer the one who can provide comfort. You can be civil and respectful, but you aren't going to be the good guy or gal. You need to trust your date's ability to bounce back, just as it's up to you to recover from rejections you experience. That's the nature of separation. Like I said, it sucks. But, hopefully, only for a little while.

> *"We keep going back, stronger, not weaker, because we will not allow rejection to beat us down. It will only strengthen our resolve. To be successful there is no other way."*
>
> —Earl G. Graves, who founded the magazine Black Enterprise in 1972, and has received honorary degrees from 28 universities.

chapter 36

Why Do I Keep Dating You?

There's no such thing as a little freedom. Either you are all free, or you are not free.
—*Walter Cronkite*

Sometimes we just find ourselves in a relationship. The first date goes well, we date again, and, we wake up one day in a relationship. We may ask ourselves, "How did I get here?" It's time to take an honest inventory of how you got to this point and whether you want to keep going.

Settling or Satisfied?

So, how's it going? Are you happy? Bored? Maybe you haven't really thought about it. We get into relationships for a variety of reasons, not all of which serve us. Let's look at some of these reasons and see which fit:

It's easy. Your relationship may feel natural and easy. You get along, like the same things, it just flows. If you had a prior relationship that was conflict-ridden, this may feel wonderful. For the most part, easy is good. Partners should like being partners. You may have that soul-mate kind of familiarity that leaves you without the need to explain everything.

On the other hand, easy can mean safe, predictable, and, well, boring. Oscar Wilde said that uncertainty is a prerequisite for romance, which may be why easy relationships are often called friendships. If easy means the absence of challenge and stimulation, you may be settling.

I'm hooked on the sex. Great sex is not a problem. Feeling addicted is. Like that drink that tastes great at night and hurts in the morning, some relationships provide pleasure at a cost. Maybe you're excited by the body of a your younger partner, but you long for a more mature mind and spirit. Maybe you feel wonderful during the lovemaking, and lonely the rest of the time. If the sex is the only thing keeping you in the relationship, you are thinking too small. You may be afraid you can't have passion *and* depth. Think again. Settling comes out of a belief in scarcity. True satisfaction comes when we believe in abundance.

I'm afraid. Maybe it just feels good to have *someone*, and you're afraid that's the best you can do. Maybe you're avoiding being alone. If you're shy, you may be seeking refuge from the stress of meeting new people.

Other kinds of fears may be related to your partner. For example, you may fear your partner's reaction if you say you are leaving, or be just be afraid of whether he or she will be okay.

From the Mouths of Baby Boomers

"When you've been through a painful marriage, are you willing to hold out for something wonderful? Most people don't do it. It's the same as building the business you've always wanted to, insisting on a job you love. Everybody settles. It's a lack of faith, lack of belief in what's possible. It's all the same energy—work in a factory, marry the dork."

—Class of '72

"If you're looking for someone to capture or reign you in, GO AWAY. If you're looking for someone to share your freedom with, come on!!"

—Class of '76

I'm needed. Being needed can make us feel powerful and important. But once you start to feel responsible for another person's functioning, you've built yourself a trap. If you find yourself in a care-taking role with a needy partner, the biggest challenge for you will be to let go of the illusion that you are indispensable. And just as you are letting go, your partner may pull out all the stops and emotionally blackmail you with threats of self-harm. We'll talk about how to get out of that trap in the next section.

It's good. Let's not overlook the obvious: You might just be staying in your relationship because it's good. You continue to be drawn to each other, spending time, sharing what happens, backing or challenging each other as needed, and coming to the table when there's a problem. It's not perfect—no relationship is, but it's alive and working.

Getting "Unsettled"

If your relationship has felt soothing, for whatever reason, it may be exactly what you've needed—for awhile. As we discussed in Chapter 33, some relationships help us heal and transition. But if you've started to feel like you're settling, it's time to get unsettled.

One way of getting unsettled is to ask for more from the relationship you're in. A younger relative of mine confided in me about her relationship. She was torn because she was very attached to the guy she was with, but also craved more excitement. She had been thinking about other men and getting confused over her dilemma. I suggested that, if she really wanted excitement, she might try being honest. Her eyes widened and revealed that she had not considered this possibility. She opened up to him and revealed a part of herself she had kept undercover. She found excitement in being honest, he revealed a maturity that surprised her, and the relationship was stirred up, but not shaken.

I find it ironic that we often play a relationship safe to avoid losing it, and end up taking the life out of it *so we have no alternative but to leave.* If you're harboring thoughts of leaving anyway, what's the harm in pushing the relationship a little? You may be surprised. And if it doesn't work, you can still leave.

Unsettling Woman

If there's one woman who challenged our tendency to settle, it was Erica Jong. She risked being crass and offensive as she challenged the limits on women's freedom, especially in their relationships with men. In her 1973 blockbuster novel, *Fear of Flying*, she writes about Isadora Wing, and her wild struggle to unsettle from her marriage to her second husband, Bennett:

> "Bennett was marked by death, up to his neck in it … If he had turned to me, if he had let me comfort him, I might have borne it with him. But he blamed me for it. And his blame drove me away. But I was afraid to go away. I stayed and grew more secret."

In an afterward written in 2002, Jung comments on her heroine: "Isadora wants love, but how can she recognize love when the madness of sex is blinding her?" It seems that until Isadora can find serenity, and approach men from that place of calm, she will not really be free. She gets her first tastes of that freedom while taking a soothing bath in the apartment of her estranged husband:

"I floated lightly in the deep tub, feeling that something was different, something was strange, but I couldn't figure out just what it was. … I hugged myself. It was my fear that was missing. … Perhaps I had only come to take a bath. Perhaps I would leave before Bennett returned. Or perhaps we'd go home together and work things out. Or perhaps we'd go home together and separate. … But whatever happened, I knew I would survive it. Surviving meant being born over and over. It wasn't easy, and it was always painful. But there wasn't any other choice except death."

The other way to get unsettled is to end the relationship. In order to do this, we need to face what got us settled in the first place.

Usually, it comes down to fear. You may be buying into that "bird in hand" advice or the worry that there aren't any good ones out there. You may be afraid that you can't replace the few good things the relationship offers, or just plain afraid of being alone. As long as you are controlled by fear, you are not free to say "no" to a relationship, but worse, you are not free to say "yes." The reality is, we don't have a hold on anything. Life is a mystery. Cling, and you may feel safe, but you avoid life.

We've talked about dating with the assumption of abundance, and how our expectations shape reality. As much as we can work to get our heads in the right place, sometimes it comes down to *acting* as if we're not afraid, rather than eliminating fear. The action of saying no to what we don't want is a very powerful one and, in my experience, it does not go unrewarded.

Let's say you decide to leave. It may be the act of breaking up that you fear. Maybe you're afraid of the emotions your partner might experience. Yet, your partner has a right to his feelings, and it doesn't feel good to be rejected. There's a difference between hearing the feelings and getting hooked by them. You can be compassionate while staying resolute.

If you have reasons to anticipate a violent reaction, don't mess around. Develop a safety plan *before* you break up. You may need to have your talk in a public place (arrange to have a friend pick you up) or by phone so you aren't alone together when you break the news. Don't hesitate to call a domestic abuse hotline (look at the beginning section of your phone book under community services), for advice and a back-up plan.

More often, though, we are afraid of harming rather than being harmed. When you are hooked by the emotional blackmail—threats of self-destruction or even suicide, you may need some help untangling yourself. Consult a therapist. The challenge really is about you letting go of responsibility you never should have owned. A suicide threat of this kind is usually an aggressive and manipulative act. Yet, it can be real. And it's the not knowing that really sucks. Sometimes the simplest answer is to call the bluff. Call 911, report the threat, and let the police check it out. If she's crying wolf, she may be more reluctant next time. If it's real, she'll get access to help. You can refer your partner for help, express your desire for her to choose life, but—bottom line, you can't control her actions.

When a friend of mine was entangled with a man she was concerned could be suicidal, she asked her therapist, "But what if he commits suicide?" The therapist calmly said, "Then that would be his responsibility." These words freed my friend from her imprisonment, and she had the courage to be honest with him. He didn't kill himself. In fact, he grew. And so did she.

If It's Working, Celebrate!

Sometimes we question things when they're going well. It's like some guilty part of ourselves is a little worried about this thing called happiness. Erma Bombeck described guilt as "the gift that keeps on giving."

> "No work of love will flourish out of guilt, fear, or hollowness of heart, just as no valid plans for the future can be made by those who have no capacity for living now."
>
> —Alan Watts, Zen philosopher, author, and unintentional spokesman for the '60s counterculture movement.

Push your guilt aside and accept the real gift right in front of you. Appreciate how good it feels to have someone in your life that you enjoy being with. Does it get any better than that?

When we get what we want, we can get a little nervous. Accepting a gift means relying on something outside of ourselves, something we don't control. We could lose it. It's your choice whether to focus on that possibility or to embrace what you have now. When you receive the gift you've been asking for, say "thank you." Then, celebrate!

chapter 37

Why Do I Keep Sampling?

Brad (Rock Hudson): Jonathan, before a man gets married, he's uh—this tree—he's like a tree in the forest. He—he stands there independent—uh, an entity onto himself. And then he's chopped down. His branches are cut off, he's stripped of his bark, and he's thrown into the river with the rest of the logs. And then this tree's taken to the mill. And when it comes out, it's no longer a tree. It's the vanity table, the breakfast nook, the baby crib, and the newspaper that lines the family garbage can.

Jonathan (Tony Randall): No-no. No, if this girl weren't something special, then maybe I'd agree with you, but with Jan, you look forward to having your branches cut off.
—Pillow Talk, *1959*

There's a lot to be said for sampling. We learn best through experience, and experiencing different people helps us figure out what we want. Just as we learn our food preferences through tasting, we learn our people preferences through dating.

But after we've had a number of dates, we may find ourselves wondering what's up. We may wonder if it's "normal" to be dating so long without settling down. Forget about what's normal! We Boomers have become much too diverse of a group to lump into categories. But we can look into our motives for continuing to sample the options, and whether what we're doing is getting us what we want.

Enjoying the Ride, or Afraid to Love?

Maybe you like meeting new people, exploring new relationships. Shopping can be a lot of fun. We've talked about appreciating dating in its own right, rather than as a means to an end. If you're doing that, good for you!

But maybe you're a little worried about the fact that no one seems quite right to you. Maybe you feel like "Georgy Girl," forever shopping but never stopping to buy. Let's look at some reasons behind the tendency to sample and see what fits:

I'm having fun! This is when dating is the best. You love the process of dating, and aren't worried about the outcome. Maybe you missed out on dating much the first time around, and you're in no hurry to get it over with. As long as you're honest about your intentions (or *lack of* intentions), you can avoid spoiling your fun with misunderstandings and guilt. Enjoy!

I'm afraid. Fears of becoming exclusive with someone can stem from a number of sources. You may be afraid to settle into a relationship, because you made a bad choice in the past. And as long as you don't decide, you can imagine a perfect person coming your way. Or maybe you're worried about getting hurt again. If you are afraid to love, you may find yourself looking for faults that give you a reason to leave. Or maybe you are afraid of conflict, and run at the first sign of it. Whatever the source, if your sampling has more to do with fear than enjoyment, you are not really free.

I love the chase. We talked a little about the game of Chase in Chapter 32. We play the Chase game because it provides challenge, uncertainty and a kind of thrill. When you can't seem to move beyond the chase, you may be addicted to the excitement and adrenaline rush the game provides. Once you've "conquered," you're bored. As with all addictions, you pay a price for the high. You may feel empty when you're not playing, and you miss out on the sustaining gifts of a relationship.

"Why?"

Pillow Talk, released in 1959, was the first movie to team the strong personalities played by Doris Day and Rock Hudson, along with the neurotic sidekick, played by Tony Randall. In this following scene, Jonathan (Randall) is challenging Brad (Hudson) to stop his game of chase and settle down. He doesn't get too far:

Jonathan: You ought to quit all this chasing around—get married.

Brad: Why?

Jonathan: *Why?* You're not getting any younger, fella. Oh, sure, it's fun, it's exciting, dancing, nightclubbing with a different doll every night … but there comes a time when a man wants to give up that kind of life.

Brad: Why?

Jonathan: Because he wants to create a stable, lasting relationship with one person. Brad, believe me—there is nothing in this world so wonderful, so fulfilling, as coming home to the same woman every night.

Brad: Why?

Jonathan: Well, if you want to, you can find tricky arguments for anything.

I'm still looking. It may just be that you haven't found someone who excites you yet. Good for you for staying with it! You aren't doing yourself or your partner a favor if you go into a relationship halfheartedly. In real life, it's not usually about being torn between two or more lovers. (Although if you are, relish it!) More often, you date a lot of people that don't do it for you. Then someone comes along, and everything changes. Remember, it only takes one. And there's someone out there for you.

I'm not ready. Dating can be a wonderful transitional phase while we prepare to be in a relationship. It's a way to learn about our preferences, get used to the idea of being with someone, and ease ourselves and our loved ones into the next phase. As the poet X. J. Kennedy put it, "The purpose of time is to prevent everything from happening at once." The same can be said of dating.

Allowing a Relationship

If you identified fear as the primary reason you keep dating new people, what do you think is getting in the way of allowing yourself to be in a relationship? Maybe there is someone you've dated who you have strong feelings for, but you won't allow yourself to go there. In fact, you may spend more time with dates that don't stir up a lot of feelings, because that feels safer. So, while you may pride yourself on being a "free spirit," you're not free at all. You are not free to love.

Yet, as Brad Allen's line suggests, the concern about loss of freedom can reveal a difficulty negotiating our needs in a relationship. Of course it's easier to get what you want when you're alone, but then you're alone. If you allow your desires to disappear once you're a couple, that is a problem. But what makes couples really cook is the interaction of desires—the process of stirring together individual desires and creating something better. Check out Chapter 30 again if you want some tips.

Maybe you've been hurt—badly. So rather than risking the loss of love, you cut it out from your life to start with. You don't risk losing love—you insure it. Over and over, I see people choosing a kind of death as a way of *avoiding* death. Life and love are always a risk.

Sometime, without realizing it, we punish ourselves for a past loss by not allowing ourselves another chance. We chastise ourselves for "not knowing better," and pay penance by blocking our own joy. Tune in to the unkind thoughts you are having toward yourself, and change your tune. We all deserve room to make mistakes, and often it's the very "mistakes" we make that lead us to new and better things.

If heaven is sitting right in front of you—take it! Allow yourself to be loved again, or maybe for the first time. Free the intensity of your own feeling, and love wildly. Let your spirit be truly free.

Dating as a Lifestyle

Our culture has been both complicated and enriched by the variety of lifestyles Boomers are living. The '50s ideal of the "nuclear family" is no longer the only acceptable unit for adult relationships. Gay and lesbian couples live in committed relationships, step parenting and adoption blend new family units, single moms and dads raise healthy children, couples choose not to have kids, and people choose to stay unattached.

For some of us, the point of dating is not to find a partner, but to share experiences while we remain single. You may get your primary rewards through your career, family, or the richness of your friendships. Maybe you've spent a good part of your life with a partner, and want to live out the next chapter as a single person. If the love of your life has died, maybe you are sustained by that relationship and don't crave another one.

From the Mouths of Baby Boomers

"I've never been settled-down kind of person. My ex and I share custody, so I have time with my kids, and time where I'm free to do whatever I want. I think the kids have a great deal, because my ex and I are both ready and excited to see them, and they get each of us all to themselves. I just want somebody to hang out with from time to time, but guys sometimes see this as a challenge and want a relationship. I just want someone to go out with, to have sex, I *don't* want to talk on the phone. Sounds like a pretty good gig, doesn't it?"

—Class of '81

"I finally figured out that what he's addicted to is the conquest. It was really revealing last time I talked to him. He told me how wonderful it had been to see me at the concert, told me how much he still loves me. He said that his girlfriend was worried about my being there. Then he said, 'I told her she shouldn't be worried. The temptation is in somebody new, not in somebody I've already dated.' There it was. I told him that he had just given me a good reality check and hung up."

—Class of '70

If you plan to remain single, your primary responsibility is to be honest about that with the people you date. For most of us, however, we don't really know where life will take us. And that's part of the fun.

Give yourself permission to change your mind.

The fact that we all have our own path is what makes us so interesting. If you're confused about your motives, ask this simple question: Am I doing this out of fear or desire? The rest is up to you.

> *"The Pope is single too. You don't hear people saying he has commitment problems."*
>
> —*Garry Shandling*

chapter 38

Why Do I Keep Dating the Same Person (in Different Forms)?

Most people do not really want freedom, because freedom involves responsibility, and most people are frightened of responsibility.
—Sigmund Freud

"He looks different." "She's nothing like my ex." "So why does our relationship feel the same? Why are we having the same fights?"

If your new relationship is feeling like an old one, you may be caught in something called repetition. Let's look at how repetition works and how you can make it stop.

> ### Buy Beech-Nut, By Gum!
>
> If anyone knows the power of repetition, it's the advertising industry. And one of the most repeated commercial slogans of the '60s was the catchy, "Buy Beech-Nut, By Gum!" An early version of this commercial had clay animals singing the phrase in a repetitive kind of fugue, alternating male and female voices, and sticking in an occasional variation, such as "by gee" or "by gosh." By the end, you knew the phrase was burnt into your brain.
>
> In the later '60s, the commercial's repetition came in the form of a popular tune. Frankie Valli and The Four Seasons sang the Beech-Nut version of their hit "Let's Hang On." The last phrase stuck in our heads: "That rush of gushing flavor hangs on—hangs on, hangs on—to what it's got." Then, to top it off, the classic jingle pops in "Buy Beech-Nut, By Gum!"
>
> Hmm, I could use a little gum right now.

The Comfort of Repetition

Freud became an icon in the '60s because, like us, he questioned the constraints of culture—and he talked a lot about sex. He also seemed to know a lot about the human psyche, which may have been our *second* favorite topic. One of his challenging discoveries was the concept of *repetition compulsion*. Freud suggested that, for a variety of reasons, people are compelled to repeat the failures of early relationships. While the idea seems absurd, we've all seen it happen.

We repeat old scenarios for a variety of reasons. One is that repetition provides comfort. Even if our interactions with a partner are negative, they are familiar, and familiar is comfortable. Repetition can also give us a sense of mastery. It's like a dance we were pulled into at one time. If you learn the steps, you start to believe you're in the lead, even if the dance was never yours to begin with. The third reason people repeat is to heal. Underneath the replay is the hope that, this time, it will come out differently. And if we can resolve an old conflict in a new relationship, somehow it transforms the old one, too.

So, what's the answer to repetition compulsion? Like Freud's answer to everything, it is to *become conscious*. Repetition, like blinking, often happens without our awareness. Once we see what we're doing, we're in a position to change it.

If It's a Pattern, Look at Yourself

If you find yourself saying, "Why is every person I date _____ (a jerk, needy, selfish)," you aren't just saying something about your dates. You are revealing something about the repetition you create. We often prefer to see ourselves as fated, doomed, conspired against, than to see how we're drawing old realities back into our lives. But as long as we avoid owning these patterns, the patterns own us.

Let's use an example to illustrate how we can leave old patterns behind:

Jane Doe's father had an extramarital affair. Then, lo and behold, her husband has an affair. She finally frees herself of that relationship, and now she's dating a guy who, well, she suspects might be having an affair. The pattern of disloyalty she witnessed as a child keeps getting repeated in her adult relationships. What should Jane do?

The tricky task for Jane will be to acknowledge her part in the pattern without beating herself up. As we've discussed, there are both healthy and unhealthy reasons for repetition. For one thing, her repetition is revealing that her father's affair was a pivotal event for her, and her life keeps alerting her of that fact. Maybe she really needs the time to work with a therapist and talk about what she went through, to have someone else witness what she felt, and to develop the empathy for herself that will inspire her to attract better men. If your pattern keeps confronting you with old feelings, it may be time to take those feelings seriously.

From the Mouths of Baby Boomers

"I've been married three times. My first wife had a history of abuse. I had no coping skills to deal with that. My second wife had also suffered abuse, and I couldn't make that work either. The woman I'm married to now is still a reflection of that pattern, although her abuse was less severe. The amazing thing is that, in all three cases, the abuse was by the mother and the father didn't protect them. I've learned that I'm a rescuer type, and that I need to be restrained about my rescuing. The level of abuse has diminished in each relationship. Maybe I'm learning."

—Class of '64

The other challenge for Jane is to notice both how she picks men and, then, what she expects from them. Maybe she picks men prone to affairs, but she may also play the role of someone who gets betrayed by affairs. If the person you are with feels familiar in negative ways, step back a little. Pretend you're a neutral party and observe. Ask your date if she is really feeling what you're *assuming* she's feeling. Ask mutual friends for perspective. And shift your role. If you expect your date to be needy, you may withhold your own needs and inadvertently create a needy partner. Try putting your own needs on the table. Your date's capacity may surprise you!

Finally, Jane needs to let go of the comfort of dating the same man in different forms. Men like dad are familiar and predictable. Allowing herself to date someone who feels less familiar in the right ways—and then allowing that person to be *who he is*, rather than a projection of the past—will be Jane's adventure. To the extent that Jane can generate a new vision of the man she wants, nurture that vision and find people who live her vision (it may be time to leave the Jilted Women's Support Group!), she will start getting comfortable with a new reality.

Maybe this time Jane won't end up with a Dick. Or maybe she'll end up with a *better* Dick.

Go, Jane, go!

> "'Your whole body, from wingtip to wingtip,' Jonathan would say, 'is nothing more than your thought itself, in a form you can see. Break the chains of your thought, and you break the chains of your body, too.'"
>
> —*from* Jonathan Livingston Seagull, *by Richard Bach*

The Fear of Getting What We Want

The idea that we avoid what we want may seem like another absurdity, but look around. We run into people everyday who seem to revel in complaining about what they don't have, while avoiding every opportunity to get it. Imagine having exactly what you want in a partner. Do you worry you'll have nothing to talk about? Do you worry whether your friends and family will still love you? Do you feel guilty?

Jane (from our example) may feel guilty about getting a better man than her mom. Dick may feel guilty about having a better relationship than his parents. Leaving behind old patterns can feel like leaving behind people we care about. And that can be a lonely feeling.

Yet, an alternative reality is as close as your own mind. Feed yourself with healthy images of relationships, get to know people who have found good people, and practice believing that you can get what you want. If guilt pops up, don't shrink back. We aren't doing others a favor by reinforcing their own worst experiences. If we challenge others to do better for themselves, we may help them feel less alone in *their* alternative reality. Risking happiness is a form of activism. As Nelson Mandala put it, "As we let our light shine, we consciously give other people permission to do the same. As we are liberated from our fear, our presence automatically liberates others."

chapter 39

Dating and Kids

*The name of the game is Secrets are Dangerous,
But Too Much Truth Is A Burden. Your job is
to find the middle ground.*
—from Sex and The Single Parent, *an excellent
dating-while-parenting guide, by Meg F. Schneider
and Martine J. Byer.*

When we first dated, most of us were living at home and had
our parents providing for our basic needs. When you have your
own kids, the situation is entirely reversed. Now you're the
provider, the parent, as well as the one doing the dating. Let's
look at how we can effectively superimpose these realities.

> ### The Son in Shining Armor
>
> It's not unusual to see a new conservatism in your older kids once you start to date. A friend of mine had her sons checking for any sign of deviance in her dates, down to the shoes on their feet. When she and her son were at a summer gathering, a man wearing a backwards baseball cap came over to talk to my friend. As soon as her son noticed, he walked right over and confronted him: "You need to leave now because this is my mom and I don't want you talking to her." The guy laughed it off at first, but the protective son persisted in front of his dumbfounded mother, "I said you need to leave." The man did leave, and when my friend asked her son what in the world he was thinking, he said, "A backwards baseball cap is a very bad sign."

When (and How) Do I Involve the Kids?

There's a very helpful concept in developmental psychology called "signal anxiety." It's the idea that if we signal a child to something that is likely to produce anxiety, it helps the child prepare and reduces the actual anxiety. It's like when the nurse prepares a child for a shot by saying, "Now you're going to feel a quick, sharp prick on your arm." The nurse accurately describes the sensation, so that when the child gets the shot, he or she is already familiar with the experience. Note that, by describing the sensation itself rather than loading it with subjective interpretations, such as—"It's going to hurt" or "It's no big deal," the child is free to have his or her own response.

This concept can be very helpful when we consider how to talk to kids about dating. Signaling children *before* they become affected by your dating can prevent excessive anxiety, as well as feelings of confusion or betrayal that can come if a child is surprised. As we discussed in Chapter 6, *how* you talk about it will vary depending upon the age of the child.

While we want to signal our children, we don't want to overwhelm them. Telling too much too soon can burden them with information they aren't ready or able to process. And dating openly, especially if you are shopping around, can leave children feeling insecure about attachments, and may expose them to needless feelings of loss when relationships end. You are also entitled to a boundary of privacy around your dating life. When your children are with the other parent, or older and living on their own, you have a natural boundary that allows you freedom and time to consider how to involve them.

Working the tension between involving and protecting kids is a creative process that will depend on many factors, including your own parenting style. A good rule of thumb is that, if the kids will know anyway, due to a date stopping by, an intercepted phone call, or changes in your behavior, signal them. For example, if a date will be coming by to pick you up, a young child just needs to know that you are going to spend some time with a nice friend. Older children can be assured that you are "just dating"— that you are wanting to meet new people, and that you enjoy going out with friends your own age. Make a friendly introduction at the door, and that's it! Keep in mind that the more casual you are about it, the less likely they will be alarmed. Kids are sponges for unspoken feelings, so try to deal with your own anxiety and guilt *before* you talk to them.

No matter how well you handle things, be prepared for anything— meltdowns, withdrawal or, most surprising of all, smooth sailing! Remember the Brady Bunch wedding?! This might be a good time to review "Helping Kids Adapt," in Chapter 6.

Kids and Attachment

Let's say you've become exclusive with one partner. Your kids are aware that she is the only one who calls or comes over. Maybe your "friend" has joined you at your child's soccer game, or even kicked the ball around with her. Your children will want to know what's going on, and are likely to ask: "Are you in love?," Are you getting married?" Just like you, your kids can develop hopes and fantasies of a future together, or magical wishes to restore something broken by the divorce. Conversely, your child may need reassurance that you are not going to replace them.

In responding to questions about a special friend, you'll need to step back from your feelings and be conservative in your response. Even if you are sure you're in love and can't imagine being with anyone else, keep these feelings in check when you talk to your child. Unless you have a wedding date set—in which case you'll have plenty to talk about, tell your child the realities only:

1. You and your friend have become close and you like spending time together.
2. You're still getting to know each other.
3. You don't know if you and this person will decide to stay together or not.

Even when you take precautions, kids are likely to get attached to someone who becomes a familiar presence in their lives. And if you separate from that person, they will feel some loss.

From the Mouths of Baby Boomers

"My ex and I live in the same town, so our son goes back and forth easily. As nice as this is, it became a problem when I started dating. When my son was at his dad's, I'd have to say, 'Make sure you call first if you plan to come home.' It didn't feel good to require him to do that, but it was the only way for me to preserve some privacy."

—Class of '74

"It's confusing for the kids. It's hard enough for them to see you *dating*. They really don't want to think of you as having sex with that person. Thinking of you having sex with daddy is gross enough!"

—Class of '71

"On one of my first dates with Rob, we ran into my former husband and his girlfriend. They left the restaurant. My kids got a hold of it and thought it was very funny and I believe they teased their dad about his not being able to be in the same restaurant with me. Then he had to prove how macho he was. At the next family gathering, he and his girlfriend literally followed Rob and I wherever we went to the point that we were squirming! I think it was our payback for finding it initially humorous. I know, on a serious note, that it becomes much easier for the kids when parents are talking and cordial. My children appreciate that we can be in the same room and speak to each other."

—Class of '64

This can be an emotional double-whammy for you, especially if you are confused about the break-up. It is essential that you have your own source of support that can help you buoy yourself up before you have to deal with your kids. You can admit feeling sad, but mostly, your job is to attend to what your kids feel and to help them adapt to the change. Your ability to do this demonstrates that you are resilient and that you remain available to them as a parent.

Sleeping Arrangements

In Freudian terms, never will the id and superego be more at war than when you consider whether to let your date sleep over when the kids are home. Your pleasure-seeking impulses (the id) will say go, while your moral enforcer (the superego) will say no. Your id will resent your kids, and your superego will flood you with guilt for your resentment. The ego, which is supposed to help the two work together, may start flashing "tilt!" under the pressure.

To help sort out your feelings about sleepovers, start by fast-forwarding to the implications. Consider the following:

- Will I really be able to enjoy it if my kids are sleeping next door? How will I deal with an interruption (requests for water tend to increase with the presence of a guest)?
- Am I ready to address questions about why he's staying over? Do I want my kids focusing on my sex life?
- Am I ready for my kids to see us as a couple, sleeping where Mom and Dad used to sleep?
- What do I want my kids to learn about sex? Do I want them to see me switch sexual partners? If I only bring one special person to the bedroom, what happens if we break up?

It is much better for you to be honest with yourself, and deal with the implications for your kids, than to pretend there's no conflict and find yourself—and your kids—feeling uncomfortable about something that you want to be wonderful. If you can't figure out a way to manage it, enjoy the creative challenge of finding other places to be intimate: That's part of what made it so fun when we were young!

If you decide to have your partner overnight, it will be much less traumatizing to the kids if it happens gradually. A natural progression might include: spending more and more time together, spending more time in your home and with the kids, sharing affection (tastefully!) in front of the kids, allowing your partner to stay late several evenings, including the partner in your kids' bedtime rituals, then having her sleep over. This way, you teach your kids that sex comes in the context of a loving relationship. Bringing your partner into your home in this way does establish you more as a family, however, and that means attachment ...

Nobody said this would be easy. But, as we discussed in Chapter 6, taking on the challenge of loving your kids while finding love is worth every ounce of energy we put in.

chapter 40

My Date Has a Mate!

I think he [the married man] is much maligned. It isn't his wife who doesn't understand him. She understands him perfectly! It's his girl friend. And what she doesn't understand is how come he doesn't get a divorce.

It's simple. He doesn't want one. Because of the children, because of the community property and because in many cases he doesn't really dislike his wife. He may be tired of her and tired of her understanding him perfectly, but basically they are pretty good friends. ... To be fair, probably every married man (and woman) has thought of divorce, and perhaps seriously enough to say 'what if' to an attorney. But between the thought and the final decree lies an area as broad, stormy, and unnavigable as the Straits of Magellan.

—Helen Gurley Brown, *from* Sex and the Single Girl, *1962*

So, you're having the time of your life. Your date treats you like royalty, hangs on your every word, and is head-over-heels crazy about you. One small glitch: Your date is married. If you find yourself in this situation, you're not alone. Married daters can be very seductive, and many a Boomer has gotten hooked. Let's look at how this happened and where you can go from here.

How Did This Happen?

If you thought dating again felt like being in the *Twilight Zone*, this is a really freaky episode. But what's probably the most freaky is how normal your relationship feels. It may be like comparing a real high on weed to the publicized horrors of "Reefer Madness." A married lover becomes a real person to you—a person you can understand, and the air gets let out of the sleazy images you have carried around. The person you're dating doesn't come off as a cheater, just someone who is unhappy, lost, and looking for the same things as everyone else.

But as your wayward date becomes humanized, you begin to suffer a little brain damage. You start to experience a split in reality where your lover's words take precedence over his actions. Unable to see the other life of your date, you begin to believe that he is devoted to you. In fact, you believe that he is devoted in a way that no one else has been.

Our susceptibility—yes, it's usually women—is completely unrelated to our level of intelligence. I have talked to women at the top of their profession who have suffered this brain damage. An unhappily married person is able to be devoted in a way a single person is not. As "the other" woman or man, you become the symbol of freedom, of excitement, of everything the one back home is not.

And this reality can be intoxicating. Who doesn't love to hear that they are the most amazing person on the planet—the most beautiful, intelligent, stimulating, fun? Who doesn't secretly enjoy being favorably compared to other prospects? You are everything, the only one, the focus. Wave these sweets in front of someone who has felt deprived for a long time—and entitled to a good time, damn it, and you have the makings of the affair.

The real paradox here is that the person making you feel like the *only* one already *has* someone. Now maybe your date is on the way out of that relationship (or says so), but today, he is still in it.

From the Mouths of Baby Boomers

"It was heartbreaking. I remember thinking, 'I just met the man I always wanted to meet and it's too late. He's married.' It felt so real to me. It took me awhile, but I finally broke away. Then he came back to me. He had left his wife, and he did ask me to marry him. But before that could happen, he went back to her. Then I talked to other women and realized that my story wasn't unique at all. I couldn't be a part of his world. I met all of these men like that: 'Oh, you're God's gift...' I didn't get it. I guess the difference was, *I* didn't have two personalities."

—Class of '75

"I've been there. But look, when you're having your cake and eating it too, what incentive is there to change things?"

—Class of '82

Love at a Price

So what's wrong with feeling valued and special and getting the royal treatment? Absolutely nothing. These are good gifts. The only problem is that you are not getting these gifts free and clear. The problem is not that you're expecting too much, but that you need to expect *more*. Here are some of the forces undermining the good feelings you're getting:

- Guilt. It helps to see the wife (or husband) back home as a monster, but usually, at some level, you know that your pleasure is coming at someone else's cost. And guilt taints your own pleasure, so that you may start to see pleasure as bad. That's when you're really hurting yourself.

- Part-time love. Because the wife (or husband) is the publicly-recognized partner, your relationship can't be front-and-center. You aren't likely to be shown off, or get to show off your love interest. The times when most couples are out playing—i.e., weekends may be the very time he needs to be home. And don't count on him being available for your birthday. Again, the implication for you is that it taints the good feelings. You start to associate pleasure with something that needs to stay hidden and peripheral in your life.

- Lost time. All the time you are holding out for the possibility that your married date will become available, you are missing out on the opportunity to meet people who are crazy about you *and* single.

Expecting More

So, what if you could have the adoration you're experiencing now—or better, adoration not based on a reaction to a bad relationship, and also have the one providing it? Would you take the offer?

The answer to this question is important, because the fact that you can't really have your lover could be serving you in some way. Maybe you're afraid of having a full-fledged relationship, or just don't feel ready. Maybe you like getting the cleaned-up version of your date, and leaving the three-dimensional version to the spouse. In this case, you probably just need to ask yourself if this is the way you want to build in that needed distance. Or maybe the danger and thrill of a secret relationship excites you. Be honest with yourself, and remember: Your problem is not in what you want, but in how you've gone about getting it.

Usually, however, the reason we get stuck in this kind of relationship is that it meets a lot of needs, and it's hard to imagine we could have these needs met in a legitimate relationship. Yet, if that is what you want, you have to push aside your fear and go for it. Here are the steps you can take:

1. Get very clear about what you want and don't want. Write it down in two columns if it helps. Note what you love about your current relationship, because this is key. You were willing to risk a lot to get these goodies. They say something about what has been lacking in your life. Be expansive with your desires. Ignore the voices in your head that say you're expecting too much.

2. Practice believing that you can have the more you want. Surround yourself by people who can believe with you. If you are stuck, get some help with moving past your fear and opening yourself to more.

3. Tell your date exactly what you want. You can tell him that you would prefer if you could have all this with him, but that you'll find it with someone else if need be. Then tell him you are not participating in this reduced version of the relationship. Say goodbye.

4. Throw yourself a party. You have just acted out of self-love and that's worth celebrating. If you feel more like crying, it's your party, and you can cry if you want to! Invite all the people who are proud of you.

5. Don't stop believing!

41

Could This Be Love?

You may forget the one with whom you have laughed,
but never the one with whom you have wept.
—Kahlil Gibran

You think you might be in love, and you're scared stiff. You're not alone. Up until now, you may have resonated with Dionne Warwick as she crooned out that she'd never fall in love again. Or you may question whether what you feel is really love— you've been fooled before.

But while you're freaking out, you're also flooded with a feeling of being reborn, a renewed innocence, a belief in miracles. You find yourself smiling all the time.

And just as you do that, another part of you slaps you in the face and says, "get real!" That part of you says that reality is the pain you've experienced, and what you're in now is only fantasy.

No, you're not on the Magical Mystery Tour. You are being jolted around by one of life's most elusive questions: "Could this be love?"

> ## I Love Paris
>
> No one is more vulnerable than the first person in a couple to say, "I love you." Audrey Hepburn captured this feeling as she played opposite Fred Astaire in *Funny Face*.
>
> As their characters, Jo and Dick, work on photo shoots as a model-photographer team, they develop a special intimacy. At one of their shoots, she is dressed as a bride on the grounds of a Parisian church. To get her into character, Dick talks about the kind of feelings she would be experiencing on her wedding day. All Jo can focus on is the fact that the wedding dress is not hers and no one is really waiting for her. When Jo can't shake her sadness, Dick comments, "Jo, something is wrong. She responds, "No, why?," and he continues, "You are the saddest-looking bride I've ever seen." He moves toward her, building the scene he wants to photograph: "This is your wedding day. It's the day you've been dreaming of all your life. You're going to marry the man you love, the man who loves you …." As he looks into her eyes, he gets caught up in his own words, "He's the only … and you're …," and then his lips meet hers with a loving kiss. As they come out of their embrace, she finally releases her feelings: "Oh Dick, I thought it would never happen! I never want to go home. I love Paris and I love these clothes and the little church and I love you." Making sure he heard correctly, he asks, "What did you say?" She quickly resumes her shyness and responds, "I love Paris!"

How Do I Know?

Remember those cute "Love Is …" cartoon panels that became popular in the '70s? The cartoon, featuring childlike nudes with round heads and big eyes, equated love with simple acts of sharing and kindness. But today, when we ask the question, it is everything but simple. We know that we can have *feelings* of love without the elements that make it last. We also know that what feels like love can turn on us, and what was attractive can become annoying. Many of us make a distinction between being "in love," that overpowering, chemistry-laden desire to be together, and "loving," a more stable and giving kind of love. Most of us want a relationship that has both.

As the "Love Is …" sayings revealed, love is many things. We have all probably experienced love in different forms with different people. But when you ask, "Could this be love?," you are asking whether this is *the* love—the love you want to invest your life energies in. Consider the following elements of loving relationships, and the answer will become clearer:

- While not sufficient, *feeling* in love is essential. It's the chemistry and the invisible magnetism between you that provides the pleasure and satisfaction that sustains a relationship through its ups and downs. The desire to be together is often so strong that you can't imagine living apart. This is very different than making a good, logical case for being together. I've talked to women and men who had married perfectly nice people and later wanted out. These individuals knew they could probably work things out if they tried, but the motivation wasn't there. When I asked about their initial attraction, the response became predictable, "Well, that wasn't a big part of the relationship." More often, the motivation was security, the desire to have a family, or the need to be loved.

- Both of you feel lucky to have the other in your life. A certain level of mutual idealization indicates that you both feel you have something to learn from the other person. According to Jung, it means that you are each holding desired qualities for the other, and you come together to recover them. As long as the couple engages in that journey, they can experience transformation through the relationship, each becoming more than they were individually. If, on the other hand, these opposite qualities become more polarized, conflict and distance can result. Which way it goes depends on the nature of the commitment, which we'll explore later in this chapter.

  What doesn't work is to "settle," to match up with someone because it's safe, because you feel superior, or because you are needed. In these cases, you sacrifice love for security.

- You both are willing and able to change. Yes, I know you've heard that it's a bad idea to get into a relationship with the idea of changing the other person. This is only partially true. We have to start by loving each other as we are. But if love does not change us, it is ineffective. If there is one element I can pin to the failure of relationships, it is the unwillingness of partners to evolve. We are designed to change, and we choose relationships to help us change in the direction we desire.

If you work through conflicts with your partner and you both come out better for it, you're doing well in this area. Keep in mind that this can only happen when both of you feel safe in the relationship, and know you can speak the truth without feeling threatened. That doesn't mean your partner won't get angry. A relationship that doesn't make you both mad from time to time isn't worth its salt. For individuals, the willingness to change, and accept change in your partner, requires both a healthy sense of self and a dose of humility.

- You know each other and still want to be together. It's easy to love someone who looks great and only shares good times with you. As we discussed in Chapter 28, true intimacy comes from sharing what we usually *don't* let others see. Once you've been through a variety of arguments, a crisis or two, and have seen each other at your worst, you're in a better position to judge the strength of your love. A friend of mine said he needed to see his relationship through the four seasons before he would feel ready to make a decision about it. Time will expose your secrets and your vulnerabilities, and real love will take them in along with everything else.

- You choose love. We often feel passive in relationship to love, as if love will choose for us. When we take this approach, love will drag us all over the map. In every relationship, the *feeling* of love comes and goes, and hate shows up, too. The choice of love becomes a foundation that underlies the normal fluctuations in our feelings.

Ultimately, the question "Could this be love?," isn't a question at all. It's a choice.

The Question of Commitment

If we've become guarded about love, we may openly mistrust marriage and commitment. Many of us feel deceived by the promise of what commitment was supposed to be. We grew up thinking of commitment as a one-time event that was supposed to insure a happy future. In fact, we equated marriage and commitment. Marriage sealed the deal, and then it was "happily ever after."

This model teaches that the only requirement of commitment is to stay together—no matter what. And many couples do. No matter if they hate each other or never talk to each other—they are together. Problem is, marriage was never meant to *be* the commitment. Marriage is a public statement of commitment, a religious ceremony, a legal status, and a celebration. And there is evidence that when a commitment, such as the commitment to exercise—is made publicly, people feel more accountable to fulfill the commitment.

But commitment asks much more than for two people to stay together. A healthy commitment is simply a promise to come to each other when something is between you. As simple as it sounds, it's not always easy to fulfill, because coming together means continually opening yourselves to change. This is the fundamental difference between the one-time-event version of commitment and the process version. The first assumes that change is a threat, and the second assumes change is a reality, and the true gift of relationships.

So, how does commitment work in real life? Let's say you and your partner have a fight. You can choose to take the conflict outside of the relationship, and bolster your defenses. This path may be quite gratifying, as you find others who will agree with your perspective and support your feelings. You may even fall in with a lover who *completely* understands. By taking this path, you have protected yourself from change.

The other path may involve talking to others, but in an entirely different way. In this case, you choose people who love you and your partner, and can help you see things more objectively. This doesn't mean you can never bitch about your partner (a certain amount of this is healthy!), you simply choose to do it with people and in places where your commitment is understood. And talking to a trusted friend does not replace going into the fire with your partner.

When you are truly committed, you consistently make yourself vulnerable. And it's that very vulnerability that fosters love. This doesn't mean we won't get defensive—we all do. But we learn. And it's often the lessons we resist the hardest that we end up being the most grateful for.

From the Mouths of Baby Boomers

"We were *very* cautious. We made a series of short-term contracts to help us plan. Could we agree that we could be there for each other for two weeks? At the end of the two weeks, we made a contract for another two weeks. After that, we asked if we could count on the other for a month? At the end of the term, we would re-evaluate the status of our relationship: were we committed to being exclusive, spending too much time together, sleeping at her house too often, that kind of thing. After a month, we went for six months. By that time, it was just a game for us, we knew."

—Class of '76

"It's not that we don't fight—we do. But we forgive each other. What's different is that we can get humor back so fast—and love back so fast."

—Class of '72

The Vulnerability of Loving

Love always makes us vulnerable, because if we have love, we can lose it. Many of us *have* lost love, maybe more than once. We might have felt invincible when we were singing, "Love, Love, Love" with the Beatles, but that feeling got left behind with the band's high-button jackets and skinny suits.

I learned a wonderful concept from a pastor friend of mine. He said that the challenge of adulthood is to give up the childish simplicity of our beliefs, to wrestle with complexities and doubts, and then to eventually come around to a new naiveté, one that does not deny, but transcends doubt. I think this is also true of love. We know more now than when love was all we needed. We've learned a great deal about ourselves and relationships, and hopefully you've learned a few things from this book. The challenge of love is to learn everything we can, and then to throw it all up in the air, take the leap, and once again believe in love.

> *"Desire fulfilled is sweetness to the soul."*
>
> —*Proverbs 13:19*

Designing Your "Pitch"

Step 1

Whether you need it for a personal ad or just want to carry it with you, a pitch can help you advertise the best of what you have to offer. Complete the following sentences, writing down your spontaneous responses. Don't worry about repeating yourself or completing every item. At the end, we'll pull out your pitch:

1. Growing up, I always had a knack for:

    _____

    _____

    _____

    _____

2. People say that I am:

    _____

    _____

    _____

    _____

3. What I love about me is:

_____

_____

_____

4. My favorite movies are:

_____

_____

_____

5. My favorite books are:

_____

_____

_____

6. I collect:

_____

_____

_____

7. My travels include:

_____

_____

_____

8. I would love to visit:

_____

_____

_____

9. My most awesome experiences include:

_____

_____

_____

10. What I still want to experience is:

_____

_____

_____

11. I like people who are:

_____

_____

_____

12. To me, the best relationship is:

_____

_____

_____

13. What I like about my looks is:

_____

_____

_____

14. I have the most fun when I'm:

_____

_____

_____

15. What bugs me is:

_____

_____

_____

16. I wonder about:

_____

_____

_____

17. What makes me sexy is:

_____

_____

_____

18. The best thing about my family is:

_____

_____

_____

19. I admire:

_____

_____

_____

20. My ultimate dream would be:

_____

_____

_____

21. What I like about my life is:

_____

_____

_____

22. I have overcome:

_____

_____

_____

23. My style could be described as:

_____

_____

_____

24. I am proud of:

_____

_____

_____

25. My idea of romance is:

_____

_____

_____

26. My favorite band/musician/musical style is:

_____

_____

_____

27. I am looking for:

_____

_____

_____

28. What I believe is:

_____

_____

_____

29. What relaxes me is:

_____

_____

_____

30. I love:

_____

_____

_____

31. I would like to live:

_____

_____

_____

32. My best friends have always been:

_____

_____

_____

33. I like to watch:

_____

_____

_____

34. I like to play:

_____

_____

_____

35. I like to shop for:

_____

_____

_____

36. I like to express myself creatively through:

_____

_____

_____

Step 2

Now go back and circle themes that repeat themselves or responses you really like. Put it all together in a sentence or two that describes you:

_____

_____

_____

_____

_____

_____

Step 3

Finally, see if you can find a word or phrase that captures your best selling point. Go ahead and try out a few until you get it:

_____

_____

_____

_____

_____

My Pitch!

appendix **B**

Who Attracts You?

Answer the following questions, and you'll start to get a good idea of who you're looking for. When that person shows up, you'll be ready!

The Four P's

1. Physical: Paint a Picture

I am drawn to people with (describe each feature):

_____ hair (e.g., wispy, long, shaggy, dark)

_____ eyes

_____ skin

_____ build

_____ height

_____ clothing

_____ jewelry, accessories

_____ style

People (friends, celebrities) I am physically attracted to include:

_____

_____

_____

_____

These celebrities are similar in the following ways:

_____

_____

Conclusion 1: I would sum up my preferred "look" as:

_____

_____

2. Personality: Animate the Picture

I am turned on by people who are:

socially _____

emotionally _____

sexually _____

And who have a(n):

_____ mind (e.g., curious, decisive)

_____ attitude

_____ inner world

_____ sense of humor

_____ approach to life

_____ approach to relationships

I am attracted to the personalities of the following people:

_____

_____

_____

_____

The above people are similar in the following ways:

_____

_____

Conclusion 2: My preferred personality style is:

_____

_____

3. Professional: Add a Lifestyle

I am attracted to people who:

Work in the field of _____

Wear _____to work

Have a(n) _____attitude toward work

Have received _____education

Have a _____ kind of intelligence

Have gained experience in _____

Express themselves through _____

Have a _____ sense of responsibility

Travel _____

Make a _____ salary

Work _____ hours

Need _____ freedom

Take _____ risks

Real-life and/or fictional characters whose life work turns me on:

_____

_____

_____

_____

The above people are similar in the following ways:

_____

_____

Conclusion 3: My preferred professional style is..

_____

_____

4. Philosophical: Add Depth

I am attracted to people who:

Believe _____

Are exploring _____

Like to talk about _____

Are fed spiritually by _____

Practice _____

Serve others by _____

Are politically _____

Have insight into _____

I am attracted to the thinking, values, or spiritual presence of these people:

_____

_____

_____

_____

The above people are similar in the following ways:

_____

_____

Conclusion 4: The soul I am seeking is:

_____

_____

Bring It All Together

Look at the four conclusions you came up with, and briefly describe your desired date:

_____

_____

See if you can capture the essence of this person in a single word or phrase. Try some:

_____

_____

_____

_____

This is it!

Congratulations! You have created a custom-made formula for your chemical match. Have fun testing it out!

Creative Dates: A to Z

A

Air show
Airplane take-off watching
Al fresco dining
Amusement park
Antiquing
Apple-picking
Arcade play
Archery Tournament
Architecture tour
Art gallery crawl
Art museum
Aquarium
Auction
Author reading
at book store

B

Badminton
Baseball game
Ballet
Ballroom dancing

Beach walk or jog
Basketball game
Bicycling
Bingo
Birding
Bluegrass jam or
festival
Blues club or festival
Board games
Boat show
Boating
Bocce ball
Boogie boarding on
the surf
Bookstore browsing
Bowling
Broomball
Breakfast
Brewery tour
Bubble bath (probably
not a first date)

C

Carnival

Carriage ride

Campfire with s'mores

Canoeing

Casino gambling or show

Car show

Card party

Cat Show

Cave exploration

Church

Church music concert

Circus

Civil War Battlefield visit

Coffeehouse

College: lectures, plays

Comedy club or open mike night

Community speaker

Community theatre

Cornfield maze

Cooking dinner together

Cooking class

Country drive

Croquet

Cruising in a convertible

Culinary road trip (check out Jane and Michael Stern's *Roadfood*)

D

Dance lessons

Dancing

Deep-sea fishing

Demolition derby

Dinner theatre

Dirt biking

Dog Walking

Dog Show

Drive-in movie

Driving range

E

Eating at a food festival

Estate sales

F

Fair

Farmer's market

Ferry ride

Film festival

Finger-painting

Fireplace with hot cocoa and popcorn

Fireworks

Five-course dinner

5k run

Fly fishing

Football game

Frisbee

Frisbee golf

G

Garage sales

Garden tour

Go-cart racing

Golf

Golf tournament

H

Hayride
Haunted house tour
Helicopter ride
Hiking
Horse race
Horseback riding
Hot-air balloon ride
Hunting deer with a camera

I

Ice cream
Ice skating
IMAX movie
In-line skating
International festival

J

Jamming on musical instruments
Jazz club, concert or festival
Jet ski

K

Karaoke
Kayaking
Kite flying

L

Lecture on interesting topic
Laser tag
Lessons: painting, surfing, whatever!
Letterboxing (look it up, it's cool!)

Limo tour of the city
Line dancing
Live music
Live theatre
Local festivals, from the "Aquatennial" in Minneapolis to the San Francisco Zoo's "Valentine's Day Sex Tours"

M

Mall walk
Martini bar
Massage together at spa
Miniature golf
Modern art exhibit
Monster truck rally
Moped or motorcycle ride
Morning bakery run
Moonlight walk
Mountain biking
Museum visit
Musical

N

NASCAR Race
National park
Necking

O

Odd attractions and museums, such as the world's largest ball of twine or the Spam museum (check out *Eccentric America* by Cheri Sicard)
Old movies at home

Omnitheatre
Opera
Orienteering
Oxygen bar

P

Paddle boating
Parasailing
Parking
People watching games: life stories, celebrity look-alikes
Performance art
Picnic
Piano bar
Pier fishing
Planetarium
Plant a tree or garden together
Playground playing and reminiscing
Poetry slam
Powered parachuting
Private dining room at restaurant

Q

Quirky shops

R

Racquetball
Rainy day walk
Rambling
Reading favorite passages to each other
Riverboat cruise
Rock climbing

Rooftop or top-story restaurant
Running

S

Sailing
Seasonal activities, carve a pumpkin or build a snowman
Scenic trails and vistas
Science museum
Scuba diving
Sculpture garden
Shell gathering
Sketching in the park
Skiing, downhill or cross-country
Sledding
Snorkeling
Snow picnic
Snowboarding
Snowmobiling
Spiritual retreat
Square dancing
Squash
Star gazing with (or without) telescope
State park
Storm Chasing
Street dance
Sunbathing
Sunrise watch (coffee and croissants optional)
Sunset watch (porch swing optional)
Sushi bar
Symphony
Synagogue

Swimming
Swing dancing

T

Tango lessons
Tea and scones at a tearoom
Temple
TV Show Audience
Tennis
Tennis tournament
Three Stooges movies
Tour historic sites
Tubing down the river

U

Underwater park

V

Vintage movies at home
Vineyard tour and tasting
Volleyball

W

Walk in the park, on the
beach, anywhere
Water park
Water skiing
Water fight
Waterfall hike
Wash cars together and get
soaked
Weekend excursion
White-water rafting
Wine tasting
Work out together,
then go out

X

X-game tournament

Y

Yard sale

Z

Zoo

appendix D

Dating Services by State

Alabama

Mobile:

MatchMaker
International
6157 Airport Boulevard
Mobile, AL 36608
(251) 343-0102

Montgomery:

MatchMaker
International
2834 Zelda Road
Montgomery, AL 36106
(334) 270-0025

Alaska

Anchorage:

People Store
Anchorage, AK 99501
(907) 258-1500

Singles Network
Anchorage, AK 99503
(907) 566-6641

Arizona

Chandler:

Dinner for Six
2079 West Periwinkle
Way
Chandler, AZ 85248
(480) 699-3606

Lake Havasu City:

Coffee and A Date
2010 McCulloch
Boulevard North
Lake Havasu City, AZ
86403
(928) 855-3306

Mesa:

Renaissance Singles
Introductions
Mesa, AZ 85201
(480) 615-4248

Selective Beginnings—
Herpes Dating Service
2753 East Broadway
Road, Suite 101-502
Mesa, AZ 85204
(602) 230-4117

Phoenix:

Arizona's Most Eligible
Singles Directory
5225 North Central
Avenue
Phoenix, AZ 85012
(602) 265-1990

Bonnie the Matchmaker
Phoenix, AZ 85003
(602) 996-0056

Calculated Couples
Phoenix, AZ 85034
(602) 230-4172

Latinas Arizona
1777 West Camelback
Road
Phoenix, AZ 85015
(602) 277-3220

New Beginnings
410 North 44th Street
Phoenix, AZ 85008
(602) 333-0100

Social Six
PO Box 51242
Phoenix, AZ 85044
(480) 753-5011

Prescott:

Introductions
Prescott, AZ 86301
(520) 420-4422

Scottsdale:

Arizona Soulmates
35365 North 93rd Way
Scottsdale, AZ 85262
(480) 575-8000

Premiere Connections
5665 North Scottsdale Road
Scottsdale, AZ 85250
(480) 946-2824

Ten Minute Dating
35365 North 93rd Way
Scottsdale, AZ 85262
(480) 575-8000

TwinSpirits
6496 North 79th Street
Scottsdale, AZ 85250
(480) 443-9917

Tucson:

Equally Yoked
5515 East Grant Road
Tucson, AZ 85712
(520) 882-9778

Soul Connect Dating Firm
900 East River Road
Tucson, AZ 85718
(520) 407-1883

Tucson Fun & Adventures
Inc
Tucson, AZ 85701
(520) 256-3866

Arkansas

Fort Smith:

Single Search of
Arkansas/Oklahoma
4117 Grand Ave. Suite 40
Fort Smith, AR 72904
1-800-706-8051 (toll-free)

Little Rock:

Between Us
Little Rock, AR 72201
(501) 490-4095

North Little Rock:

Business Class Professional
Service
North Little Rock, AR 72122
(501) 821-1704

California

Alhambra:

AA Dating Agency
33 East Valley Boulevard
Alhambra, CA 91801
(626) 300-8238

Unique International
Service
1441 East Valley Boulevard
Alhambra, CA 91801
(626) 282-3381

Zhen Xin Dating Service
421 East Mission 26
Alhambra, CA 91776
(626) 289-7033

Anaheim:

B.P.D. Consulting
2034 East Lincoln, Suite 344
Anaheim, CA 92806
(714) 632-3841

Arcata:

Chances Are Dating
Network
PO Box 485
Arcata, CA 95518
(707) 826-9373

Bakersfield:

Dinner 4 Six
PO Box 42092
Bakersfield, CA 93309
(661) 837-2277

Benicia:

Pacific Romance
PO Box 1245
Benicia, CA 94510
(707) 747-6906

Beverly Hills:

Dianne Bennett
Matchmaker
Beverly Hills, CA 90210
(310) 859-6929

Gianna Professional
Matchmaking
Beverly Hills, CA 90210
(310) 557-3556

Kelleher & Associates
Matchmaking
Beverly Hills, CA 90210
(310) 271-6500

Meet Me Cafe
105 North Robertson
Boulevard
Beverly Hills, CA 90211
(310) 659-4083

Pair-Us Agency
292 South La Cienega
Boulevard
Beverly Hills, CA 90211
(310) 360-0035

Winkler Debra Personal
Search
9595 Wilshire Boulevard
Beverly Hills, CA 90212
(310) 777-6900

Campbell:

Baydates Dating Service
Campbell, CA 95008
(408) 377-8111

Carlsbad:

Athletic Singles Association
2725 Jefferson Street #9
Carlsbad, CA 92008
(760) 434-4700

It's Just Lunch
Carlsbad, CA 92008
(760) 268-0004

Chico:

Dinner 4 Six
PO Box 1492
Chico, CA 95927
(530) 345-2020

Chino:

Latter Day Ideals
Chino, CA 91710
(909) 590-9700

Concord:

Christian Connections
4701 Clayton Road
Concord, CA 94521
(925) 827-9695

Video Introductions
4701 Clayton Road
Concord, CA 94521
(925) 676-2399

Corona:

Genesis Matchmaking
Service
1451 Rimpau Avenue
Corona, CA 92879
(909) 272-4846

Covina:

Singles Connection
Covina, CA 91722
(626) 332-1776

Daly City:

Bay Area Best Eligible
Singles
PO Box 7
Daly City, CA 94014
(415) 469-5683

Del Mar:

Barbara Summers Healthy
Professional Singles
Del Mar, CA 92014
(858) 793-7776

Bay Area Best Eligible
Singles
PO Box 7
Daly City, CA 94014
(415) 469-5683

Encino:

Great Expectations Services
for Singles
17207 Ventura Boulevard
Encino, CA 91316
(818) 788-7878

Escondido:

30 Plus Singles Parties
Escondido, CA 92025
(760) 746-4537

San Diego Singles Parties
Escondido, CA 92025
(760) 746-4537

Fresno:

Progressive Computing
5588 North Palm Avenue
Fresno, CA 93704
(559) 650-2700

Hawthorne:

It's Just Lunch
Hawthorne, CA 90250
(626) 345-9922

Huntington Beach:

Confidential Christian
Introductions
16168 Beach Boulevard
Huntington Beach, CA
92647
(714) 375-0400

Irvine:

Asian Soul Mates
2061 Business Center Drive
Irvine, CA 92612
(949) 252-8887

Equally Yoked for South
Coast Christians
Irvine, CA 92602
(949) 660-0566

Great Expectations
18818 Teller Avenue
Irvine, CA 92612
(949) 476-1986

Millionaires Club
Irvine, CA 92602
(949) 852-0666

The Nikki Morgan Agency
8001 Irvine Center Drive
Irvine, CA 92618
(949) 450-1555

Together Introduction
Services
18300 Von Karman Avenue
Irvine, CA 92612
(949) 910-0090

La Jolla:

Debra Winkler Personal
Search
La Jolla, CA 92037
(858) 535-1555

Lafayette:

Catholic Singles Network
3454 Hamlin Road
Lafayette, CA 94549
(925) 283-8339

Laguna Beach:

Kelleher & Associates
Laguna Beach, CA 92651
(949) 494-7744

Livermore:

2 Heart Won Love
3819 East Avenue
Livermore, CA 94550
(925) 371-2725

Long Beach:

It's Just Lunch
Long Beach, CA 90802
(562) 983-9944

Los Altos:

Meeting for Good
Los Altos, CA 94022
(650) 949-4611

Los Angeles:

Adam & Steve Gay Video
Introductions
Los Angeles, CA 90010
(323) 936-1666

Affinity Exchange
Los Angeles, CA 90001
(323) 663-3378

California Singles
4801 Wilshire Boulevard,
Suite 302
Los Angeles, CA 90024
(323) 857-1622
(310) 475-7447

Filipino Singles Club
3545 Wilshire Boulevard,
Suite 219
Los Angeles, CA 90010
(213) 386-4732

Greater Relations
10345 West Olympic
Boulevard
Los Angeles, CA 90064
(310) 432-6300

It's Just Lunch
1880 Century Park East
Los Angeles, CA 90067
(213) 627-9999

John the Matchmaker
Los Angeles, CA 90001
(323) 512-8836

Loveworks Dating Coach &
Consultants
Los Angeles, CA 90001
(310) 442-9700

Meet A Mate
11022 Santa Monica
Boulevard
Los Angeles, CA 90025
(310) 914-3444

Options Dating Service
6399 Wilshire Boulevard
Los Angeles, CA 90048
(323) 653-6764

Perfect Match
4619 Beverly Boulevard
Los Angeles, CA 90004
(323) 465-0879

The Date Doctor
PO Box 34911
Los Angeles, CA 90034
(310) 559-3806

Worldwide Introductions
International
South Fairfax Avenue, Suite
290 363
Los Angeles, CA 90036
(213) 769-5260
1-800-485-7691 (toll-free)

Malibu:

Pretty People 2000
11940 Whalers Lane
Malibu, CA 90265
(310) 457-4377

Marina:

Foreign Relations
Marina, CA 93933
(831) 917-6246

Marina Del Ray:

Athletic Singles Association
Marina Del Rey, CA 90292
(310) 302-9332

Ultimate Encounters Match
Making Service
Marina Del Rey, CA 90292
(310) 305-7560

Martinez:

Equally Yoked Christian
Singles
Martinez, CA 94553
(925) 228-5255

Mill Valley:

Jewish Connection
Matchmaking Services
Mill Valley, CA 94941
(415) 388-0118

Kelleher & Associates
Mill Valley, CA 94941
(415) 381-3192

Mission Viejo:

Pair Us Agency
Mission Viejo, CA 92691
(949) 598-2926

Monterey:

Central Coast Introductions
98 Del Monte Avenue
Monterey, CA 93940
(831) 647-9100

Moorpark:

It's Just Lunch
Moorpark, CA 93021
(805) 523-3000

Mountain View:

Table for Six Total
Adventures &
Entertainment
444 Castro Street
Mountain View, CA 94041
(650) 934-0800

Newport Beach:

Athletic Singles Association
3848 Campus Drive
Suite 203
Newport Beach, CA 92660
(949) 753-3515
(310) 827-5680

Debra Winkler Personal
Search
Newport Beach, CA 92660
(949) 760-6600

It's Just Lunch
1300 Dove Street
Newport Beach, CA 92660
(949) 251-9494

North Hollywood:

City Singles of Southern
California
North Hollywood, CA 91601
(818) 766-9530

Oakland:

California Chinese Service
320 10th Street
Oakland, CA 94607
(510) 663-3508

Pacifica:

Dining Encounters
700 Carmel Avenue
Pacifica, CA 94044
(650) 359-8500

Palmdale:

Town and Country Dating
Club
Palmdale, CA 93550
(661) 947-9338

Palo Alto:

Singles Supper Club-Single
Gourmet
PO Box 60518
Palo Alto, CA 94306
(650) 327-4645

Pasadena:

It's Just Lunch
Pasadena, CA 91101
(626) 345-9922

Placentia:

Singles Connection
Placentia, CA 92870
(714) 528-2588

Reseda:

Christian Introductions USA
PO Box 370070
Reseda, CA 91337
(818) 881-5882
1-877-215-3787 (toll-free)

Riverside:

It's Just Lunch
Riverside, CA 92501
(909) 275-9494

Laura Mitchell
Introductions Inc
4371 Latham Street
Riverside, CA 92501
(909) 782-2012

Roseville:

Equally Yoked Private Social
Club for Christians
Roseville, CA 95661
(916) 722-3463

It's A Date
Roseville, CA 95661
(916) 789-9489

Sacramento:

Great Expectations
2277 Fair Oaks Boulevard
Sacramento, CA 95825
(916) 927-2700

Kelleher & Associates
Matchmaker
Sacramento, CA 95814
(916) 925-4111

The Right One
1300 Ethan Way
Sacramento, CA 95825
(916) 565-0180

San Bernardino:

Singles Connection
San Bernardino, CA 92401
(909) 882-2800
1-800-585-3283 (toll-free)

San Diego:

Christian Singles
San Diego, CA 92101
(619) 563-1853

Great Expectations
3465 Camino Del Rio South
San Diego, CA 92108
(619) 283-6400

Great Expectations
10525 Vista Sorrento
Parkway
San Diego, CA 92121
(858) 558-9178

It's Just Lunch
225 Broadway
San Diego, CA 92101
(619) 232-8999

Progressive Computing
Customer Service
San Diego, CA 92111
(858) 707-7700

Right One
8989 Rio San Diego Drive
San Diego, CA 92108
(619) 291-2380

The Pair-Us Agency
San Diego, CA 92101
(619) 298-7442

Soul Purpose Christian
Singles
2525 Camino Del Rio South
San Diego, CA 92108
(619) 291-7404

You and Me Latinas
111 Elm Street
San Diego, CA 92101
(619) 233-0284

San Francisco:

Asian American Connection
Inc
2344 Judah Street
San Francisco, CA 94122
(415) 933-6888

Good Partner Dating Service
3410 Geary Boulevard
San Francisco, CA 94118
(415) 379-9908

How About Lunch
San Francisco, CA 94102
(415) 281-5845

Introductions by Marsha:
Personal Intros for
Professionals
San Francisco, CA 94102
(415) 351-1508

Jewish Connection
San Francisco, CA 94102
(415) 351-1508

Kelleher & Associates
Matchmaker
San Francisco, CA 94102
(415) 409-4111

Quality Partners Inc
San Francisco, CA 94102
(408) 294-4848

Table For Six Total
Adventures
291 Geary Street
San Francisco, CA 94102
(415) 782-0680

San Jose:

Arlene's Matchmakers
San Jose, CA 95101
(408) 985-2815

Premier Matches
San Jose, CA 95101
(408) 288-8820

San Luis Obispo:

Central Coast Introductions
San Luis Obispo, CA 93401
(805) 549-7572

San Rafael:

Love Paula Consultant
Love Paula Ms
San Rafael, CA 94901
(415) 464-1171

Right One
2175 Francisco Boulevard
East
San Rafael, CA 94901
(415) 259-0742

Santa Ana:

Gay Connection
Santa Ana, CA 92701
(714) 836-6338

Santa Barbara:

Central Coast Introduction
351 Hitchcock Way
Santa Barbara, CA 93105
(805) 687-3949
1-877-989-3283 (toll-free)

Match Makers
1216 State Street
Santa Barbara, CA 93108
(805) 555-1212

Santa Clara:

8 Minutes Date
Santa Clara, CA 95050
(408) 296-3288

Great Expectations
3255 Scott Boulevard
Santa Clara, CA 95054
(408) 982-3700

Lifetime Partners
1765 Scott Boulevard
Santa Clara, CA 95050
(408) 554-8100

Santa Monica:

Big Difference
Santa Monica, CA 90401
(310) 398-5113

Santa Rosa:

Shalaine the Matchmaker
Santa Rosa, CA 95401
(707) 539-2338

Sausalito:

Kelleher & Associates
Matchmaker
Sausalito, CA 94965
(415) 332-4111

Sherman Oaks:

Double Dating Syndicate
15250 Ventura Boulevard
Sherman Oaks, CA 91403
(818) 382-6363

Excellence Agency Match
Making Service
Sherman Oaks, CA 91403
(310) 858-2626

Stockton:

The Right One
4609 Quail Lakes Drive
Stockton, CA 95207
(209) 477-9211

Studio City:

Greater Relations
4370 Tujunga Ave #150
Studio City, CA 91604
(818) 784-3840

Tarzana:

Great Expectations Services
for Singles
18801 Ventura Boulevard
Tarzana, CA 91356
(818) 344-5553

Thousand Oaks:

Cupid's Coach
1691 Bellshire Court
Thousand Oaks, CA 91361
(805) 371-9557

Elite Connections Inc
Thousand Oaks, CA 91360
(805) 493-5129

Pacific Island Connection
PO Box 4601
Thousand Oaks, CA 91360
(805) 492-8040

Torrance:

Video Date USA
438 Amapola Avenue,
Suite 205
Torrance, CA 90501
(310) 320-0512

Valley Village:

Equally Yoked Christian
Singles
12125 Riverside Drive
Valley Village, CA 91607
(818) 754-0002

Van Nuys:

Marriage Minded
Van Nuys, CA 91401
(310) 276-5828

Single Search Los Angeles
6314 Van Nuys Boulevard
Van Nuys, CA 91401
(818) 787-4304

Walnut Creek:

Equally Yoked Christian
Singles
1475 North Broadway
Walnut Creek, CA 94596
(925) 944-8871

First Impressions Dating
33 Quail Court
Walnut Creek, CA 94596
(925) 938-0497

Great Expectations
1280 Civic Drive
Walnut Creek, CA 94596
(925) 944-4900

Total Adventures &
Entertainment
1700 North Broadway
Walnut Creek, CA 94596
(925) 279-9333

West Hollywood:

Loveworks-Dating
Consultant & Author Renee
Piane
732 North Doheny Drive
West Hollywood, CA 90069
(310) 274-8004

Westlake Village:

Elite Connections
1220 La Venta Road
Westlake Village, CA 91361
(805) 496-9610

Whittier:

Introductions By Sage Inc
8208 La Sierra Avenue
Whittier, CA 90601
(562) 698-7171

Lesbian Dating Club
Whittier, CA 90601
(562) 696-4424

Colorado

Aurora:

The Love Connection
13618 East Nevada Place
Aurora, CO 80012
(303) 495-7075

Colorado Springs:

Cupid's Arrows
PO Box 63175
Colorado Springs, CO 80962
(719) 527-6997

People People People
Western Place
Colorado Springs, CO 80915
(719) 591-8820

Perfectly Matched
4465 Northpark Drive
Colorado Springs, CO 80907
(719) 260-1000

Right One
19 North Tejon Street
Colorado Springs, CO 80903
(719) 329-0077

Denver:

Christianintroductions
1660 South Albion Street
Denver, CO 80222
(303) 765-2820

Date-A-Thon Inc.
6000 East Evans Avenue
Denver, CO 80222
(303) 691-1726

Dinner 4 Six
1221 South Clarkson Street,
Suite 100
Denver, CO 80210
(303) 777-0700

Dinner 4 Six
5031 S Ulster St Bldg. 3,
Suite 300
Denver, CO 80237
(303) 721-3300

Equally Yoked
7600 East Eastman Avenue
Denver, CO 80231
(303) 755-5166

Institute for Spiritual
Partnership
2745 Prairie Ridge Court
Lafayette, CO 80026
(303) 926-9339

It's Just Lunch
Denver, CO 80202
(303) 292-2600

L'Chaim the Jewish Single's
Resource
300 South Dahlia Street
Denver, CO 80246
(303) 394-3370

La Clef D'or Dating Service
469 South Cherry Street
Denver, CO 80246
(303) 321-1668

Tango Personals
Denver, CO 80202
(303) 563-4848

Englewood:

Equally Yoked
14 Inverness Drive East
Englewood, CO 80112
(303) 799-4673

Parker:

Christian Singles Network
Parker, CO 80134
(720) 842-5272

Peyton:

Seeking Someone Special
PO Box 359
Peyton, CO 80831
(719) 683-5944

Connecticut

Cromwell:

Your Perfect Match
PO Box 59
Cromwell, CT 06416
(860) 665-7339

Danbury:

For Single's Only
Danbury, CT 06810
(203) 778-8673

Fairfield:

Viaggi Consultant Service
38 Post Road
Fairfield, CT 06824
(203) 319-1063

Farmington:

Relationship CO Inc
3 Brick Walk Lane
Farmington, CT 06032
(860) 677-7687

New Haven:

Jewish Dating Service
New Haven, CT 06510
(203) 777-6666

Rocky Hill:

Great Expectations
2189 Silas Deane Highway
Rocky Hill, CT 06067
(860) 257-3336

Stamford:

Great Expectations Services
for Singles
78 Southfield Avenue
Stamford, CT 06902
(203) 327-2066

Introductions by the Looking
for Love Team
Stamford, CT 06901
(203) 323-8248

It's Just Lunch
Stamford, CT 06901
(203) 327-3100

Jewish Dating Service
Stamford, CT 06901
(203) 325-9935

Singles Network
111 Prospect Street
Stamford, CT 06901
(203) 730-9669

West Hartford:

Jewish Dating Services
1260 New Britain Avenue
West Hartford, CT 06110
(860) 920-5340
(860) 561-3250

Westport:

Viaggi Consultant Service
38 Post Road West
Westport, CT 06880
(203) 227-4062

Delaware

Frankford:

Eastern Shore Singles
Connection
Road 367
Frankford, DE 19945
(302) 537-5122

Wilmington:

It's Just Lunch
1 Commerce Street
Wilmington, DE 19801
(302) 651-9999

District of Columbia

Ann Wood the Matchmaker
1313 29th Street, Northwest
Washington, DC 20007
(202) 234-0670

It's Just Lunch
1001 Connecticut Avenue
Northwest, #719
Washington, DC 20036
(202) 466-6699

Telecompute
2233 Wisconsin Avenue
Northwest
Washington, DC 20007
(202) 328-3546

Florida

Altamonte Springs:

Friends Connection and
Introductions Inc.
283 Cranes Roost Boulevard
Altamonte Springs, FL
32701
(407) 831-3800

Boca Raton:

Destiny Connection Inc.
Boca Raton, FL 33428
(561) 394-3800

Events & Adventures
4800 North Federal
Highway
Boca Raton, FL 33431
(561) 353-0535

It's Just Lunch
1900 Glades Road
Boca Raton, FL 33431
(561) 347-9022

Latin Introductions of
America
Mykonos Court
Boca Raton, FL 33487
(561) 997-9263

Brandon:

Single's Preference
121 Lithia Pinecrest Road
Brandon, FL 33511
(813) 651-1956

Clearwater:

Great Expectations
15500 Roosevelt Boulevard
Clearwater, FL 33760
(727) 532-0236

Universal Dating Service
609 McLennan Street
Clearwater, FL 33756
(727) 461-3806

Deerfield Beach:

Gary and Deborah Davis
Computer Dating System
513 North West 46th Avenue
Deerfield Beach, FL 33442
(954) 725-8455

Debary:

Introductions III
2851 Enterprise Road
Debary, FL 32713
(386) 668-3722

Destin:

Matchmaker International
10221 Emerald Coast
Parkway West
Destin, FL 32550
(850) 763-0202

Fort Lauderdale:

Country Club Singles
3343 West Commercial
Boulevard
Fort Lauderdale, FL 33309
(954) 717-9000

Love Of Asia Vietnam
6278 N Federal Hwy, 459
Fort Lauderdale, FL 33308
(941) 629-4765

Options Dating Service
211 Southwest 2nd Street
Fort Lauderdale, FL 33301
(954) 527-0208

Rainbow Intros
3096 South Oakland Forest
Drive
Fort Lauderdale, FL 33309
(954) 485-0250

Fort Myers:

Class Act Referrals
Fort Myers, FL 33901
(239) 226-4262

Fort Walton Beach:

Matchmaker International
Fort Walton Beach, FL
32547
(850) 664-6022

Gainesville:

A Dating Services
Gainesville, FL 32601
(352) 376-6222

Mix & Match Services Inc
3805 Northwest 17th Street
Gainesville, FL 32605
(352) 373-7272

The Matchmaker
1801 Northeast 23rd Avenue
Gainesville, FL 32609
(352) 373-7272

Gonzalez:

The Ultimate Dating System
PO Box 812
Gonzalez, FL 32560
(850) 937-0615

Hialeah:

Club de Solteros
1790 West 49th Street
Hialeah, FL 33012
(305) 823-3600

Hollywood:

Great Expectations
1920 East Hallandele Beach
Blvd
Hollywood, FL 33019
(954) 455-9255

Great Expectations
3400 Lakeside Drive
Hollywood, FL 33027
(954) 443-9006

Jacksonville:

Fabulous Dinner
Connections
Jacksonville, FL 32202
(904) 880-1876

Lakeland:

USAmate
2941 West Campbell Road
Lakeland, FL 33810
(863) 816-2353

Maitland:

Great Expectations
1001 North Lake Destiny
Road
Maitland, FL 32751
(407) 475-0910

Melbourne:

Selective Singles
Melbourne, FL 32901
(321) 725-4448

Miami:

A Singles Resource Center
Miami, FL 33125
(305) 448-5683

Casfel Florida Inc
2355 Salzedo Street
Miami, FL 33134
(305) 445-8144

Global Select
3915 North Meridian Avenue
Miami Beach, FL 33140
(305) 672-0655

Latin Euro Introductions
Miami, FL 33125
(305) 858-7766

Love American Style
9745 Southwest 72nd Street
Miami, FL 33173
(305) 412-3800

Naples:

Class Act Referrals
Naples, FL 34102
(239) 774-0712

Palm Beach:

Latin Connections
101 Bradley Place
Palm Beach, FL 33480
(561) 832-0800

Palm Beach Gardens:

Together Dating
4440 PGA Boulevard,
Suite 306
Palm Beach Gardens, FL
33410
(561) 626-4566

Pensacola:

Cupid Connection
Pensacola, FL 32501
(850) 476-6536

MatchMaker International
5700 North Davis Hwy, #219
Pensacola, FL 32503
(850) 476-0202

Port Charlotte:

Singles Finders
Port Charlotte, FL 33952
(941) 743-8152

Sarasota:

Great Expectation Inc
4141 South Tamiami Trail
Sarasota, FL 34231
(941) 926-8788

Relationship Coach The
1343 Main Street
Sarasota, FL 34236
(941) 330-2141

Singles USA Inc.
2687 Floyd Street
Sarasota, FL 34239
(941) 362-3442

Tampa:

A Pair of Hearts
5415 Mariner Street
Tampa, FL 33609
(813) 287-5083
(813) 289-5683

Lunch Date
3218 W Cherokee Ave
Tampa, FL 33611
(813) 902-8100
(813) 837-5874

Progressive Computing LLC
238 East Davis Boulevard
Tampa, FL 33606
(813) 250-9666
(813) 976-4744

Soul Mates
Tampa, FL 33602
(813) 814-1364

South of the Border
Introductions
14905 Southfork Drive
Tampa, FL 33624
(813) 931-1992

Steve & Sheela's On-Your-
Toes-Video Dating Social
Club
Tampa, FL 33602
(813) 273-8111

West Palm Beach:

Social Connections
West Palm Beach, FL 33401
(561) 596-2422

Winter Haven:

Bringing People Together
Inc.
39 3rd Street Southwest
Winter Haven, FL 33880
(863) 293-0028
(863) 293-7277

Winter Park:

Dinner Dates
Winter Park, FL 32789
(407) 339-3283

Selective Singles
Winter Park, FL 32789
(407) 788-0010

Georgia

Arlington:

Christian Filipina
412 Morgan Road
Arlington, GA 31713
(229) 725-3991

Atlanta:

Affairs of the Heart
142 Mitchell Street
Southwest
Atlanta, GA 30303
(404) 524-3352

Eight at Eight
PO Box 250682
Atlanta, GA 30325
(404) 888-0988

Ebony Connections
Atlanta, GA 30303
(404) 524-7874

European Connections
& Tours
PO Box 888851
Atlanta, GA 30356
(770) 458-0909

Great Expectations Services
for Singles
1975 North Park Place
Southeast
Atlanta, GA 30339
(770) 956-9223

It's Just Lunch
230 Peachtree Street
Northwest
Atlanta, GA 30303
(404) 588-2700

Lunch Date
1100 Circle 75 Parkway
Southeast
Atlanta, GA 30339
(770) 933-1660

Options Dating Service
1447 Peachtree Street
Northeast
Atlanta, GA 30309
(404) 815-0321

The Right One
7000 Central Parkway NE
Suite 230
Atlanta, GA 30328
(678) 443-9911
1-800-818-DATE (toll-free)

The Right One
7000 Central Parkway
Northeast
Atlanta, GA 30328
(678) 443-9911

Traditional Matchmaker Inc.
3210 Peachtree Road
Northwest
Atlanta, GA 30305
(404) 266-1416

Augusta:

The Relationship Company
3540 Wheeler Road
Augusta, GA 30909
(706) 667-0291

Dalton/Calhoun:

Matchmaker International
Dalton & Calhoun, GA
30701
(706) 629-7007

Decatur:

It's Time
PO Box 372851
Decatur, GA 30037
(404) 373-5019

Savannah:

MatchMaker International
315 Commercial Dr,
Suite D-1
Savannah, GA 31406
(912) 352-0022

Tucker:

DateChek
4426 Hugh Howell Road
Suite B314
Tucker, GA 30084
(770) 413-9943
1-800-343-6641 (toll-free)
Dating Service

Hawaii

Honolulu:

Right One
615 Piikoi Suite 1504
Honolulu, HI 96814
(808) 593-0668

Shalaine Inc., Matchmaker
1750 Kalakaua Avenue
Honolulu, HI 96826
(808) 941-5799

Kailua Kona:

Sunshine International
PO Box 5500
Kailua Kona, HI 96745
(808) 325-5977

Idaho

Boise:

People Store
5105 West Overland Rd
Boise, ID 83705-2635
(208) 426-0600

Perfect Match
7950 King Street
Boise, ID 83704
(208) 375-0270

Renaissance for Singles
671 E Riverpark Lane,
Suite 140
Boise, ID 83706
(208) 345-0777

Illinois

Alton:

Christian Singles Fellowship
Outreach
726 Henry Street
Alton, IL 62002
(618) 462-7100

Bloomington:

Heart To Heart Express
Introduction Service Inc
2302 East Oakland Avenue
Bloomington, IL 61701
(309) 662-2210

Champaign:

Professional Introductions
508 W Clark St #1
Champaign, IL 61820
(217) 359-5833

Single's Advantage
119 North Prairie
Champaign, IL 61820
(217) 355-9200

Chatham:

Intriguing Introductions
Chatham, IL 62629
(217) 483-3558

Chicago:

Black Dating Network
Chicago, IL 60607
(773) 723-4161

Connections Club
600 West Van Buren Street
Chicago, IL 60607
(312) 466-1000

Eight at Eight
PO Box 147251
Chicago, IL 60607
(312) 583-0888

Friends First
200 North Michigan Avenue
Chicago, IL 60601
(312) 541-0574

Great Expectations
1 East Erie Street
Chicago, IL 60611
(312) 943-1760

It's Just Lunch
70 W Hubbard St., #200
Chicago, IL
(312) 644-9999

Lavalife
55 West Monroe Street
Chicago, IL 60603
(630) 571-9898

Lavalife
501 63rd
Chicago, IL 60607
(312) 894-0016

Match Making by Annie
500 North Michigan Avenue
Chicago, IL 60611
(312) 595-0402

Platonic Partners
2920 West Altgeld Street
Chicago, IL 60647
(773) 772-8425

Premiere Connections
62 West Huron Street, #2E
Chicago, IL 60610
(312) 943-7750

Selective Search Inc
2 East Oak Street
Chicago, IL 60611
(312) 396-1200

Selective Singles Social Club
233 East Erie Street
Chicago, IL 60611
(312) 944-9898

The Right One
333 North Michigan Avenue
Chicago, IL 60601
(312) 236-1800

Downers Grove:

Interactive Media Group
501 63rd Street
Downers Grove, IL 60516
(708) 599-7700

East Peoria:

People Store
125 Thunderbird Lane
East Peoria, IL 61611
(309) 698-0835

Evanston:

Spark Services
1603 Orrington Avenue,
#700
Evanston, IL 60201
(847) 475-9955

Hinsdale:

Interactive Media Group
55 West Monroe
Hinsdale, IL 60521
(630) 571-9898

Island Lake:

Hitching Post
Island Lake, IL 60042
(847) 526-2929

Itasca:

It's Just Lunch
Itasca, IL 60143
(847) 222-9000

Jerseyville:

Forever Yours Christian
Dating Service
848 South State Street
Jerseyville, IL 62052
(618) 498-1400

Lake Zurich:

Absolute Perfection
Matchmakers
159 South Rand Road
Suite 216
Lake Zurich, IL 60047
(847) 382-0443

Moline:

Date Break
4509 49th Street Court
Moline, IL 61265
(309) 797-4739

Mount Prospect:

Lifetime Partners
502 Hill Street
Mount Prospect, IL 60056
(847) 342-1376

Normal:

M & M Dating Service
406 East Locust Street
Normal, IL 61761
(309) 888-4338

Oak Lawn:

Lavalife
Oak Lawn, IL 60453
(708) 599-7700

Peoria:

The Right One
411 Hamilton Boulevard
Peoria, IL 61602
(309) 671-0505

Peoria Heights:

Heart To Heart Express
4700 North Prospect Road
Peoria Heights, IL 61616
(309) 688-6011

Rockford:

The Right One
5301 East State Street
Rockford, IL 61108
(815) 395-7000
(217) 698-3388

Rolling Meadows:

Your First Impression Inc
5999 New Wilke Road
Rolling Meadows, IL 60008
(847) 290-0306

Roselle:

Lake Street Introductions
24W713 Lake Street
Roselle, IL 60172
(630) 924-9047

Salem:

Harvey Smith's Connection
212 West Rogers Street
Salem, IL 62881
(618) 548-9188

Schaumburg:

Conscience Connections
715 East Golf Road
Schaumburg, IL 60173
(312) 627-9453

Crossroads Connections
830 East Higgins Road
Schaumburg, IL 60173
(847) 995-0368

Great Expectations
1701 East Woodfield Road
Schaumburg, IL 60173
(847) 706-9889

Heart To Heart
2040 East Algonquin Road
Schaumburg, IL 60173
(847) 303-1050

Premiere Connections
1515 East Woodfield Road
Schaumburg, IL 60173
(847) 995-9595

Soulmates
1111 North Plaza Drive,
#250
Schaumburg, IL 60173
(847) 240-6283

Skokie:

Coffee Break Dating Service
9933 Lawler Avenue
Skokie, IL 60077
(847) 329-7699

Jewish Matchmakers
Skokie, IL 60076
(847) 674-4022

Indiana

Evansville:

MatchMaker International
7201 East Virginia Street
Evansville, IN 47715
(812) 479-9800

Fort Wayne:

MatchMaker International
305 Airport N Office Park
Fort Wayne, IN 46825
(260) 490-3283

People Store
Fort Wayne, IN 46802
(260) 484-5588

Indianapolis:

It's Just Lunch
101 West Ohio Street
Indianapolis, IN 46204
(317) 951-9999

People Store
Indianapolis, IN 46201
(317) 487-0500

Together Dating Service
8910 Purdue Road
Indianapolis, IN 46268
(317) 879-9144

Lakeville:

Friends First
109 North Michigan Street
Lakeville, IN 46536
(574) 784-5676

Osceola:

Connections Inc
515 Lincoln Way West
Osceola, IN 46561
(574) 675-4030

Plainfield:

Friendship Network
Plainfield, IN 46168
(317) 838-3050

West Lafayette:

Together Dating Service
2639 Yeager Road
West Lafayette, IN 47906
(765) 464-0805

Iowa

Cedar Rapids:

Compatible Connections
5250 North Park Place
Northeast
Cedar Rapids, IA 52402
(319) 377-0040

The Right One
5925 Council Street
Northeast
Cedar Rapids, IA 52402
(319) 393-7171

Des Moines:

The Right One
Des Moines, IA 50307
(515) 221-9191

Redfield:

Shy Singles
104 Wood Street
Redfield, IA 50233
(515) 833-2599

Kansas

Olathe:

Friendship Exchange
16109 West 149th Terrace
Olathe, KS 66062
(913) 393-5967

Overland Park:

MatchMaker International
7121 W 95th St.
Overland Park, KS 66212
(913) 642-5700

Shawnee Mission:

Dating Service Information
Line
Shawnee Mission, KS 66204
(913) 498-8100

Equally Yoked Christian
Singles
1000 W 75th Street
Shawnee Mission, KS 66204
(913) 236-9653

Great Expectations
7501 College Boulevard
Shawnee Mission, KS 66210
(913) 451-3711

Hartley Connections Inc.
Shawnee Mission, KS 66204
(913) 345-1514

Kansas City Supper Club
PO Box 23622
Shawnee Mission, KS 66221
(913) 851-8400

Matchmaker International
7125 West 95th Street
Shawnee Mission, KS 66212
(913) 642-5700

Together Dating Service
6800 College Boulevard
Shawnee Mission, KS 66211
(913) 344-0777

Topeka:

Friendship Exchange
3625 Southwest 29th Street
Topeka, KS 66614
(785) 271-6292

Matchmaker International
Topeka, KS 66603
(785) 233-7400

Relationship Headhunters
Topeka, KS 66603
(785) 272-1615

Wellington:

New Elite Dating Service
769 North Hoover Road
Wellington, KS 67152
(316) 652-0651

Wichita:

People Store
Wichita, KS 67203
(316) 262-1900

Together Dating Service
8100 East 22nd Street North
Wichita, KS 67226
(316) 683-8800
(316) 683-2229

Kentucky

Bowling Green:

Perfect Pair
110 Whispering Hills Blvd.
Bowling Green, KY 42101
(270) 842-3697

Greenup:

VIP Dating Service
Greenup, KY 41144
(606) 473-5901

Louisville:

Reservation for Eight
3235 Wynbrooke Circle
Louisville, KY 40241-3126
(502) 394-0030

Paducah:

Matchmaker International
2830 Lone Oak Road
Paducah, KY 42003
(270) 554-8600

St. Matthews:

Together Dating Service
4010 Dupont Circle, # 122
St. Matthews, KY 40207-4842
(502) 895-7216

Louisiana

Baton Rouge:

Image & Body Language
Consultants
Baton Rouge, LA 70806
(225) 938-0200

Personal Intro Louisianne
8252 West El Cajon Drive
Baton Rouge, LA 70815
(225) 927-2422

Single Resources
7914 Wrenwood Boulevard
Baton Rouge, LA 70809
(225) 923-0510

Metairie:

Together Dating Service
3841 Veterans Memorial
Blvd.
Metairie, LA 70002
(504) 456-1399

Sulphur:

Match Mates Dating Service
1202 Taylor Street
Sulphur, LA 70663
(337) 527-8430

Together Dating Service
New Orleans, LA 70112
(504) 840-6550

Maine

Augusta:

Maine Connection
Augusta, ME 04330
(207) 626-5687

Biddeford:

Matchmaker
5 Alfred St, # 202
Biddeford, ME 04005
(207) 282-6800

Millinocket:

Maine Connection
76 Penobscot Avenue
Millinocket, ME 04462
(207) 723-4400

Portland:

Matchmaker
477 Congress Street
Portland, ME 04101
(207) 775-2288

Scarborough:

Successful Introductions
153 US Route 1
Scarborough, ME 04074
(207) 883-1003

Maryland

Annapolis:

It's Just Lunch
Annapolis, MD 21405
(410) 990-0966

Columbia:

Together Dating Service
5850 Waterloo Rd, Suite 120
Columbia, MD 21044
(410) 418-5030

Baltimore:

It's Just Lunch
Baltimore, MD 21201
(410) 659-6699

Lavalife NY
Baltimore, MD 21201
(410) 528-8444

Bethesda:

Dateable
7830 Wisconsin Avenue
Bethesda, MD 20814
(301) 657-3283

Encounters International
Inc
Bethesda, MD 20814
(301) 530-7759

Source for Singles
8120 Woodmont Avenue
Bethesda, MD 20814
(301) 654-8588

Bishopville:

Eastern Shore Singles
Connection
Bishopville, MD 21813
(410) 352-5844

Edgewood:

Enchanted Dreams
Introductions
Edgewood, MD 21040
(410) 612-9799

Ellicott City:

Together Dating Service Inc.
5026 Dorsey Hall Drive
Ellicott City, MD 21042
(410) 730-8866

Fort Washington:

Attachmate Corporation
12901 Chalfont Avenue
Fort Washington, MD 20744
(301) 203-8134

Frederick:

Together Dating Service
176 Thomas Johnson Drive,
Suite 205
Frederick, MD 21702
(301) 695-1723

Glen Burnie:

Matchmaking
8005 Cross Creek Dr
Glen Burnie, MD 21061
(410) 787-1919

Halethorpe:

Mates of Color Inc.
3700 Koppers Street
Halethorpe, MD 21227
(410) 368-1629

Pikesville:

Great Expectations
25 Hooks Lane
Pikesville, MD 21208
(410) 653-9003

Rockville:

Heart To Heart
Introductions
Rockville, MD 20850
(301) 762-5339

MagicSearch
15889 Crabbs Branch Way
Rockville, MD 20855
(301) 258-9494

Speed Dating
11418 Old Georgetown Road
Rockville, MD 20852
(301) 881-7110

Takoma Park:

The Social Club
Takoma Park, MD 20912
(301) 439-8300

Towson:

The Singles Society
Towson, MD 21286
(410) 825-6625

Westminster:

Exclusive Dining Services
79 John Street
Westminster, MD 21157
(410) 876-5552

Massachusetts

Andover:

Lunch Couples
Andover, MA 01810
(978) 470-0519

Arlington:

Compatible Couples
35 Gardner Street
Arlington, MA 02474
(781) 646-2046

Boston:

Creative Allies
172 Newbury Street
Boston, MA 02116
(617) 236-6996

Creative Connections
172 Newbury Street
Boston, MA 02116
(617) 236-6996

Eight Minute Dating
236 Huntington Ave, #208
Boston, MA 02115
(617) 859-8866

Gentlepeople, Ltd.
172 Newbury Street
Boston, MA 02116
(617) 492-1200

Imatch
15 Court Square
Boston, MA 02108
(617) 535-3333

Lunchdates
Statler Office Building
Boston, MA 02108
(617) 350-3161

Bridgewater:

Successful Singles
16 Central Square
Bridgewater, MA 02324
(508) 697-6944

Brighton:

Lunch Dates
425 Washington St.
Brighton, MA 02135
(617) 254-3000

Burlington:

Coffee Companions
265 Winn Street
Burlington, MA 01803
(781) 273-0522

Lunch Dates
121 Middlesex Turnpike
Burlington, MA 01803-4990
(781) 229-7710

Chestnut Hill:

Right One
850 Boylston St #407
Chestnut Hill, MA 02467-
2436
(617) 232-4800

Framingham:

Lunch Dates
254 Cochituate Rd
Framingham, MA 01701-
4627
(508) 620-1211

Hingham:

Right One Introductions
160 Old Derby St. #221
Hingham, MA 02043-4005
(781) 749-5700

Johnson City:

Computer Dating USA
25 Poplar
Johnson City, NY 13790
(617) 492-1200

Lexington:

Suitable Match
International Inc.
8 Nickerson Road
Lexington, MA 02421
(781) 863-0893

Needham:

Lunch Couples
Needham, MA 02494
(781) 449-7164

New Bedford:

Cupid's Original Match
Maker
New Bedford, MA 02740
(508) 999-7154

Marilyn Personal
Matchmaker
New Bedford, MA 02740
(508) 979-8830

New Salem:

Links for Singles
232 Neilson Road
New Salem, MA 01355
(978) 544-5465

Newton:

Creative Events &
Introductions, For Jewish
Singles
Newton, MA 02461
(617) 818-1057

Great Expectations
29 Crafts St
Newton, MA 02458
(617) 332-7755

Plymouth:

Lunch Couples
Plymouth, MA 02360
(508) 224-6322

Shrewsbury:

Right One
555 Main Street
Shrewsbury, MA 01545
(508) 845-3283

Wakefield:

Lunch Couples
Wakefield, MA 01880
(781) 224-0099

West Springfield:

Compatibles
82 Main Street
West Springfield, MA 01089
(413) 781-1008

Relationship Company
59 Interstate Drive
West Springfield, MA 01089
(413) 733-5200

Wellesley Hills:

Successful Singles
International
212 Worcester
Wellesley Hills, MA 02481
(781) 237-2064

Table for Eight
Wellesley, MA 02482
(781) 239-3370

Woburn:

Right One
3 Baldwin Green Common
Woburn, MA 01801
(781) 935-4798

Worchester:

Successful Singles
255 Park Avenue
Worcester, MA 01609
(508) 797-3006

Michigan

Bay City:

Matchmaker International
Call
Bay City, MI 48706
(989) 684-4401

Brighton:

Irene's Match Making
Service
2867 South Hacker Road
Brighton, MI 48114
(810) 225-2230

Caro:

A Way To Meet Others
Caro, MI 48723
(989) 672-4656

Detroit:

MatchMaker International
30400 Telegraph RD. #118
Birmingham, MI 48025
(248) 258-1515

Farmington:

Farmington Single
Professionals
Farmington, MI 48331
(248) 851-9909

Flint:

MatchMaker International
1289 South Linden Road
Flint, MI 48532
(810) 230-1800
(248) 614-2800

Grand Rapids:

MatchMaker International
2450 44th Street Southeast
Grand Rapids, MI 49512
(517) 381-1800

Howell:

Quick Date
1917 Park Ridge Court
Howell, MI 48843
(517) 552-0673

Lansing:

People Store
Lansing, MI 48906
(517) 394-6400

Livonia:

Video Singles Library
28200 7 Mile Road
Livonia, MI 48152
(248) 777-5555

Oak Park:

Metropolitan
Singleprofessionals
8479 Yale Street
Oak Park, MI 48237
(248) 851-9919

Okemos:

Together Dating Service
2395 Jolly Road
Okemos, MI 48864
(517) 381-0512

Royal Oak:

Strategies for Romantic
Success
1109 North Center Street
Royal Oak, MI 48067
(248) 336-0327

Saginaw:

Dating Service
Saginaw, MI 48601
(989) 771-7227

Southfield:

Compatible Connections
20245 West 12 Mile Road
Southfield, MI 48076
(248) 352-5300

Great Expectations
25925 Telegraph Road
Southfield, MI 48034
(248) 354-3210

Interactions Dating Services
27305 Southfield Road
Southfield, MI 48076
(248) 559-8500

Traverse City:

Chances Are
PO Box 1631
Traverse City, MI 49685
(231) 929-3577

Troy:

It's Just Lunch
888 West Big Beaver Road
Troy, MI 48084
(248) 273-1000

Minnesota

Andover:

Best Bet Inc.
3401 152nd Lane Northwest
Andover, MN 55304
(763) 712-0585

Baxter:

Date by Design
1650 Excelsior Road North
Baxter, MN 56425
(218) 829-4909

Edina:

Adventure Seekers LTD
6009 Wayzata Boulevard
175
Edina, MN 55416
(952) 543-3888

Minneapolis:

Aspire Inc.
Minneapolis, MN 55401
(763) 566-1212

Christian Singles
Connection
Minneapolis, MN 55401
(612) 333-5683
(952) 854-4433

Equally Yoked Christian
Singles Limited
Minneapolis, MN 55401
(763) 542-8100

Great Expectations Dating
Service
3300 Edinborough Way
Minneapolis, MN 55435
(952) 835-9590

Introplace
6600 France Avenue South
Minneapolis, MN 55435
(952) 925-3339

It's Just Lunch
120 South 6th Street
Minneapolis, MN 55402
(612) 376-7373

Jewish Dating Service
7515 Wayzata Boulevard
Minneapolis, MN 55426
(952) 542-9790

Matchmaking Connection
Minneapolis, MN 55401
(952) 895-7244

Singles Network
6600 France Avenue South
Minneapolis, MN 55435
(952) 925-6000

Together Dating Service Inc
3300 Edinborough Way
Minneapolis, MN 55435
(952) 831-3322

Webb Professional Services
7701 France Avenue South
Minneapolis, MN 55435
(952) 837-6200

Moorhead:

Date by Design
Moorhead, MN 56560
(218) 233-3283

Saint Paul:

Christian Connections
Saint Paul, MN 55105
(651) 290-2929

Reservations for Eight
Saint Paul, MN 55101
(651) 688-0175

St. Vincent:

Cupids Connections
Route 1, Box 50
St. Vincent, MN 56755
(218) 379-0010

Sauk Rapids:

Date by Design
2 2nd Avenue South
Sauk Rapids, MN 56379
(320) 251-3283

Wayzata:

Kailen Andrews Inc
Executive Matchmaking
Wayzata, MN 55391
(952) 745-0932

Mississippi

Booneville:

Dateline Services
103 Smith Drive
Booneville, MS 38829
(662) 720-9925

Hattiesburg:

Christian Connection
207 Kensington Drive
Hattiesburg, MS 39402
(601) 296-0081

Ocean Springs:

Heart To Heart
2112 Bienville Boulevard
Ocean Springs, MS 39564
(228) 818-0838

Missouri

Ballwin:

West County Singles
Activity Line
129 Woods Mill Road
Ballwin, MO 63011
(636) 391-2000

Cape Girardeau:

MatchMaker International
364 South Broadview Street
Cape Girardeau, MO 63703
(573) 335-6226

Chesterfield:

Dinner by Request
Chesterfield, MO 63017
(636) 728-1265

Independence:

Select Mates
1111 East 10 Terrace
Independence, MO 64050
(816) 252-0000

Joplin:

Preference Video
Introductions
712 East 32nd Street
Joplin, MO 64804
(417) 624-0640

Kansas City:

Avalon Communications
416 Cypress
Kansas City, MO 64124
(816) 483-9099

Digitized Communications
Systems Inc.
324 East 11th Street
Kansas City, MO 64106
(816) 283-3283

People Store
Kansas City, MO 64108
(816) 924-6100

Lebanon:

Better Chances
18998 Julie Road
Lebanon, MO 65536
(417) 532-1114

Paramus:

Perfect Match
Paramus, MO 63401
(201) 291-0880

Saint Louis:

Forever Yours Christian
Dating Service
Saint Louis, MO 63141
(314) 576-5839

It's Just Lunch
222 South Central Avenue
Saint Louis, MO 63105
(314) 863-7300

Origins Communications
10 Adams Street
Saint Louis, MO 63135
(314) 524-0007

Partners for Life
11116 South Towne Square
Saint Louis, MO 63123
(314) 416-0808

Springfield:

Equally Yoked
1721 West Elfindale Street
Springfield, MO 65807
(417) 868-8484

Preference Introductions
3158 South Campbell
Avenue
Springfield, MO 65807
(417) 881-1230

Montana

Billings:

One To One Introductions
2501 Montana Avenue
Billings, MT 59101
(406) 245-2121

Nebraska

Lincoln:

The Right One
100 North 56th Street
Lincoln, NE 68504
(402) 467-4846

Omaha:

After 5 Productions
3921 Ames Avenue
Omaha, NE 68111
(402) 933-2070

Perfect Match
PO Box 540723
Omaha, NE 68154
(402) 345-3333

Perfect Match-Client
Services
1945 North 120th Street
Omaha, NE 68154
(402) 345-3334

Nevada

Las Vegas:

Amour and More Limited
4472 South Eastern Avenue
Las Vegas, NV 89119
(702) 732-3283

Eight at Eight
7500 W. Lake Mead, 9-438
Las Vegas, NV 89128
(702) 228-8088

Great Expectations Video
Dating Service
4045 Spencer Street
Las Vegas, NV 89119
(702) 734-6000
(702) 734-7218

Interactions of Las Vegas
3885 South Decatur
Boulevard
Las Vegas, NV 89103
(702) 262-9600

Progressive Computing LLC
Las Vegas, NV 89101
(702) 798-8808

Reno:

Happy Dates
Reno, NV 89501
(775) 853-1961

People Store
Reno, NV 89501
(775) 826-8600

Reno Date Night
Reno, NV 89501
(775) 333-9205

Together Dating Service
770 Smithridge Drive
Reno, NV 89502
(775) 824-0200

New Hampshire

Bedford:

The Right One
116 South River Road
Bedford, NH 03110
(603) 622-5999

Hampton:

Dinner Match
37 Towle Farm Road
Hampton, NH 03842
(603) 929-1096

Hanover:

Compatibles Dating
Network
Hanover, NH 03755
(603) 643-1760

Manchester:

New Hampshire Singles
Network
Manchester, NH 03101
(603) 626-7997

Nashua:

Together Of NH Inc.
337 Amherst Street
Nashua, NH 03063
(603) 882-8732

Portsmouth:

Together
2456 Lafayette Road
Portsmouth, NH 03801
(603) 436-3906

New Jersey

Bordentown:

Caribbean American
Matchmakers, Inc.
PO Box 461
Bordentown, NJ 08505
(609) 298-2900

Bridgewater:

Together
1031 U S Hwy No 22
Bridgewater, NJ 08807
(908) 707-1440

Cherry Hill:

The Right One
1892 Greentree Road
Cherry Hill, NJ 08003
(856) 489-6550

Great Expectations Services
For Singles
1 Cherry Hill Office Bldg
Cherry Hill, NJ 08002
(856) 667-6673

Edison:

Great Expectations
379 Thornall Street
Edison, NJ 08837
(732) 744-0414
(732) 744-9103

Fairfield:

Perfect Match
Fairfield, NJ 07004
(201) 291-0880
(973) 394-1911

Jackson:

Mingles
Jackson, NJ 08527
(732) 928-9900

Jersey City:

Cupid's Corner
Jersey City, NJ 07302
(201) 656-5006

Linwood:

Relationships
Linwood, NJ 08221
(609) 927-7575

Together Dating Service
2021 U S Highway No 9
Linwood, NJ 08221
(609) 927-4999

Moorestown:

Jewish Connections Inc.
110 Marter Avenue
Moorestown, NJ 08057
(856) 638-0222

Morristown:

Carole Janes Singles
31 South Street
Morristown, NJ 07960
(973) 292-4748

Together Dating Service
Morristown, NJ 07960
(973) 451-1220

Mount Laurel:

Maria Mancini Matchmaker
Inc.
Mount Laurel, NJ 08054
(856) 866-8858

New Brunswick:

Right Choice Dating Service
(732) 536-8981
(732) 729-4900 New
Brunswick Area

Oradell:

Carole Jane's Singles
Oradell, NJ 07649
(201) 261-1433

Orange:

Christian Dating Service
International, Inc.
Orange, NJ 07050
(973) 674-0959

Paramus:

Perfect Match
Paramus, NJ 07607
(201) 291-0880

Parsippany:

Perfect Match of Parsippany
3799 US Highway 46
Parsippany, NJ 07054
(973) 394-1911

Passaic:

Love Match Plus
Passaic, NJ 07055
(973) 772-1665

Rahway:

Together Dating Service Inc.
727 Rapitan Road
Rahway, NJ 07065
(732) 381-9555

Red Bank:

Great Dates Unlimited
81 Oak Hill Road
Red Bank, NJ 07701
(732) 450-1243

Right Choice Dating Service
Red Bank Area
Marlboro Area
Red Bank, NJ 07701
(732) 212-9000

Ramsey:

Thirty Plus Singles
Ramsey, NJ 07446
(201) 818-1262

Rochelle Park:

Great Dates Unlimited
65 Passaic Ave.
Rochelle Park, NJ 07662
(201) 291-6767

Together Dating Service
West 340 Passaic
Rochelle Park, NJ 07662
(201) 909-9880

Saddlebrook:

The Right One
1 Park 80 Plaza West Two
Saddle Brook, NJ 07663
(201) 368-9711
1-800-818-3283 (toll-free)

South Orange:

Christian Dating Service
International
31 Eder Terrace
South Orange, NJ 07079
(973) 414-1197

Summit:

It's Just Lunch
Summit, NJ 07901
(908) 665-7855

Singles Bon Vivant
PO Box 1405
Summit, NJ 07901
(908) 273-6868

Toms River:

Together Dating Service
2008 State Hwy No 37
Toms River, NJ 08753
(732) 270-2300

Trenton:

Finally
Trenton, NJ 08618
(609) 671-1100

Together
Princeton Area
Trenton, NJ 08648
(609) 895-1969

Whippany:

American Asian Dating
Service
64 S Jefferson Road
Whippany, NJ 07981
(973) 515-3133

The Singles Center
75 North Jefferson
Whippany, NJ 07981
(973) 781-1616

New Mexico

Albuquerque:

First Connections Inc
PO Box 66677
Albuquerque, NM 87193
(505) 883-5008

People Store
4700 San Mateo Blvd
Northeast
Albuquerque, NM 87109
(505) 237-8000

Carlsbad:

There's Someone For
Everyone
120 S Canyon St
Carlsbad, NM
(505) 628-0888

Columbus:

Thompson & Associates
Pershing Avenue
Columbus, NM 88029
(505) 531-2681

New York

Brooklyn:

Personal Dates
406 Brighton Beach Ave
Brooklyn, NY 11235
(718) 332-7608

Buffalo:

MatchMaker International
331 Alberta Dr, #102
Amherst, NY 14226
(716) 835-4046

Progressive Computing LLC
775 Main Street
Buffalo, NY 14203
(716) 852-4800
(716) 852-5800

Corona:

Happy Ever After Dating
Service
54-07 102nd St.
Corona, NY 11368
(347) 385-4342

East Aurora:

Reservation for Six Inc.
East Aurora, NY 14052
(716) 655-3708

East Meadow:

Hand in Hand
East Meadow, NY 11554
(212) 988-4502

Floral Park:

Lavalife New York
Floral Park, NY 11001
(718) 269-0226

Forest Hills:

Personal Approach Inc.
10719 71st Avenue
Forest Hills, NY 11375
(718) 575-5518

Hartsdale:

A Singles Network
111 N Central Ave
Hartsdale, NY 10530
(914) 946-1801
(203) 327-3280

Islandia:

Conch Connection
200 Corporate Plaza
Islandia, NY 11749
(631) 231-3283

Jamesville:

A-1 High Expectations Video
Dating Service Inc.
4901 Jamesville Road
Jamesville, NY 13078
(315) 446-4702

Le Roy:

Date-A-Mate
7380 Griswold Road
Le Roy, NY 14482
(585) 768-6540

Levittown:

Friendly Entertaining
3601 Hemstead Turnpike
Levittown, NY 11756
(631) 265-2061
(631) 265-2723

Massapequa:

Alternative LifeStyles of
America
Lovers Lane
Massapequa, NY 11758
1-800-994-4897 Lesbian
Hotline
1-800-994-4897 (toll-free)
Gay Hotline

Merrick:

Meet Your Future
Corporation
229 Sunrise Highway
Merrick, NY 11566
(516) 771-1596

New York:

Best 4 U Consulting Co.
401 Broadway
New York, NY 10013
(212) 219-2775

Buddy System
545 8th Avenue
New York, NY 10018
(212) 500-2200

Cafe Au Lait
122 West 26th Street
New York, NY 10001
(212) 714-9784

Chatfield Introductions
17 East 70th Street
New York, NY 10021
(212) 570-2800

China American Friendship
Associates
18 West 33rd Street
New York, NY 10001
(212) 967-5393

Christen Global Dating
Service
139 Fulton Street
New York, NY 10038
(212) 634-4005

Eight at Eight
PO Box 1553
New York, NY 10028
(212) 785-5888

Exclusive Service Inc.
41 East 42nd Street
New York, NY 10017
(212) 391-2233

Fields Exclusive Service Inc.
317 Madison Avenue
New York, NY 10017
(212) 391-2233

First Impressions Inc.
22 Prince Street
New York, NY 10012
(212) 219-0923

Great Expectations Inc.
444 Madison Avenue
New York, NY 10022
(212) 223-9300

It's Just Lunch
120 East 56th Street
New York, NY 10022
(212) 750-8899

Jewish Quality Singles, Inc.
2578 Broadway, Suite 121
New York, NY 10025
(212) 663-6127
(212) 613-6236

Links
850 7th Avenue
New York, NY 10019
(212) 751-3731

M Chatfield Ltd Social
17 East 70
New York, NY 10021
(908) 781-7776
1-800-360-0364 (toll-free)

New York Urban
Professional Dating Club
302 West 79th Street
New York, NY 10024
(212) 721-2920

Options Dating Service
350 5 Avenue
New York, NY 10001
(212) 564-2274

Perfect Match
475 Park Avenue South
New York, NY 10016
(516) 409-4666

Perfect Match of New York
475 Park Avenue South
New York, NY 10016
(718) 206-4400

Personal Approach Inc.
450 7 Avenue
New York, NY 10123
(212) 967-9870

Prime Connections
Exclusive Dating for
Selective Singles
506 East 88th Street
New York, NY 10128
(212) 628-3700

Rendezvous Singles
Connection
New York, NY 10024
(212) 799-1752

Social Circles
1133 Broadway
New York, NY 10010
(212) 505-9985

Together Introductions of
Manhattan
New York, NY 10001
(718) 778-9200

Together Personal Dating
60 East 42nd Street
New York, NY 10165
(212) 973-1273

VIP Life
89 5 Avenue
New York, NY 10003
(212) 242-4755

VIP Millionaire Club
227 West 29th Street
New York, NY 10001
(212) 760-2948

Winston Denise Professional
Matchmaker Inc.
200 East 61st Street
New York, NY 10021
(212) 935-9350

New Rochelle:

Lavalife
342 Madison Avenue
New Rochelle, NY 10801
(914) 654-6660

Port Jefferson:

Single Search Suffolk
County
Port Jefferson, NY 11777
(631) 476-5801

Rochester:

Better Beginnings Personal
Introduction Service
550 Latona Road
Rochester, NY 14626
(585) 227-8400
(716) 227-8400

Relationships Inc.
Rochester, NY 14603
(585) 442-8420

Your Perfect Match
3300 Monroe Avenue
Rochester, NY 14618
(585) 385-1100

Roslyn:

Great Expectations Inc.
1044 Northern Boulevard
Roslyn, NY 11576
(516) 625-9855

Tonawanda:

Buffalo Niagara
Introductions
1868 Niagara Falls
Boulevard
Tonawanda, NY 14150
(716) 694-8585

North Carolina

Chapel Hill:

Singles Exchange
81404 Alexander
Chapel Hill, NC 27517
(919) 942-3035

Cary:

Christine O'Keefe Limited
Cary, NC 27511
(919) 380-2976

Charlotte:

Singles Exchange
4822 Albemarle Road
Charlotte, NC 28205
(704) 537-4332

Together Dating Service
5601 77 Center Drive
Charlotte, NC 28217
(704) 523-7172

Greensboro:

Together Dating Service
5 Oak Branch Drive
Greensboro, NC 27407
(336) 292-8811

High Point:

Friends Dates & Mates
High Point, NC 27260
(336) 885-3283

Matthews:

O'Keefe Christine Limited
Matthews, NC 28105
(704) 846-1331

Morganton:

Real Connections Dating
Service
3782 Lipscomb Road
Morganton, NC 28655
(828) 584-3055

Raleigh:

Great Expectations
3801 Lake Boone Trail
Raleigh, NC 27607
(919) 785-1600

North Dakota

Fargo:

Date By Design
1111 Westrac Dr, Suite 200
Fargo, ND 58103

Ohio

Akron:

MatchMaker International
3090 West Market Street
Akron, OH 44333
(330) 869-6688

Beachwood:

Millionaires Dating Club
22536 Chagrin Boulevard
Beachwood, OH 44122
(216) 765-0677

Cincinnati:

Christian Singles
International
6127 Bridgetown Road
Cincinnati, OH 45248
(513) 598-8900

Great Expectations
7890 East Kemper Road
Cincinnati, OH 45249
(513) 489-9888

Just Lunch
700 Walnut Street
Cincinnati, OH 45202
(513) 929-4499

Together
4555 Lake Forest Drive
Cincinnati, OH 45242
(513) 554-2100

Cleveland:

Companions Dating Service
318 East 4th Street Dover
Cleveland, OH 44124
(216) 292-1080

It's Just Lunch
55 Public Square
Cleveland, OH 44113
(216) 830-9999

Columbus:

Great Expectations Services
for Singles
1103 Schrock Road
Columbus, OH 43229
(614) 431-8500

It's Just Lunch
37 West Broad Street
Columbus, OH 43215
(614) 233-9999

Dayton:

Compute-A-Date
40 West 4th Street
Dayton, OH 45402
(937) 222-5503

Dating Club
40 West 4th Street
Dayton, OH 45402
(937) 228-2434

Independence:

Great Expectations
4511 Rockside Road
Independence, OH 44131
(216) 642-8855

Rocky River:

MatchMaker International—
West
22255 Center Ridge Road
Rocky River, OH 44116
(216) 221-4700

Pepper Pike:

MatchMaker International—
East
29525 Chagrin Boulevard
Pepper Pike, OH 44122
(216) 765-8600

Port Clinton:

North Coast Connections
Port Clinton, OH 43452
(419) 732-7744

Sandusky:

Christian Dating Service
1621 Sycamore Line
Sandusky, OH 44870
(419) 626-6283

Toledo:

MatchMaker International
5577 Airport Highway
Toledo, OH 43615
(419) 866-4500

Warren:

Chance of A Life Time
Dating Service
8256 East Market Street
Warren, OH 44484
(330) 856-7331

Worthington:

MatchMaker International
6797 N. High Street., #319
Worthington, OH 43085
(614) 888-0202

Oklahoma

Broken Arrow:

Singles Station
Broken Arrow, OK 74011
(918) 252-0003

Together Personal
Introductions
Broken Arrow, OK 74011
(918) 294-1888

Oklahoma City:

Christian Singles
5900 Mosteller Drive
Oklahoma City, OK 73112
(405) 810-9656

Match Made in Heaven
Oklahoma City, OK 73113
(405) 810-9653

Michael's Dating Service
217 North Harvey Avenue
Oklahoma City, OK 73102
(405) 270-0825

Single Station Dating CO
5900 Mosteller Drive
Oklahoma City, OK 73112
(405) 607-0100

Owasso:

Elite Match
15106 East 114th Street
North
Owasso, OK 74055
(918) 371-4668

Tulsa:

Match Made in Heaven
Christian Dating Service
1418 East 71st Street
Tulsa, OK 74136
(918) 491-1999

Matchmakers for Singles
4004 East 51st Street
Tulsa, OK 74135
(918) 747-5503

Singles Station
1418 East 71st Street
Tulsa, OK 74136
(918) 491-0002

Oregon

Albany:

Date Link
305 South East Ermine
Street
Albany, OR 97321
(503) 370-2344

Beavercreek:

Christian Singles Unlimited
PO Box 753
Beavercreek, OR 97004
(503) 650-1996

Eugene:

Selective Dating Services
Eugene, OR 97401
(541) 689-4394

Singles Network
96 East Broadway
Eugene, OR 97401
(541) 345-1333

Medford:

Romance Connection
1762 East McAndrews Road
Medford, OR 97504
(541) 858-0222

Portland:

Abstinence Only Dating
PO Box 3091
Portland, OR 97208
(503) 246-7311

Data
1507 Southeast 122nd
Avenue
Portland, OR 97233
(503) 255-3154

It's Just Lunch
621 Southwest Morrison
Street
Portland, OR 97205
(503) 248-9995

Modern Singles
1507 Southeast 122nd
Avenue
Portland, OR 97233
(503) 255-3154

Pals Pursuing Another
Loving Soul
10216 Southeast 41st Court
Portland, OR 97222
(503) 353-9999

Progressive Computing
Portland, OR 97201
(503) 299-9911

Soulmates
Portland, OR 97201
(503) 916-0200

Salem:

Christian Connection
Ministries
Salem, OR 97301
(503) 390-1880

Pennsylvania

Allentown:

All About Singles
5100 Tilghman St
Allentown, PA 18104
(610) 706-3234

MatchMaker International
1027 South Route 100
Allentown, PA 18101
(610) 395-5222

Audubon:

Perfect Partners
Audubon, PA 19407
(610) 630-9466

Bala Cynwyd:

Maria Mancini Matchmaker
Inc.
Bala Cynwyd, PA 19004
(610) 668-3353

Bensalem:

Single Search Pittsburgh
Bensalem, PA 19020
(215) 750-0772

Bethlehem:

MatchMaker International
2650 Schoenersville Road
Bethlehem, PA 18017
(610) 882-9717

Butler:

The Right Relationship
Located On Route 82
Butler, PA 16001
(724) 282-4400

Camp Hill:

Matchmaker International
355 North 21 Street
Camp Hill, PA 17011
(717) 737-0400

Carnegie:

Blue Moon Personal
Introductions
Carnegie, PA 15106
(412) 429-5959

Doylestown:

Together Dating
Doylestown, PA 18901
(215) 230-1976

Greensburg:

Matchmaker International
585 Rugh Street
Greensburg, PA 15601
(724) 838-8828

Harrisburg:

Compatibles Dating Service
Inc.
4807 Jonestown Road
Harrisburg, PA 17109
(717) 657-3111

Single's Network
Harrisburg, PA 17101
(717) 232-2900

Hollidaysburg:

MatchMaker International
1409 Blair Street
Hollidaysburg, PA
(814) 944-9986

Jenkintown:

Unique Introductions
Jenkintown, PA 19046
(215) 663-8663

King of Prussia:

It's About Time Master
Matchmaker
900 East 8th Avenue,
Suite 300
King Of Prussia, PA 19406
(610) 768-8058

Maria Mancini Matchmaker
Inc.
King Of Prussia, PA 19406
(610) 265-6928

The Right One
King Of Prussia, PA 19406
(610) 992-5099

Lancaster:

Dinner Etc
Lancaster, PA 17601
(717) 290-7330

Single's Network
1689 Crown Avenue
Lancaster, PA 17601
(717) 291-0100

Langhorne:

Maria Mancini Matchmaker
Inc.
116 North Bellevue Avenue
Langhorne, PA 19047
(215) 564-3383
(215) 752-2500

Mechanicsburg:

Together Inc.
5020 Ritter Road
Mechanicsburg, PA 17055
(717) 766-8220

Media:

Big But Beautiful Dating
Service
Media, PA 19063
(610) 565-1717

Monroeville:

Equally Yoked
4099 William Penn Highway
Monroeville, PA 15146
(412) 380-2500

Together Dating Service
Monroeville, PA 15146
(412) 856-1800

Newtown:

Hart 2 Hart
Newtown, PA 18940
(215) 504-9400

Maria Mancini Matchmaker
Inc.
Newtown, PA 18940
(302) 655-3300

Newtown Square:

628 Social Network
Newtown Square, PA 19073
(610) 355-9628

Philadelphia:

Dateline Dating Service
Philadelphia, PA 19102
(215) 465-4888

Dating
Philadelphia, PA 19102
(215) 976-5483

Interactive Media
Corporation
1617 John F Kennedy
Boulevard
Philadelphia, PA 19103
(215) 557-2055

It's Just Lunch
1528 Walnut Street
Philadelphia, PA 19102
(215) 772-9999

Options Dating Service Inc.
1616 Walnut Street
Philadelphia, PA 19103
(215) 985-2009

Pittsburgh:

Love Search
4501 Peoples Road
Pittsburgh, PA 15237
(412) 931-6909

MatchMaker International
200 Fleet Street
Pittsburgh, PA 15205
(412) 922-1200

Single Resources
7 Parkway Centre
Pittsburgh, PA 15220
(412) 875-2250

The Right One
7 Parkway Center
Pittsburgh, PA 15146
(412) 856-1800
(412) 928-2500

Greentree Office
1-800-968-3283 (toll-free)

Together Dating Service
2275 Swallow Hill Rd
Pittsburgh, PA 15220
(412) 429-8500

Wexford:

Gatherings
Wexford, PA 15090
(724) 933-8881

Wilkes Barre:

All About Singles
1065 Highway 315
Wilkes Barre, PA 18702
(570) 820-3283

Judy's Introduction Service
1065 Highway 315
Wilkes Barre, PA 18702
(570) 820-3283

York:

Singles Network
York, PA 17401
(717) 846-8460

Rhode Island

Coventry:

Tri State Multi Services
Coventry, RI 02816
(401) 828-6210

Providence:

Great Expectations
1 Park Row
Providence, RI 02903
(401) 861-0700

Introductions
203 South Main Street
Providence, RI 02903
(401) 331-9855

Warwick:

Right One
615 Jefferson Boulevard
Warwick, RI 02886
(401) 737-7822

South Carolina

Charleston:

Kompatible Introductions
LLC
Charleston, SC 29401
(843) 722-2272

Greenville:

Intros
37 Villa Road
Greenville, SC 29615
(864) 298-0043

Together Dating Service
100 Executive Center Drive
Greenville, SC 29615
(864) 288-0800

Hilton Head:

Hilton Head Special Select
214 Indian Trail
Hilton Head Island, SC
29926
(214) 360-1040
(843) 342-6427

Summerville:

Single Professionals'
Network, Inc.
975 Bacon's Bridge Road,
Suite 148–121
Summerville, SC 29401
(843) 824-5554
1-800-253-7358 (toll-free)
State Wide Access

South Dakota

Sioux Falls:

Mix Then Match
535 S Summit Avenue
Sioux Falls, SD 57105
(605) 334-0501

Together Dating Service
3500 South Sheldon Lane
Sioux Falls, SD 57105
(605) 338-9292

Tennessee

Brentwood:

Great Expectations
1624 Westgate Circle
Brentwood, TN 37027
(615) 329-8115

Chattanooga:

MatchMaker International
6215 Lee HWY.
Chattanooga, TN 37422
(423) 499-0050

Johnson City:

MatchMaker International
3119 Bristol Highway
Johnson City, TN 37601
(423) 282-0080

Knoxville:

MatchMaker International
5103 Kingston Pike
PO Box 10963
Knoxville, TN 37939
(865) 588-1770

Memphis:

Lunch for Two
4745 Poplar Avenue
Memphis, TN 38117
(901) 683-5484

Nashville:

Just 2 Date
Nashville, TN 37201
(615) 269-8484

Lunch Dates
Nashville, TN 37201
(615) 386-7136

Singles Network
1040 Murfreesboro Pike
Nashville, TN 37217
(615) 360-1110

Texas

Addison:

Elite Singles DFW
5100 Belt Line Road
Addison, TX 75001
(972) 404-0600

It's Just Lunch
15303 Dallas Parkway
Addison, TX 75001
(972) 851-0750
(972) 991-4161

Arlington:

Christian Single Adults
Dating Service
1112 East Copeland Road
Arlington, TX 76011
(817) 265-0606

Dating Made Easy
Arlington, TX 76001
(817) 469-6966

World Class Inc.
420 Joyce Street
Arlington, TX 76010
(817) 860-1184

Amarillo:

Singles of Society
112 West 8th Avenue
Amarillo, TX 79101
(806) 342-0048

Austin:

Christian Single Adults
Dating Service
10000 Research Boulevard
Austin, TX 78759
(512) 345-1717

It's Just Lunch
301 Congress Avenue
Austin, TX 78701
(512) 476-5566

Love & Romance
PO Box 150492
Austin, TX 78715
(512) 280-5859

People Store
Austin, TX 78701
(512) 462-1000

Single Adults Association
2213 South 1st Street
Austin, TX 78704
(512) 707-8121

Together Dating Service
8140 North Mo Pac
Expressway
Austin, TX 78759
(512) 231-1004

Beaumont:

Together Dating Service
Beaumont, TX 77701
(409) 832-7655

Dallas:

Active Successful Single of
NE
Dallas, TX 75201
(972) 238-8877
(817) 589-2262

Christian Single Adults
Dating Services
12900 Preston Road
Dallas, TX 75230
(972) 392-0753
(972) 233-0055

Eight at Eight
Dallas, TX 75201
(214) 887-8811

Equally Yoked Christian
Singles
Dallas, TX 75243
(214) 349-8222
(817) 355-1600

Executive Match
Dallas, TX 75201
(214) 752-5677

Great Connections Inc.
6009 Belt Line Road
Dallas, TX 75254
(972) 991-3283

Great Expectations
14180 Dallas Parkway
Dallas, TX 75254
(972) 448-7900

The Right One
15443 Knoll Trail Drive
Dallas, TX 75248
(972) 407-1609

Together Dating Service
4950 Westgrove Drive
Dallas, TX 75248
(972) 407-1700

El Paso:

Matchmakers Dating Service
6044 Gateway Boulevard
East
El Paso, TX 79905
(915) 778-5683

Euless:

Connections Matchmaking
Euless, TX 76039
(817) 685-6787

Progressive Computing LLC
Euless, TX 76039
(817) 280-0101
(817) 282-2500

SOLO for Singles
Euless, TX 76039
(817) 354-4647

Fort Worth:

A Connection-Singles over
Age 38
Fort Worth, TX 76107
(817) 679-0750

Active Quality Singles of
Arlington
Fort Worth, TX 76118
(817) 589-2262
(817) 284-8027

It's Just Lunch
500 Main Street
Fort Worth, TX 76102
(817) 870-9999

Singles Plus of the Far
Southwest Greater
Fort Worth, TX 76118
(817) 589-2262

Great Expectations Dating
Service
1116 Houston Street
Fort Worth, TX 76102
(817) 332-8009

Singles Plus Matching of
Grapevine
Fort Worth, TX 76118
(817) 284-8027

Grapevine:

Selective Singles
Grapevine, TX 76051
(817) 410-2240

Houston:

Great Expectations
50 Briar Hollow Lane
Houston, TX 77027
(713) 623-6495

Christiansingleweb
2411 Fountain View Drive
Houston, TX 77057
(713) 783-5683

Eight Friends Out
PO Box 540122
Houston, TX 77254
(281) 870-0827

It's Just Lunch
3050 Post Oak Boulevard
Houston, TX 77056
(713) 572-0900

Match Mate
4265 San Felipe Street
Houston, TX 77027
(713) 960-6678

TLC Worldwide Inc.
PO Box 924994
Houston, TX 77292
(713) 466-9866
(713) 896-9224

Together Dating Service
2100 West Loop South
Houston, TX 77027
(713) 621-7788

Together Membership
Services
2100 West Loop South
Houston, TX 77027
(713) 621-1067

Hurst:

Active Quality Singles
1050 West Pipeline Road
Hurst, TX 76053
(817) 590-8003

Singles Plus-Modern
Matching
1050 West Pipeline Road
Hurst, TX 76053
(817) 284-8027
(817) 589-2262

Irving:

Connection Dating Service
Irving, TX 75038
(972) 254-9728

Planet Singles
3575 North Beltline Road
Irving, TX 75062
(972) 240-8455

League City:

Faces Etc.
906 West Main Street
League City, TX 77573
(281) 554-3223

Plano:

Christian Singles Registry
Plano, TX 75023
(972) 423-6767
1-800-821-0811 (toll-free)

Richardson:

Singles Plus Modern
Matching
Richardson, TX 75080
(972) 238-8877

San Antonio:

It's Just Lunch
San Antonio, TX 78201
(210) 525-9988

Matchmaker Inc.
1407 Jackson Keller Road
San Antonio, TX 78213
(210) 344-1115

The Lonely Hearts Dateline
and Dating Services
San Antonio, TX 78202
(210) 946-5940

Sherman:

Singles Meeting-Dating
Singles
Sherman, TX 75090
(903) 868-2413

Tyler:

Christian Singles
Connection
222 West Rieck Road
Tyler, TX 75703
(903) 509-8047

Wichita Falls:

Singles Search of North
Texas
Wichita Falls, TX 76301
(940) 687-0300

Utah

Bountiful:

Social Introductions
Bountiful, UT 84010
(801) 292-3066

Midvale:

A Choice Companion
6911 S. 1300 E., #243
Midvale, UT 84047
(801) 947-9031

Murray:

Let's Do Lunch
5808 S 900 East
Murray, UT 84121-1644
(801) 266-5600

Ogden:

Latter Day Ideals
Ogden, UT 84401
(801) 627-9888

Salt Lake City:

Dining To Meet You Inc. &
Travel
PO Box 526438
Salt Lake City, UT
(801) 485-8358

Vermont

Brattleboro:

Relationship Group
139 Main Street
Brattleboro, VT 05301
(802) 258-2338

Montpelier:

Compatibles Dating
Network Inc.
Montpelier, VT 05602
(802) 223-3111

Saint George:

Ice Breakers
400 Cornerstone Drive
Suite 213
Saint George, VT 05452
(802) 288-9100

Williston:

Compatibles Dating
Network
771 Essex Rd,
Williston, VT 05495-7187
(802) 872-8500

Virginia

Alexandria:

Compatible Interests Dating
Alexandria, VA 22304
(703) 212-8600

Dinner At 8
PO BOX 19154
Alexandria, VA 22320-0154
(703) 838-8038

Ashburn:

Asian & American Dating
Service
Ashburn, VA 20147
(703) 723-2900

Chesapeake:

Virginia Speed Dating
1035 Land Of Promise Rd
Chesapeake, VA 23322
(757) 421-4057

Falls Church:

Equally Yoked Christian
Singles
6201 Leesburg Pike
Falls Church, VA 22044
(703) 538-4900

Together Dating Service
7700 Leesburg Pike
Falls Church, VA 22043
(703) 827-9090

Upscale Connections
Falls Church, VA 22046
(703) 204-1111

Fredericksburg:

Introductions of
Fredericksburg
1320 Central Park Blvd
Fredericksburg, VA 22401
(540) 786-1444

VaDate4U
PO Box 5156
Fredericksburg, VA 22403
(540) 310-9916

Glen Allen:

It Takes 2
4050 Innslake Drive,
Suite 110
Glen Allen, VA 23060
(804) 967-9911

Herndon:

Christian Dating Service
2940 Harvest Glen Court
Herndon, VA 20171
(703) 715-0583

Newport News:

Introductions Inc.
732 Thimble Shoals
Boulevard
Newport News, VA 23606
(757) 591-2200

Hampton Roads Date
Exchange
526 Dartmoor Dr.
Newport News, VA 23608-
8043
(757) 890-9717

Richmond:

Face To Face
Richmond, VA 23219
(804) 270-0300

Virginia Speed Dating
Richmond, VA 23219
(804) 266-3747

Roanoke:

Together Dating Service
3140 Chaparral Drive
Roanoke, VA 24018
(540) 774-6228

Sterling:

Athletic Singles
18 Hopton Court
Sterling, VA 20165
(703) 404-9626

Vienna:

Date2Match International
9783 Oleander Avenue
Vienna, VA 22181
(703) 281-1396
1-800-484-7583 ext.6014
(toll-free)

Great Expectations for
Singles
8601 Westwood Center Dr.,
200
Vienna, VA 22182-2217
(703) 847-0808

Heart To Heart
Introductions
8230 Old Courthouse Road
Vienna, VA 22182
(703) 506-2111

Options Dating Service Inc.
2108A Gallows Rd
Vienna, VA 22182
(703) 848-0887
1-800-360-3283 (toll-free)

Virginia Beach:

Equally Yoked
5660 Indian River Rd, # 113
Virginia Beach, VA 23464-
5240
(757) 523-5200

Great Expectations
208 Golden Oak Court
Virginia Beach, VA 23452
(757) 306-6000

Introduction Dating Service
780 Lynnhaven Pkwy, # 450
Virginia Beach, VA 23452-
7345
(757) 886-1200

Washington

Auburn:

For A Lifetime Christian
Introductions
11405 Se 290th Pl
Auburn, WA 98092
(253) 876-7768

Bellevue:

Events & Adventures
12021 Northup Way,
Suite 201
Bellevue, WA 98004
(425) 746-4534

Great Expectations Service
For Singles
3180 139th SE
Bellevue, WA 98005
(425) 641-1200

Renaissance
12301 Northeast 10th Place
Bellevue, WA 98005
(425) 450-0082

Bellingham:

Renaissance For Singles
1200 Harris Avenue
Bellingham, WA 98225
(360) 756-5151

Everett:

Selective Singles
Everett, WA 98208
(425) 347-5133

Friday Harbor:

Dating Mating Service
60 1st Street
Friday Harbor, WA
(360) 378-6033

Kent:

For A Lifetime
Kent, WA 98031
(253) 876-7768

Lacey:

Olympia Singles Dating
Service
PO Box 5969
Lacey, WA 98509-5969
(360) 412-6949

Renaissance for Singles
Lacey, WA 98503
(360) 456-4234

Mill Creek:

Green Mates Vegetarian
Singles Network
PO Box 13563
Mill Creek, WA 98082
(425) 338-1888

Portland:

Abstinence-Only Dating
P O Box 3091
Portland, WA
(503) 246-7311

Seattle:

Connector
2921 East Madison Street
Seattle, WA 98112
(206) 323-6666

Emerald Cities Rainy Day
Dating Service
5601 Renton Avenue South
Seattle, WA 98118
(206) 715-5563

Equally Yoked Christian
Singles
Seattle, WA 98101
(206) 575-2424

Express Dating
2612 23rd Avenue West
Seattle, WA 98199
(206) 352-3259

Relationships to Savor, Inc.
PO Box 21092
Seattle, WA 98111
(206) 682-4514

Renaissance for Singles
Seattle, WA 98101
(206) 839-1116

Speed Dating
6036 Seward Park Avenue
South
Seattle, WA 98118
(206) 721-9100

Spokane:

Christian Singles
Spokane, WA 99212
(509) 230-1671
1-877-604-6519 (toll-free)

Matchfinders for Singles
1210 N Argonne, Suite A
Spokane, WA 99212-2611
(509) 242-0159

Tacoma:

Renaissance for Singles
2115 South 56th Street
Tacoma, WA 98409
(253) 473-3151

Intro's
15 Oregon Ave, Suite 304
Tacoma, WA
(253) 839-0479

Washougal:

Heart and Soul Connection
181 Pohl Road
Washougal, WA
(360) 837-1150

West Virginia

Charleston:

MatchMaker International
410 Washington Street East
Charleston, WV 25301
(304) 345-6554

Wheeling:

Matchmaker International
Wheeling, WV 26003
(304) 233-2201

Wisconsin

Appleton:

Dating Technology
International
1004 S Olde Oneida St.
Appleton, WI 54915
(920) 954-6776

The Right One
47 Park Place
Appleton, WI 54914
(920) 733-9411

Eau Claire:

Renaissance for Singles
3119 Golf Road
Eau Claire, WI 54701
(715) 836-7714
(715) 836-9006

Green Bay:

Renaissance for Singles
Green Bay, WI 54301
(920) 432-2345

The People Store
1800 West Mason Street
Green Bay, WI 54303
(920) 497-9031
(920) 720-9083

Hartland:

Datalogics
Hartland, WI 53029
(262) 367-9470

The People Store
Hartland, WI 53029
(262) 367-9470

Madison:

The Right One
437 South Yellowstone Drive
Madison, WI 53719
(608) 274-5252

Milwaukee:

Single Attractions Dating
Service
933 N Mayfair Rd, # 212
Milwaukee, WI 53226
(414) 774-7764

Wausau:

Renaissance for Singles
605 S 24th Ave # 20
Wausau, WI 54401
(715) 842-0414

Together
605 S 24th Ave, # 20
Wausau, WI 54401
(715) 842-1173

Wauwatosa:

Great Expectations
1033 N Mayfair Rd # 100
Wauwatosa, WI 53226
(414) 777-5780

Wyoming

Cheyenne:

Cheyenne Dating Service
1219 West 31st Street
Cheyenne, WY 82001
(307) 772-7551

Torrington:

WYO Nebraska Singles
208 East Valley Road
Torrington, WY 82240
(307) 532-2678

index

The times, they are a-changin'

The *Boomer's Guide* series offers practical knowledge and advice about the really important things in life, geared specifically to the needs of baby boomers. You know—those of us now 40- or 50-something who have teen- or college-age children, aging parents, maturing marriages (or perhaps a new single status), looming retirement, investment and property responsibilities, new health and fitness concerns, and a realization that we are finally becoming our parents.

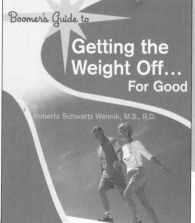

Boomer's Guide to
Getting the Weight Off... For Good

Roberta Schwartz Wennik, M.S., R.D.

1-59257-160-3 • $16.95

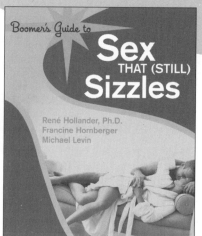

Boomer's Guide to
Sex THAT (STILL) **Sizzles**

René Hollander, Ph.D.
Francine Hornberger
Michael Levin

1-59257-155-7 • $16.95

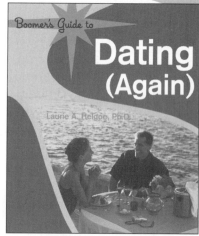

Boomer's Guide to
Dating (Again)

Laurie A. Helgoe, Ph.D.

1-59257-164-6 • $16.95

Coming Summer of 2004:

Boomer's Guide to
Divorce

ALPHA

From the publishers of *The Complete Idiot's Guide®* series